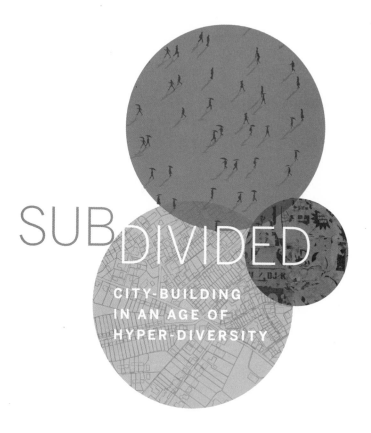

SUBDIVIDED

CITY-BUILDING IN AN AGE OF HYPER-DIVERSITY

EDITED BY

JAY PITTER AND **JOHN LORINC**

Coach House Books, Toronto

Jay Pitter dedicates this book to Kirsten Breanna Azan
John Lorinc dedicates this book to Joan York and Vera Halmos

first edition

 Canada Council   Conseil des Arts
for the Arts   du Canada

Published with the generous assistance of the Canada Council for the Arts and the
Ontario Arts Council. Coach House Books also acknowledges the support of the
Government of Canada through the Canada Book Fund and the Government of
Ontario through the Ontario Book Publishing Tax Credit.

LIBRARY AND ARCHIVES CANADA CATALOGUING IN PUBLICATION

Subdivided : city-building in an age of hyper-diversity / edited by Jay Pitter and
John Lorinc.

Includes bibliographical references.
Issued in print and electronic formats.
ISBN 978-1-55245-332-2 (paperback).

1. Cultural pluralism--Ontario--Toronto--Case studies. 2. City planning--Social
aspects--Ontario--Toronto--Case studies. 3. Toronto (Ont.)--Ethnic relations. 4. Toronto
(Ont.)--Social conditions. I. Pitter, Jay, 1971-, editor II. Lorinc, John, 1963-, editor

HN110.T6S82 2016   305.8009713'541   C2016-902092-4

Subdivided is available as an ebook: ISBN 978-1-77056-443-5 (EPUB),
ISBN 978-1-77056-458-9 (MOBI), ISBN 978-1-77056-444-2 (PDF).

Purchase of the print version of this book entitles you to a free digital copy. To claim
your ebook of this title, please email sales@chbooks.com with proof of purchase or
visit chbooks.com/digital. (Coach House Books reserves the right to terminate the
free digital download offer at any time.)

CONTENTS

Introduction
Jay Pitter

I remember three things about second grade: the powdery aftermath that candy cigarettes left above my lips; the itchy floral dress my mother made me wear on special occasions; and my teacher, an Irish-Canadian man with curly hair that resembled an afro. It was the late 1970s – an unlikely decade for reasonable fashion or snack options, and an era when it was even more unlikely for a teacher and a student from vastly different experiences to forge an enduring relationship.

Our narrative begins in an elementary school located between a residential subdivision in Toronto's east end and the public housing community where I grew up. I was a gregarious, feisty little girl who often spoke out of turn. One day, while I was telling a story in the back of the class, Mr. Frank[1] stopped the lesson and said, 'It really doesn't make sense for both of us to speak at once. Is there something important you'd like to share with everyone?'

Typically, an eight-year-old would be silenced by such a question. But I confidently shared my tale. What came next was profoundly transformative. Mr. Frank acknowledged the value of my voice and, perhaps more importantly, provided a safe space for me to be heard. This was especially significant to me because I often felt unsafe as a child.

From that moment forward, our lives intertwined. He encouraged me to be a part of the larger classroom community, which progressed into excursions to the theatre, ballet, library and frequent pizza lunches. During summer vacations, Mr. Frank sidestepped the intimidating characters who patrolled the perimeter of my neighbourhood to bring me books and reminders that it was crucial for me to imagine myself beyond its narrow margins.

As I think back to this relationship, which shaped my life, I see how it could exemplify multiculturalism, as championed by Liberal Prime Minister Pierre Trudeau. It was an instance of how the lives of two people situated in opposite social locations – Black and white, male and female, child and adult, poor and economically stable – intersected meaningfully within the context of a fast-growing city. It *seems* like a story that supports our proclamation that diversity does, in fact, work. Yet as I observe today's teeming city-region, I know that such stories, and the intricate forces that create them, are far too rare to validate the efficacy of diversity and the paint-by-numbers politics of urban identity. It isn't that diversity is bad; it's inherent in the urban project's built environment and natural ecology. But when it comes to the human beings who collectively make up a global city like Toronto – a place with accelerating social, economic and ethnocultural divisions – the over-emphasis placed on diversity is lazy social shorthand, an attempt to smooth over ragged edges we struggle to understand. Civic leaders endlessly repeat the catchphrase 'Diversity is our strength,' as if it could resolve our issues or conclude difficult discussions.

Cities and Social Diversity

Cities are a constant negotiation of distance and difference. Across time, people have cast their hopes toward these collectively conceived places of possibility that are at once immutable and fragile. Within a few city blocks, towers of industry and influence preside over cars and cyclists competing for space, parkettes constrained by concrete and pedestrians navigating the new homeless – entire families huddling atop street grates.

As a result of unprecedented migration and intensification, we are building global cities in which we literally live on top of one another. We have created a complex convergence of stories that reveal growing social disparities. More than ever, many urban dwellers exist in a daily dissonance of economic despair and polarized ideology, while others revel in an affluent world of chic boutiques, high-end restaurants and impossibly expensive homes.

In recent decades, we've wrongly deployed the language and paradigm of diversity to address – or in some instances avoid – a complicated range of issues arising from, among others, improper policing, NIMBYism, gendered violence, transit inequality and an increasingly precarious urban labour force.

While there isn't a single agreed-upon definition or approach to diversity, the phenomenon is generally understood to be a way of defining and responding to the increasing number of 'others' within cities. Of course, *everyone* is diverse: we are all distinct and different. However, in the language of municipal policy and planning, someone like me – a visible 'minority' and woman – has come to be understood and widely accepted as 'diverse' while my teacher turned lifelong mentor – a white male – would be considered 'normal,' the centralized status. Unspoken notions of power, differently valued bodies, spatial entitlement, and economic and social capital are all implicit in a term we have come to consider virtuous.

Using this flawed framework, which reinforces rather than redresses social power dynamics, we've developed public policy, business-based programs and mandated workplace training to increase our collective capacity to deal with difference. In fact, diversity is so knitted into Canada's national identity and its values that, for some, any critique of this rhetoric amounts to a challenge to our collective sense of respectability. But while we've been focused on embracing the identities of 'others' and celebrating their differences, the economic disparities between city dwellers – and not just in Canada – have greatly increased.

In an urban context, accelerating income disparity has created an insidious form of social segregation within and across neighbourhoods. Here in Toronto, the most culturally diverse city in the world, University of Toronto sociologist David Hulchanski's 'Three Cities' research[2] has shown how, over the past two generations, wealthy and poor neighbourhoods have become increasingly concentrated and isolated from one another, producing a social geography that offers a ground-level rebuke to the redemptive rhetoric extolling the virtues of diversity.

Conversations focusing on social disparity are on the rise. In his 2006 book, *The Trouble with Diversity: How We Learned to Love Identity and Ignore Inequality*,[3] American literary theorist Walter Benn Michaels argues that by emphasizing the celebration of difference – primarily cultural difference – for the past three decades, we've ignored the more uncomfortable matter of economic inequality.

Michaels reminds us that race is merely a social construct with no meaningful scientific legitimacy. But our preoccupation with racial or ethnocultural categories precludes a more fluid and holistic way of seeing the world, one that allows us to identify ourselves with other points of reference, such as economics, passion, politics, belief and the kind of society we value. My reading of his work is not without reservation. Race and economic inequality are obviously not mutually exclusive, nor do we live in a post-racial society. However, his deliberations raise important and uncomfortable questions that should prompt us to strive for a discourse that goes beyond diversity's superficial rhetoric, policies and celebrations.

If Not Diversity, Then What?

In recent years, a few city-builders across North America and Europe have begun to use the term *hyper-diversity* to describe the social realities of these places we call urban regions. As a 2014 study commissioned by the European Union[4] explains, urban hyper-diversity refers to an intense diversification of the population in socio-economic, social and ethnic terms, but also with respect to lifestyles, attitudes and activities. While theoretical frameworks are not wholly equipped to describe the beauty, contradictions and messiness of our lives, the concept of hyper-diversity enables us to move beyond the oversimplifications of diversity and identity politics and explore more deeply what, exactly, it means to live in twenty-first-century global cities like Toronto.

Refreshingly, the term implicates all of us, not just those whom we've come to categorize as 'others.' This approach is a good start because history has taught us that imposing labels on others, even in seemingly benign ways, is an oppressive act, one that prevents us from truly seeing and meeting each other on equal ground. Without prescribed categories or policies that reinforce divisions while negating social disparities, we are forced to be more observant to what legal scholar Kimberlé Crenshaw describes as 'intersectionality'[5] – a theory that calls for us to acknowledge the multiple parts of our identities, constructed, as they are, in relation to the social environments in which we function.

The notion of individual beings comprised of multiple, intersecting identities that shape the way they experience the world disrupts the neat boxes on census documents and employer diversity forms. It is also a fundamentally urban idea, one that enables us to confront disparities across hyper-diverse cities. In addition to recognizing how various elements of our identities impact the way we navigate spaces, inequitable systems and social environments, intersectionality requires us to acknowledge that our cities contain diversities within diversities within diversities. They are deeply complicated places.

A vivid illustration of urban hyper-diversity, and the fluidity of our identities as city-dwellers, occurs each June, during Toronto's Pride Parade, following a year of programming and dialogue. Fundamentally, Pride is a place-making initiative that galvanizes queer people and their supporters to recognize the right to be their full selves in public. Yet to take in the festivities is also to understand that there is no such thing as a homogenous LGBT+ community. Rather, Pride is a festival of multiple, nested and overlapping diversities, with stages for French, Filipino, South Asian and Caribbean LGBT+ communities and special marches for those who identify as transgendered and lesbian.

There are also spaces for ethno-racial youth and for individuals involved in punk and emo culture. Equally important, a large number of parade attendees are not members of the LGBT+ communities. More than ever, loved ones, friends and colleagues attend the parade to show their solidarity. Some members of the queer community, moreover, avoid the event for fear of disclosure or feelings of alienation.

It's also true that Pride has been critiqued in recent years for its corporatization, the subtle decisions about which floats and stages get sponsorship dollars and which don't, and the lack of equal space for members of the communities it strives to reflect. By using a hyper-diversity lens, we are able to assess multiple social and economic aspects of the parade, which can help us to understand the intricacies of communities that are wrongly perceived as monolithic, wherein all members have equal social power. This more complex and nuanced framework – the notion that our identities are fundamentally fluid, considering our social and economic contexts – can help us to actively co-create city-building processes that respond deftly to rapidly changing urban neighbourhoods.

The timing couldn't be better, because our insistence on the apparent strength of our diversity has caused us to ignore these shifts. Two decades ago, the notion of a gender spectrum was implausible, and no one could have envisioned how digital culture would define a generation and ultimately change the way our cities function. Individuals are boldly redefining notions of identity and demanding more of urban spaces and city-building processes.

In my own place-making practice, I often encounter these complexities, which reflect the emerging hyper-diversity of cities. I recently met a young activist who is Asian, lesbian and an active member of her church. She challenges systems and works to carve out spaces for herself and others who embrace identities that have historically been at odds. Another young activist committed to uncovering Indigenous peoples' history and contributions in cities leads walking tours and is creating an archive to educate the public. For her, this place and its meanings are even more complex, fraught with unspeakably painful histories and erased contributions – but also incredible teachings and hope for a reconciled future. Her work extends beyond cultural archiving and is situated in place-making and policy development. These next-generation leaders expect to be centralized in city-building processes and defy imposed boundaries of space and identity.

Even for folks of my generation – Canadians who came here at an early age or are first-generation – our stories became a series of hyphenations, partially spoken in our grandparents' dialects. For years, I struggled with the seemingly incongruent details of my lived experience and the ways it has caused me to sometimes hover between and across spaces. And it's no surprise. My two most significant role models are my Caribbean mother, who taught me fortitude through her struggle to move us out of public housing, and an Irish-Canadian mentor, who modelled unconditional love. My story would not be possible anywhere but here. I love the city in all its promise. Still, I always carry with me an uneasy awareness of the stark disparities inscribed in our neighbourhoods, our cultural venues and our workplaces. I have numerous social and professional networks, yet they rarely intersect. Why is that, and what does it say about our city?

The experience of living and observing disparities across urban spaces is a reality for a growing number of city dwellers. Despite that, the relatively small number of designers, investors and decision-makers who have historically driven city-building processes don't have the breadth of insight to address this degree of hyper-diversity. If metropolitan communities are predicated on the equal participation and vision of their citizens, the challenge that a global region like Toronto faces is actually an opportunity – to embrace an inclusive, creative and nuanced approach to city-building. This book presents a small yet compelling sample of those perspectives and voices.

A Conversation

I will never forget my final conversation with the teacher who became a beloved mentor. We sat across from each other in an Irish pub near Spadina and Bloor with pints of beer and a lot of history and mutual respect between us. I had recently recorded a radio commentary about him, which he'd heard on his way up to the cottage with a friend. He told me how proud he was to hear our story in the car and that I was the daughter he thought he'd never be permitted to have. You see, my mentor was a privately gay man who lived in a time that dictated his identity and restricted him from expressing his full self across urban spaces. Like that little girl who constantly spoke out of turn, he, too, was lodged in the margins. I imagine that's why he risked so much for me.

At the time, I didn't realize the differences between us, nor how incredibly progressive he was. Although he and I met long before we began to recognize the hyper-diversity that is redefining our cities, he intuited the need to address the social inequalities I'd undoubtedly encounter rather than focus on my 'diversity.' Besides emphasizing literacy, he gave me opportunities to explore urban spaces and leadership roles outside of my community. Through our conversations and explorations, he provided me with the tools to overcome social disparities and become a citizen of the city.

His example has informed the work I do now. Whether leading national engagement strategies, design equity charrettes or neighbourhood walks, I stress the importance of facilitating difficult conversations across difference – conversations intended to create social cohesion, belonging and equity.

From the moment that urban affairs writer John Lorinc invited me to collaborate on this anthology, it was clear that our partnership would be marked by this same kind of conversation. My first response was 'I'm not interested in writing a book about diversity; that's boring.' John wasn't at all taken aback. Like me, he wanted to dig into something more complex, something that would animate what we'd both addressed in different ways in our city-building work and personal lives. We agreed to go beyond traditional notions of identity and unpack the ways that diversities within diversity could disrupt and improve current models of city-building.

Before we began to set up interviews or determine the book's contents, we wanted to really talk to potential contributors. We listened for perspectives and professional insights that revealed an understanding of the city in all its complexity. Once we settled on the contributor cohort, it was important to expand the discussion and share our resources and networks. Coach House Books was immediately supportive and arranged for an on-site tour of their tiny yet powerful press – in this digital era, there's something remarkable about seeing an actual book printed on a Heidelberg press. The excitement of our words being set in ink was palpable in that tiny room.

Yet we've always known this book was not just for reading. *Subdivided* aspires to encourage urgent and difficult conversation. The chapters that follow span issues such as hostile police and public relations, transit equity, new approaches to social housing, the emergence of digital gated communities, the complexity of culture and mental health, the shortcomings of youth arts funding, the lack of representation in municipal government, fights over the development of non-traditional religious institutions and the way Indigenous communities experience urban places. The pieces are both analytical and often deeply personal, written by contributors with exceptional insights and deep investment in the topics they address. We want *Subdivided* to prompt thoughtful but spirited discussions about the issues that increasingly confront the global cities now deeply defined by an unprecedented degree of hyper-diversity.

The case for conversation and inclusive city-building has never been more urgent.

Identity and the City:
Thinking Through Diversity
Beyhan Farhadi

My story has an infinite number of beginnings, though I usually recount it as if there were only one. It depends on the time and place, on the audience and my mood, and on an imagined present and anticipated future.

It might begin in Edmonton, Alberta, where I was born to immigrant parents. Or Atlanta, Georgia, which marks a transition from their inevitable divorce. Or in Flemingdon Park, Toronto, where my mother did the best she could with very little. Or in Malvern, with my father, from whom I am now estranged. The story might end in Port Union, where I now live with my two children and my partner, and then pick up as if it were beginning again.

My story also pulls collective memory from Istanbul, Mombasa and Mumbai. It romanticizes Costa Rica, Spain and Thailand. If you wish, I can deliver it in Spanish. In my story, I am the rebellious, hurting teen, or the promising academic; I am the lover, daughter, mother, teacher, mentor, writer, friend, foe, menace, rabble rouser, intellectual and model citizen – though in my utopia, I am afforded the space to be all these things at once. It is a narrative of both places and people. I rarely tell it the same way twice.

It's an urban story.

With more than half of the world's population living in cities, the urban is always in our imagination, even if we don't live there. Whether it is in the way we project our desires onto the cityscape, in search of all it can offer us, or in the way we feel we know cities we have never seen, the imagination provides us with as much knowledge about the urban as our claim to or rejection of city living.

I approach this broad understanding of the urban as a human geographer and an urbanite. I consider the role of the city in our stories, taking it as the site of our location, destination and throughway. How do the settings of our stories limit us by organizing social life into categories of identity while simultaneously providing us with the capacity to imagine people and cities as dynamic organisms in constant flux, defying categorization?

By drawing on the lived experiences of four people in Toronto – Abu Zaid, Avi, Danielle and Farhiya – this essay illustrates the role the city plays in shaping people as well as the role of people in shaping cities. I have used narrative as a method of getting at the complexity of identity – not to disregard the histories it is tethered to, but as a means of opening up spaces for a more plural and therefore satisfying understanding of identity.

What shifts in our framework might be required to think about gender, class, religion, sexuality, ethnicity, race, ability, nationality, [insert identifier here] – not as separate, not as intersectional, but existing at the same time, in ways that exceed any one categorization? If one of the conditions of success in professional and personal practice is asking the right questions, we must consider the possibility that there are questions we never thought to ask. My hope is that these stories provoke such 'unthinkable' questions, and that the work of responding thoughtfully gives space, as the city itself does, to a plurality of answers.

Abu Zaid

I was born in South Africa and I lived there for twenty years. This is the foundation of my identity. This is who I am, from South Africa to Syria to Canada. Living through the first twenty years of apartheid, I knew I was read by the colour of my skin, not by my religion. I knew then that we had to defend ourselves and fight to be understood as human.

When we came to Canada and 9/11 happened, I realized I was not only a visible minority but also a Muslim. So I was dealing with it again, after trying to live free of apartheid, after trying to assimilate in Canada. Now I have to defend myself as a Muslim – not so much as a brown person, but as a Muslim. And then I went home with my sexuality, and now it seems like it's all three that I have to defend.

If you were to look at Abu Zaid, the only thing you would know for certain is that he is a brown man. Unless he was in Syria, in which case he might be read a Black man, or South Africa, where he would be read a mixed man. Abu Zaid spent the first two decades of his life in Johannesburg during apartheid, which was one of the most explicit examples of how urban planning and development can deploy racialized identity to organize bodies in the city.

Cities are pedagogical; they map our place in the world. Abu Zaid remembers having to learn his place very early in his life, and having that knowledge reinforced through spatial exclusion. Though his family attained modest wealth, it did not provide any social advantage; the political instability and the restrictions placed on the family's mobility contributed to their decision to leave.

When he arrived in Toronto, Abu Zaid recalls the benefits of accessing employment services targeted toward visible minorities; in fact, he credits one agency with helping him land his first job in Canada with a provincial ministry. Because of this experience, Abu Zaid went on to earn a research position in a Toronto hospital. When his contract expired some years later, he left the country for Syria – where he had a solid familial network – in order to consider his next path, both spiritually and personally. There he was introduced to the woman who would later become his wife.

Abu Zaid eventually returned to Canada to raise his family. However, after he'd fathered two children, his relationship with his wife deteriorated dramatically. Because of his earlier success in accessing services as a newcomer, Abu Zaid reached out again to agencies for support against the abuse he was experiencing. But this time he was constrained, because he fell outside the parameters of service provision. What once benefited him as a visible minority and newcomer now failed him as a man and father.

The abuse was one of controlled manipulation, with the system as the executioner. It was silent and so powerful that it gripped me beyond my capacity to fight back. My wife used family court, where she knew she had an advantage, to threaten me regularly. If I didn't do what she wanted, I couldn't see my kids. I had no money to defend myself with a lawyer and I couldn't get help from aid shelters [which only served women], or the police. And my religion and culture – my beard and my look – stereotyped me as a typical dominant Muslim male. There was no support. It wasn't even considered abuse.

Abu Zaid was eventually able to meet his needs for support and familial mediation through his local mosque, though he notes that as a gay man, he would no longer be eligible for the backing of his religious community. Ironically, he was later able to leverage his sexual identity to gain support in the justice system as a father, since his claim to injury was based on discrimination by his ex-wife because of his sexuality.

Abu Zaid does not conform to the trope of 'coming out.' His relationship with his wife, and subsequent women, were ones he felt invested in and fulfilled by at the time. However, a formative moment for his sexual evolution was marked by a return from a trip to South Africa, where he celebrated his fortieth birthday.

After coming from vacation, I was stronger, bolder and, being forty, determined to live. To live for me, even if it was in the closet. I did meet people on social media and different sites, but this was not enough. I wanted to belong in my own way to a community. So when I got back to Toronto, I was sitting around one night, thinking about what I was going to do with my life. I decided to get dressed and I actually drove down to the [Gay] Village, and got out and just started walking. I walked and looked and I just ended up at one of the clubs there. Then I finally met people, and that's how it just happened. Yes, it is a double life, but nothing I can't handle for now.

Abu Zaid describes being gay as an identification that doesn't betray his sexual experiences with women. It's something that 'just happened.' Coming out in this context had less to do with his need to assert something essential about his identity than about responding to the demands others made on him to conform to particular roles. His need to find belonging in a community where he could express his sexuality was a search for place rather than for an identity placeholder. Though there are limitations to sexual communities,

Abu Zaid said that his need to belong outweighed the prejudices that often accompany conditions of belonging.

As a result, his family, which once served as a safeguard from racial and religious discrimination, has now become a site of risk because he fears persecution based on his sexual orientation. Family is at the core of Abu Zaid's value system. And while family is typically framed as a standard of heterosexuality, Abu Zaid's identity exists in constant negotiation with his roles as a son, brother, father, employer and partner. His story resonates with theories of eminent queer scholars, such as Eve Kosofsky Sedgwick[1], who argued that the opposition between heterosexuality and homosexuality is insufficient to understand the spectrum of human sexuality. The closet is perhaps too limiting a metaphor to capture the complex and contradictory spatial configurations of sexual expression, especially in the city.

When I first approached Abu Zaid with the parameters for the conversation, he responded by organizing his experiences in the spheres of work space, public space and home space, though his memories bled between all three. When he recounts his experience as a gay, racialized, Muslim man, what these terms meant changed in relation to where he was and whom he was with. He spoke frequently about the need to consider his children, who have a strong relationship with their grandparents and extended family. He also spoke about his fears for the future; he's currently engaged to be married to his partner, Kevin, and understands the challenges he'll soon face:

> I have to think about being disowned, which also means I lose my privileges of being an owner and walk away with nothing. I will be punished. I'll have to look for a job, a career. I'll have to network. In the suburbs, I can't find that. In the mosque, I can find a job, networks, but I can't disclose my sexuality. Or I can go to organizations for LGBTQ people downtown and network … but they might reject me as a Muslim. I have three access points as a minority, a Muslim and a gay father. But there isn't a service that deals with all three of those things. Do you think it can exist? It can, but I don't think anyone has done that – just taking you as you, people in this situation like me, networking together and helping each other.

Abu Zaid concludes our conversation with a utopian vision of service provision unencumbered by the mandates of identity, yet delivered by people who can speak to similar life experiences and who would understand his particular challenge. The setting for this vision is the city, where he experiences greater freedom to live across his identifications – as a man in a partnership with another man; as a father to two teenage children; as an employer; as a racialized Canadian whose sense of self is rooted simultaneously in South Africa and Syria; and as a Muslim who professes a deep love for his faith. Each identifier on its own eclipses not only the complexity of Abu Zaid's sense of self, which sits in tension with his sense of family and duty to his children, but also the ways in which his needs within these constraints fall short of the promise of the 'diverse city.'

Avi

> I am wary of group identifications. I am an architect. I am from Israel. I am Jewish by culture, and there is a connection to the land, even though I may not like that connection. I come from a country that's based on group identification and there's not as strong a sense of individualism. If a member of one group enters the space of another group, doesn't threaten them as individuals – but rather their sense of the group – it leads to people dying, and it's happening right now to both sides – disproportionately, for sure, but still, people are dying because of group identifications, either religious or cultural or both. I hate it. That's one of the reasons I wanted to leave, to go to an entirely unfamiliar place, to spend my savings to integrate.

Israel dominates the atmosphere in my conversation with Avi, though he takes great pains to situate his experiences broadly along his professional trajectory in architecture, which has given him a breadth of vocabulary when talking about building cities, and about the networks he's developed in Toronto – volunteering, going to graduate school and founding a successful non-profit that supports important social and environmental causes through art.

Avi discusses his experiences attending school and finding work, as well as the social, emotional and bureaucratic challenges as an immigrant to Canada. However, within the context of our conversation, I understand why his experiences in his country of origin resonate so loudly: there is perhaps no greater current-day example of the ways in which identity is bound to place than Israel. And while Avi is fiercely individualistic and wholly ambivalent about cultural identification, he has inevitably been shaped living twenty-four years in a country that, in his terms, has become synonymous with the word *conflict*.

Avi's story undoes the sort of romanticism inherent in urban framings of diversity by pointing to the ways in which identity categories, when linked to migration, are often steeped in histories of violence and intolerance, political instability and economic precarity. These histories are simultaneously rooted in attachments to land and communal/familial infrastructures that provide sources of positive emotion and support for populations.

What's more, his narrative reveals that the way a person experiences the urban is tied intimately to their framing of home in relation to migration. For instance, he speaks of moving freely through the city, feeling relatively safe in most places, and his drive to meet his personal and professional goals, which is partly determined by the bureaucratic urgency of settlement in the context of citizenship, and partly informed by the advantage of being a white, straight male, allowing Avi to move inconspicuously through space. Avi recognizes these aspects of his freedom, and notes that he is often read as French. He captures his diversity as one that – in the context of a white Canada – is an 'other that looks like you.' His ability to pass, belied by language barriers and the social dynamics of a second-language accent, sits in tension with his experiences as an immigrant.

The city plays a significant role in the integration of both migrants and refugees. Public institutions, such as libraries, schools and service agencies, have to attend to the unique needs of newcomers, which include getting acquainted with the city. This carries a particular urgency for those intending to acquire citizenship because of the pressure to establish personal networks, locate long-term housing and employment, and negotiate the language barriers and social codes inherent in encountering any new place. However, identity categories, determined by nationality, often frame the context for mediating the relationship between the newcomer and the city. Upon moving to Toronto, Avi turned to volunteer opportunities instead of Jewish social groups and centres. This is not to say Jewish cultural centres couldn't provide him with support and opportunities to network; rather, he didn't identify with the Jewish collective that these organizations were serving.

Avi understands urban space not just in terms of the built environment, where proximity to amenities and work determines its structure, but also in terms of the opportunities for collaboration and connectivity. Though the city has traditionally been understood as an organization of neighbourhoods and cultural enclaves, Avi conceptualizes the city in terms of networks connected by accessible modes of transportation. His sense of place is mediated by barriers of time.

> I'm more invested in a neighbourhood in the west end because I'm doing art there and I joined community meetings. In my own neighbourhood, I'm not doing anything. In a city that has a metro, a subway or other modes of rapid transport, barriers of distance disintegrate. If I owned the property I live in, I'd be more invested in it. I think I'd feel more secure. In terms of being involved in the community, my ideal is when arts and community come together.
>
> I don't want to get political; I'd rather do something that makes people happy. I can be polarizing and aggressive, but when I do this sort of positive, fun community work, politics can be aside. There are some things that left and right share. Everybody likes to have fun, and I prefer to focus on that.

Many cities have focused on transit-oriented development, and Avi's recollection of his experience integrating as a newcomer challenges us to consider how the time freed up by efficient forms of transit shapes the composition of our communities. This is very much dependent upon a capitalist economy that determines the experience not just of time, but of space. For instance, Avi references the way property ownership may affect his capacity to feel invested in his neighbourhood, as well as the way his sense of community is determined by the activity he is engaged in, rather than where he lives.

The lack of political representation was also a significant factor in Avi's sense of place in the city – not only in terms of his disengagement within his own neighbourhood, but also in the ways he navigates bureaucratic systems.

> *I understand that immigrating to Canada is getting harder and harder. [The difficulty of navigating bureaucracy] might be a way to let people fall between the cracks. I really don't know. The hoops immigrants have to go through, such as flagpoling. And I don't have any political representatives. I didn't vote.*
>
> *I don't think anyone is representing permanent residents. Even in my profession, there is a union, but they're not representing me yet. I don't have time to advocate for everything I would like or need, to make sure my interests are served. Some of my interests coincide with citizens and the agendas that some of the politicians are setting, but I can't vote for them.*

As of the 2006 census, permanent residents in Toronto comprised roughly 18 percent of the city's population, and yet their lack of representation raises important questions about how access to citizenship determines the engagement of people with their city. What is at stake when people living in the city are unable to access the institutions that determine their quality of life – in what ways does this erode the urban? And what is the benefit of diversity if it is unable to *assert itself* into the conversation of city-building? More importantly, in what ways does immigration, and the alienation that can ensue from a lack of political representation, determine the quality of diversity in the city?

Danielle

> *When I say I'm from Canada, I get the response 'No one is really from Canada.' Actually, I am. My mother is Indigenous – her ancestors are the original peoples of this land. And my father, his French roots go back to the 1600s. My parents' ancestors have deep roots*

in a Canadian context. I do not identify as Métis. I am a Status, First Nations and French woman.

What is nationality? There are some Indigenous advocates who never refer to being Canadian. Personally, I reference my Indigenous nation first and then I identify with my French roots, but I also put it in the context of land and territory before nationality. Often, I introduce myself referencing family roots: my Anishinaabe (Ojibwe) family are from the Great Lakes region – Lake Superior, to be exact – and I continue to describe the greatness of this lake and territory.

I tie my identity to the land where I grew up, then Canada as a country. Sometimes I say I'm from Turtle Island, which is a reference to North America, and specifically Canada. Yet in other countries I identify very much as Canadian and as an Indigenous woman from Canada.

Danielle's story raises a fundamental question about the role of the city within the context of nation-building: if diversity is *our* strength and if the pronoun *our* connotes a relation and belonging to a city, who is excluded or rendered invisible from this formulation? According to University of Winnipeg social geographer Evelyn Peters, Canada's First Peoples have always posed significant challenges to urban planning and development,[2] even though of those identifying with one of Canada's Aboriginal groups, 34 percent live in cities.[3]

The internal migration to cities by First Peoples – who comprise the fastest-growing segment of the Canadian population – is a provocation to conventional processes of city-building, particularly because the structure of governance in cities does not incorporate Indigenous interests – and the inherent right to self-determination – into its administration.

In our utopian imagining of the diverse city, we don't assimilate or 'melt together' into a fusion of culture, although those who migrate to the city will inevitably struggle to integrate into the urban fabric without being absorbed by it. For First Peoples, this is a contentious, if not violent, negotiation. Particularly for First Nations communities, who constitute approximately 60 percent of First Peoples in Canada,

assimilation not only represents an encroachment on the constitu-
tionally protected right to sovereignty, but it also contrasts against a
vastly different relationship to the land.

In this context, First Nations peoples – more than half of whom
live in cities – are not merely stakeholders in the project of city-
building. Rather, they are rights holders within the context of national
relations. When Danielle discusses her national identity, it requires
that beneficiaries of Canada's colonial project[4] drastically reconfigure
an understanding of citizenship and its relationship to land when
thinking about the city. This involves an understanding of the diversity
that exists within First Peoples, who possess distinct laws, forms of
governance, economic systems, social structures, languages and
cultures; more importantly, it requires a conscious re-evaluation of
the ways in which traditional territories of First Peoples continue to
shape the imagery of our city.[5]

How would our understanding of planning, development and land
use change if we sought out and valued Indigenous worldviews and
knowledge in all their diversity? Danielle understands land spiritually,
psychically, physically, socially and culturally as a founding source of
her identity and a strength of her nation. This may be why she considers the urban to be a 'strange concept.'

*'Urban' is a curious word to me: what is that? My professional life
is rooted in urban thinking, but the communities I work with, serve
and think about are not necessarily urban. What is urban? Is it
because you live and exist in a city centre? Sometimes being up
north in the context of work does challenge me and makes me feel
urban. Growing up in the north, I do relate more to – and love
being in – the outdoors. I feel a connection.*

*Fortunately, I live in a part of the city that is close to a ravine
and surrounded by trees and birds and gardens and greenery, and
I think definitely a part of me is rooted in a closeness to nature,
and I embrace this more than wanting to be part of the urban landscape. The urban life to me is intense, fast-paced, always moving. I
really don't know what the connection to my identity is within it.*

'Urban' is a strange concept. I imagine some people would consider me very urban and others perhaps not so.

Danielle's struggle to define the urban is informed by her ambivalent location within it, whereby she is pressed to reconcile her identity as First Nations with her professional life in Toronto. She recalls being compelled to learn more about her culture only after coming to the city, partly because her roots became a site of appropriation in various situations (such as during her employment, where she was pressed to identify as 'Aboriginal' in order to qualify for her role) and partly because her cultural history was something First Nations people have been conditioned to suppress after European contact.

In the city, I became another person on the sidewalk. People couldn't figure out what my background was. Sometimes that was a nice thing – being able to meld in – but it became more evident there was a need for and importance to becoming a voice for and in support of Indigenous peoples, though this was probably shaped by my professional experiences, where I often had to be a voice for my race.

Recalling her arrival in Toronto in her early twenties, Danielle spoke about how exasperated she sometimes felt (and continues to feel) having to educate people about the history of Indigenous peoples and her background, noting the change she observed in the attitude of acquaintances or co-workers when she told them she was Anishinaabe. In work contexts, she felt she had to downplay the politics of her identity while simultaneously being constrained by it.

In professional spaces, it can be a challenge. I really can see why I'm a part of that professional space, because it is often based on identity as opposed to skills and knowledge. It's hard sometimes. I worked for a cultural institution, a position I initially was not interested in, but when I was appointed, I had a sense the people who worked there believed I only was hired for the job based on my ethnicity rather than my skills, experience and knowledge. I found this really disappointing, as my challenge became to overprove and overwork … It goes back to race becoming an issue as opposed to just being a person.

Identity, in the context of her employment, became a site of great contention for Danielle. On one hand, she expressed her naïveté about her desire to effect change contrasted against being pigeonholed into a role because of her race.[6] Danielle described her frustration with being hired for titles such as 'Aboriginal Officer,' which ironically contributes to the systemic racism that diversity recruitment is meant to defuse. She also talks of her disappointment with most of her colleagues, who were unable to treat her with the same respect they afforded her non-Indigenous counterparts.

Having to constantly navigate uncomfortable situations and toxic conversations, Danielle eventually decided to start her own business: 'I felt like a block of stone, and slowly I was being chipped away at, chipping pieces of who I was, my personality and my identity.' Working on her own afforded Danielle an opportunity to utilize her extensive education, professional experience and skill sets without having those attributes mitigated, questioned or discredited because of her race and nationality.

Her story suggests the challenge is perhaps not just about asking different questions, but also about ensuring that those from diverse backgrounds are wholly incorporated into structures of city-building without the qualifier of identity categories.

Farhiya

What is 'home'? Is home a piece of land? Is home with a group of people? Is home in my heart? Is home where I feel most safe? Is home with my family? I don't know what home is anymore. The places that make me most happy are where I gravitate toward, and sometimes that doesn't look like traditional notions of home. Sometimes that looks like performing spoken-word onstage. Sometimes that looks like showing my graphic art online.

I don't know where my home is, and that's part of the third-culture complex. How do you navigate when you don't feel like you belong here and you don't feel like you belong there. Where do you belong?

Farhiya's narrative captures the struggles of being a third-culture person – like others in this essay – and reinforces important questions for future city-builders: how do we meet the needs of a population living between worlds? And how do these acts of living affect the cultures of which that population is a product?[7]

One result of globalization, where we see mass movement of people across places, is that conventional ideas of belonging – particularly in the context of citizenship – are undergoing a conceptual crisis as an emerging generation grapples to find words to express identities that evade the language of traditional group affiliations.

Contrary to the suggestion that third-culture people are uprooted, however, Farhiya did not express any confusion about who she was or where she fit in. Instead, she spoke with clarity about her identity within this third space, as well as of the need to make a place for herself and for others emerging from this culture. As a cultural border-crosser, Farhiya outlined her activism as a process of survival and healing and an act of solidarity and creative production in places where she feels ejected. It is a process as painful as it is aspirational.

Farhiya immigrated to Toronto with her family as a young girl from Somalia in 1990, right before the outbreak of the Somali Civil War. She describes her arrival to a largely white community as both socially and culturally violent. In her schooling experience in particular, her status as an outsider was crudely reinforced by both teachers and students.[8] Farhiya recounts being referred to as a 'slow and stupid student' during elementary school, largely because of a vision impairment that went unnoticed until Grade 2. Further, she had to confront racial epithets, and her religious and cultural practices – celebrating Eid, dressing in traditional clothing, eating Somali food – were often met with hostility and ridicule.

As more Somali people migrated to an area in the west Toronto suburb of Etobicoke famously known as Dixon City,[9] Farhiya noticed a change in geography, marked by the appearance of coffee shops and Somali restaurants, as well as the flight of smaller businesses and shopping markets that couldn't cater to the changing ethnic and economic demographic of the community.

Farhiya speaks of Somalia as a nation of poets who cope with trauma and tragedy through storytelling and social organizing. In this way, she describes the function of coffee shops in particular as social and cultural sites of connection in a community with few public spaces in which to gather. This spatial reconfiguration is coupled in her accounting by the poor treatment of her community, who were both exploited and marginalized by unwelcoming and inhospitable establishments.

Living in a city where the racialized are made to feel unwanted resulted in a strong identification with her Somali origins. However, Farhiya's return to Somalia decades later proved painful, as she not only experienced similar patterns of exclusion, but also had to come to terms with the ways in which her country of settlement had shaped her identification as Canadian.

> I am hesitant to claim the Canadian nationality because I am made to feel like I don't belong here, so much so that I cling to my Somali flag. As much as I like to dismiss my Canadian-ness, I'm very Canadian. When I'm in Somalia, the social norms and cultural practices – it's hard for me to accept them because I'm Canadian.
>
> And that's the dilemma: where the home you're in now, you don't belong here, and your native home, you don't belong there either. So there's this third identity that has been given birth to. It's painful.

Farhiya exercises activism vigorously both online and off-line. Shortly before her visit to Somalia in 2013, she began a journey of self-discovery and healing by sharing her story of survival online. Survival for Farhiya – her persistence in existing – is an act of resistance in the face of what she refers to as several layers of trauma, from mental illness and the brutality of being 'othered,' to sexual violence and bullying.

Farhiya describes the backlash that frequently accompanies her resistance, particularly within the Somali community, where survivors are pressured to stay silent and perpetrators of sexual violence are protected through the shaming of their victims. In response, Farhiya starts many such socially forbidden conversations, which she hosts across her social media platforms; through her artistic practice, which gives Somali women priority; and in the production of workshops that facilitate the management of violence and trauma through creative production and self-care.

Unlike the sorts of networks we envision in cities, which are connected through physical infrastructure, Farhiya points out the ways in which off-line infrastructure lacks the capacity to accommodate the global rearrangements of our social world.

> *I was very lonely for many years. It was a decade in silence. But once I shared my story, it went out to parts of the world where I didn't think they would feel my pain, and I'm always meeting young girls who are doing big things. How can we work together, how can we collaborate? I created beautiful networks because of that.*
>
> *I'm in a place on my platform, where, if I ever need something, such as a person with a specific skill set, nine out of ten times I'll get contacted. We're so isolated, but social media is connecting us together. I have so many activist supporter friends who are in different pockets of the world, and we are pushing these topics out as a community.*

Farhiya is quick to point out the ways her online work informs and inspires her work off-line, whether it is through the production of art or the facilitation of workshops. Her work as an educator and artist can't be clearly distinguished from her activism. Her curation of online space is a response to the absence of diverse representations of Somali women in particular, as well as the lack of welcoming physical spaces in the city to accommodate Black bodies more generally.

Online, Farhiya describes the safety of creation blended with the physical landscape of 'back home' – 'it's both land and imagination.' I would argue that this spatial blending, which is the creative place-making of a third space, underscores the cultural crisis facing global cities. In thinking about building for the future, Farhiya cites the need for non-profit shared spaces for marginalized communities – for example, the Nia Centre for the Arts and the TAIBU Community Health

Centre in Toronto – to be commonplace rather than anomalies. She also expresses her frustration with the lack of public resources available to conduct the work of place-making, particularly after she turned thirty, when she could no longer access funding set aside for 'youth.'

Considering the 'public' as society and, more broadly, the global community, Farhiya's desire to build physical infrastructure that is as dynamic and creative as its digital counterpart points to the gap between the economic, social and cultural worlds across which we imagine and live out our spaces *as* place. Within this context, I envision her labour, both online and off-line, as a public service in the interest of building more inclusive, creative and healthy communities.

'Diversity Is Our Strength'

To say that diversity is our strength – as Toronto repeatedly does – makes an assertion that runs contrary to our innate discomfort with change. Difference requires us to change how we interact with others who are, by definition, not like us. It means we are often uncomfortable, anxious, stressed, displaced, uncertain or afraid of unpredictability when interacting with people from places, cultures and social spaces with which we are unfamiliar.

Diversity that doesn't begin with confronting the pain of change can't acquire strength.

While this sample of conversations isn't sufficient to determine a pattern, the subtext suggests that the turn of some toward group identification (which also guards against difference) is influenced by the reaction of other groups to difference and change. This reaction, when conditioned by fear and informed by histories of occupation, frames the person in the position of 'difference' as a danger or a threat at worst, and at best as an unpleasantness.

For those frequently brown and Black bodies at the receiving end of this response, group identification operates as a survival mechanism against the violence of rejection and ejection. It will be vital for future diversity planning to view group attachments and their accompanying identity categories not just as personal descriptors but as a response to the hostility that diversity can foster.

For Harvard political theorist and urban planning scholar Susan Fainstein, diversity as a guiding principle for city planners – not just in Toronto but across the globe – is taken for granted, often at expense of democracy, equity, growth and sustainability.[10] In her theory of the 'just city,' Fainstein explains that these sets of values are necessary to human development and that often a focus on diversity over other areas results in trade-offs. For example, she notes that diversity could be at odds with democracy if group interests outweigh common interests and that economic growth, especially when tied to urban revitalization, does not presuppose social equality. For Fainstein, it is vital to foster our capacities in all areas – within national policy contexts – to create the conditions for a just city.

If we think about the ways that communities are constituted not through traditional identity categories, but through more diffuse and circumstantial conditions of membership, diversity planning can be engaged in as a process toward a just city, rather than as a tool or an endgame. This undertaking is not just about the distribution of the majority versus the minority, nor is it a blunt analytical instrument at the scale of the city;[11] rather it is about the ways we move between and within the contexts of the personal, professional, social and cultural spaces we occupy.

These four stories, graciously shared by Abu Zaid, Avi, Danielle and Farhiya, serve as a foil to Toronto's slogan 'Diversity is our strength,' by exemplifying the ways that the official notion of diversity as a singular, monolithic concept is belied by the messiness of identity. Diversity, then, is neither a strength nor a weakness, neither an asset nor a deficiency. Rather, it is an intricate, manifold sense of self and other, with the capacity to both liberate and contain. Within this context, stories, as a method of inquiry, engage not just with the *stuff* of diversity, but also the very psyche of what is urban. If we pay closer attention to the stories we tell ourselves and the stories that others tell us about city life, perhaps we can begin to tap into the rich experiential resource of diversity, in all its complexity.

Doing Immigrant Resettlement Right
Doug Saunders

For five decades and for almost two million immigrants, Greater Toronto got lucky: it became the world's premier urban immigration success story, almost without trying. People arrived from places of poverty and found just the right kind of housing at the right price point in the right neighbourhoods with the right economy. Governments helped, but Toronto's success was mostly self-built by the immigrants and their children. Yet in coming decades, and for the next millions of newcomers, Greater Toronto will have to get skilled. In its policy, urban planning, transportation, education and architecture, the Toronto of the current century will have to work much harder to turn itself into the ideal landing pad it was during the last one.

Throughout the twentieth century, and especially after World War II, Toronto's inner core became a profoundly successful machine for the integration and inclusion of large communities of immigrants. Hundreds of thousands of people, often arriving from rural poverty, came to the city from southern and eastern Europe, southern China, the Indian subcontinent and the Caribbean. They followed a familiar pattern within the city's quilt of ethnic neighbourhoods – 'arrival cities,' as I describe these immigrant-created cities within cities.

They settled, in clusters of similar ethnicity and language, into the then-unfashionable Victorian and Edwardian housing districts downtown. Taking advantage of relatively low property prices, these newcomers first rented and then purchased their dilapidated housing – immigrants to Toronto were overwhelmingly likely to buy housing. Taking advantage of lightly enforced planning, zoning and licencing practices, they set up shops, restaurants, rental ventures and an impressive range of businesses in their residential districts, often right in their houses. These dense, low-cost districts happened to be immediately adjacent to large middle-class neighbourhoods, which provided both employment and consumers, so the immigrants' small-business ventures were often successful. They used the rising value of their houses, the stable salaries of their blue-collar jobs and the successes of their businesses to finance the post-secondary education of their children and often a move into the suburbs. So the Poles, Italians, Greeks, Chinese, Indians, Portuguese, Pakistanis, Vietnamese and Trinidadians frequently found themselves entering the middle class within one generation, if not sooner.

Paradoxically, the very success of this twentieth-century Toronto model has now rendered it all but inaccessible to many of the immigrants of the twenty-first century. No longer are the high-density red-brick districts of downtown Toronto an affordable bargain for new immigrants. (Even though immigrants today tend to start at an income and education level higher than those of their earlier predecessors, they still generally start out poor and lacking in resources by Canadian standards.) The arrival cities of our century are now overwhelmingly located in the suburbs – and especially the slab-apartment suburbs of Etobicoke, North York, Scarborough, York Region and especially Peel Region. These places have become the landing pads for almost all new immigrants to Greater Toronto and, therefore, for almost half the immigrants who come to Canada each year.

Those districts have formed quilts of low-income immigration-settlement communities, often organized by language, culture and place of origin, just as the classic downtown neighbourhoods were. Both immigration and poverty, in Greater Toronto, are now suburban phenomena. Research by University of Toronto urbanist David Hulchanski shows that in 'downtown' Toronto today (i.e., in the pre-amalgamation City of Toronto), 28 percent of residents are foreign-born and 82 percent are white. In the inner suburbs, 60 percent are foreign-born and 34 percent are white – an almost complete reversal of the pattern of the postwar decades.

Downtown, almost 40 percent of families earn more than $100,000 a year and six out of ten have university educations. In the inner suburbs, only 10 percent have six-figure family incomes and three in ten have university degrees. This income disparity is not necessarily a fixed attribute, though; assuming that much of the poverty of the suburbs is immigrant poverty rather than the more intractable inter-generational poverty of the native-born, these low incomes may be seen as an initial step on the ladder of economic integration. In fact, historically, the low incomes of first-generation immigrants have generally been transitory. The process of arrival involves passing through a period of low income and education, typically for one generation (and sometimes for two), before these families build up the social and actual capital, the education and employment and business success, necessary to obtain the more secure and sustainable incomes and educations of established middle-class Torontonians.

This was the path followed by the waves of new Torontonians of the last century, anyway. Yet that path may not be as easy to follow for current immigrants. They are not just entering a new suburbanized geography; these newcomers must also find work in a service-oriented and often informalized economy. The secure working-class labour that gave many last-century new Torontonians their start – jobs that came with long-term employment guarantees, pensions and wages capable of supporting a mortgage – is far less prevalent in Ontario's post-industrial economy: while 70 percent of employed Canadians still hold secure full-time jobs, immigrants often start in less secure service-industry employment. Likewise, the entrepreneurial opportunities that gave a great many immigrant families their platform for success are less easy to find in the suburbanized geography that awaits today's immigrants. There is a risk that the current tranches of newcomers may not be able to experience the rapid social and economic mobility of earlier arrivals, or, in the worst case, that some might become trapped in spaces of intergenerational poverty, failed economic and spatial integration, and continued isolation from the established economic and social networks of Toronto.

Immigration as a Trajectory

Avoiding these fates requires a new way of thinking about the immigration experience: not as a fixed and static point, or a landing, but rather as a dynamic trajectory, one that leads from some place of origin – a village or city in another country – through the 'arrival city' district and its economies, into an imagined destination within the established city, with its fully realized economic, educational, political and cultural life. This dotted line is a tangible reality in the minds of most immigrants. Because international immigration is an expensive, disruptive and risky endeavour for individuals and families at any income level, it is rarely undertaken without a specific plan and set of ambitions in mind.

To ensure that the new, suburbanized arrival city can be as successful as the old, downtown one, it's worth thinking about the integration experience as a trajectory that can be interrupted if the required resources are absent or inadequate. Immigrants may seek to integrate themselves, but that mission can be derailed, with profoundly disruptive results.

The factors that make an urban neighbourhood ideal as an accessible bottom rung on the ladder of urban integration – in particular, factors that have given that very neighbourhood unusually low housing costs – often later become obstacles that prevent future upward mobility. This is especially true with the inner-suburb immigration experience, in which settlement occurs in surroundings that feature low population densities, limited transportation links and sparse public resources, and that are designed for bedroom-community automobile commuters rather than entrepreneurial new immigrants. In these neighbourhoods, policy and institutional barriers collude with the poorly designed physical environment to prevent isolated migrant residents from progressing beyond a phase of arrival and survival.

Here is where policy interventions can be most successful: identifying missing rungs and then improving the factors that caused them to be missing. A one-time policy intervention intended to remove a barrier to the long trajectory of integration can restore the pathways of social and economic mobility, and the processes of social and political inclusion. Such interventions are considerably less costly than the future multigenerational price of dealing with communities suffering from failed integration and entrenched marginalization.

The Barriers to Success

Immigrants need dense, high-intensity neighbourhoods
Integration takes place, first and foremost, at the neighbourhood level. When immigrants arrive in a new city, they gravitate to neighbourhoods with affordable housing, access to economic

opportunities and networks of established migrants from the same country, region or culture who can assist with settlement and integration.

Due to the 'suburbanization of migration,' many migrants settle in neighbourhoods that feature broad clearances between buildings; long, winding streets; and large courtyards with unmonitored entry points. In these districts, strict postwar zoning regulations segregate residential, commercial and industrial areas, leaving vacant buffer zones between them. Empty corridors and blocked sightlines foster a perception of danger, deterring the social and commercial activity of residents, especially women.

Empty spaces can become sites of illegal and threatening behaviour, gangs and extremism. These insecure conditions discourage migrants from making the property improvements or small-business investments that advance their integration (and such housing developments are usually all-rental, with no pathway to ownership, further discouraging investment and improvement). Safe environments for investment require not only secure multi-use spaces and a community-sourced police force, but also sufficient density.

The low density of these neighbourhoods, however, hinders both entrepreneurial activity and the access to public transit upon which many newcomers rely. This reality is glaringly evident in the most distinctly Canadian form of housing, the suburban slab-apartment complex, which has become the premier form of settlement housing in the new century. Greater Toronto has over 2,000 of these 1960s and 1970s towers in its periphery, and they have become the signature landing pads for new immigrants.

Such 'tower in the park' developments – a form made famous by the Swiss architect Le Corbusier – are popular with immigrants for their large, clean apartments. But their built form creates serious obstacles. They are typically located at such distances from employment zones and each other that they prevent vibrant economic and social networks from flourishing. Without increased density, these suburban or high-rise districts are unlikely to benefit from better transit options, which help migrants access distant labour markets, or increased foot traffic, which sustains immigrant entrepreneurs. There is plenty of evidence that this generation of suburban immigrants are seeking small-business spaces: the 1950s-era two-storey strip malls that often populate these neighbourhoods have become thriving sites of polyglot commerce, culture, food service and social activity. With greater density and better transit, these retail footholds could become the next generation's equivalent to Spadina Avenue's Chinatown or College Street's Little Italy: places that draw people from across the metropolis.

Immigrants need spaces they can reshape and transform

The adaptation of urban property for multiple uses – residential, retail, light industrial and food service, often simultaneously – is central to the experience of immigrant success. Immigrants may transform a formerly residential-only street into a food-service, retail and residential street; the lower floor of an apartment block into a commercial and service-office space; a corner or public square into informal retail in the form of a market. And these uses may change over time as the economic shape of the community, and its interface with the larger urban economy and social life, shifts and adapts.

These transformations are far less easy to execute in the suburban arrival city. Building complexes often lack either the physical spaces or the land-use permissions to transform space in this way, so building permits and business licences may be hard to obtain. What's more, the low population density of these developments and their (related) dearth of frequent public-transit connections means they lack the density of customer traffic to make most street-level businesses economically sustainable.

Toronto's 'Tower Renewal' zoning category, introduced in 2013 and intended to allow variances that permit apartment-building developers and owners to create 'density between,' in the form of low-rise housing, commercial and retail construction with comparatively loose zoning restrictions, is a crucial remedy to such barriers and an intervention worth encouraging. After three years, it's not yet clear whether private-sector developers are responding to this opportunity by investing in infill density in their own developments. If the relaxation of zoning through Tower Renewal proves insufficient, it is worth looking at policies that would provide more direct incentives for developers to intensify and build up density on their existing properties – both for the sake of transit growth, and for the sake of more successful communities for newcomers and established residents alike.

Immigrants need a pathway to ownership

Ownership of housing and property can underpin newcomers' successful integration, which explains why property ownership rates among immigrants often exceed those of non-immigrants; home ownership has been the chief route to middle-class stability for Canadian immigrants for more than a century. As a result, the gentrification of Toronto's classic 'ethnic' neighbourhoods was mostly beneficial to formerly poor immigrants, who were able to participate in the housing-value increase and use it to their advantage and their children's. These benefits, however, require access to property markets, or at least a combination of secure tenure and mechanisms that capture increases in land value. The reality is that the new suburban arrival city has far fewer pathways to ownership. Rental-only complexes (both in private-sector and social housing) predominate, while average home prices almost everywhere are beyond the reach of non-elite immigrants.

It is time to start viewing the inaccessible housing market as a serious barrier to integration, and make a concerted effort to overcome it, by creating pathways to ownership through flexible loan instruments and incentives to establish ownership paths in rental and social housing; by offering incentives to construct lower-price housing in suburban districts; by introducing requirements, as seen in other cities, to include a proportion of affordable housing in all new condo developments; and by making lower-cost housing part of the larger initiative to increase population density in inner-suburban arrival-city districts.

Immigrants need transit connections

For migrants to integrate rather than simply settle, they need physical access to the city's resources. A targeted transportation intervention to increase migrants' access to urban centres can remove long-term barriers to social mobility.

A transit journey of an hour or more, involving multiple modes of public transportation with unreliable connections and unpredictable arrival times, can have a sequence of detrimental effects. The residential segregation created by poor transit connections has been shown to increase dramatically the likelihood and duration of unemployment. Children of parents who do manage to make these commutes often cope with limited sources of support and education, and the lack of convenient transit connections also reduces access to the educational and cultural resources of the established city. These factors conspire to create preconditions for social and economic isolation, discourage second-generation integration and stall social mobility.

Transportation links are not used only for residents of the neighbourhood to seek work and education. A significant element of the migrant districts' success, given their typical emphasis on consumer-focused small business, is their ability to attract shoppers, diners and potential tenants. The classic Toronto ethnic neighbourhoods of the twentieth century were often ideally situated to attract passing foot and vehicle traffic from more prosperous districts; this was greatly aided by that era's public-transit system, centred on the streetcar (which extended into 'streetcar suburbs' such as southern Etobicoke, the Beach, Riverdale and Parkdale). Today's suburban immigrant districts, which do not benefit from this positioning, will have a hard time developing these economies until they are given strong transit systems and careful marketing: rather than warning people away from these new immigrant districts, the city should be encouraging Torontonians, and tourists, to spend time in them.

Immigrants need excellent health clinics

New immigrant communities, which have endured the considerable strains of an international migration (and in some cases the traumas of having escaped war and violence), rely heavily on public health systems. Due not only to migrants' backgrounds, but also their initially scarce resources, access to preventative medicine, public health, nutrition, psychiatric counselling and other services is crucial for their family stability and, in some cases, employability. Active public health and preventative medicine outreach to new immigrant communities can be especially effective and valuable – particularly with vulnerable populations, like some immigrant women, who tend to be overlooked by traditional health systems. Research has shown that health outreach services tailored to immigrants can significantly reduce the expensive overuse of emergency-room services and allow hospitals to function more efficiently.

Immigrants need great public libraries

In the post-paper age, public libraries have become de facto centres of integration and inclusion in Toronto: they are busier and more crucial than ever, and they are especially heavily used by new Canadians, for whom the library has become a central institution of acculturation, network formation and education. Studies in other Western countries have shown that a strong majority of new immigrant families make regular use of the library. And they use it for purposes specifically related to the needs of integration: connection to public services, formation of networks of mutual support, accumulation of fundamental cultural and linguistic knowledge and the education of their children, who may rely heavily on library computers if their parents haven't amassed enough wealth to purchase their own systems.

Immigrants need better-than-average schools

The families of immigrants who come to Canada have often fared much better, economically and culturally, than families from the same places who have migrated to European cities, in large part because their children have stayed in school. When immigrants attain educational integration – that is, they have the same average level of education as the native-born population – the impediments to cultural and social integration fall away.

But the phenomenon of 'second-generation decline,' in which the native-born children of immigrants fail to achieve the economic and integration outcomes of their parents, occurs when the male children of immigrants (for this is most often a gendered problem) leave secondary school prematurely, often at the youngest possible age. This disengagement from educational institutions usually occurs because schools, with their inflexible structures, provide some second-generation youth with strong incentives to leave the system, by separating them from their more ambitious peers, systematically sorting immigrant kids into vocational streams or ignoring their particular needs with teaching geared to a single, homogeneous education level. Such inflexibility is a significant problem in Western Europe, where second-generation early school-leaving is prevalent; there, these young men without high school completion frequently fall into economic marginality, black-market economies, petty criminality and sometimes extremism. They often appear to become less culturally integrated than their parents, retreating into atavistic cultural patterns as a defence mechanism.

Greater Toronto's schools have generally been adept at circumventing this fate, in large part by being attentive to the educational needs of diverse populations. They've avoided the most damaging educational practices, abandoning the early separation of students into vocational streams. They no longer hold underperforming students back, but advance them by age rather than aptitude. They have a greater prevalence of practices in which multiple teachers and teaching assistants offer lessons at multiple educational levels (though these practices are now being challenged by reduced budgets). And GTA schools have learned, as have most Toronto residents, that teaching practices aimed at students with mixed levels of linguistic and educational attainment work better for all students. Research in Canada and the U.S. has shown that English-fluent children who attend classes with significant numbers of non-fluent students experience better educational outcomes than those who attend all-fluent classes. The reason? Such schools devote more resources to teaching at varied education levels and with varied learning styles within the same class, which tends to be good practice in all contexts.

Still, there is a risk that Toronto-area schools in arrival-city neighbourhoods could fall prey to a phenomenon seen in many immigrant districts in the West: a spiral of educational decline, in which the neighbourhood's more ambitious students, both immigrant and native-born, are transferred by parents to better schools in middle-class neighbourhoods, leaving behind those with fewer resources and aptitudes. In some cities, this leads to lower-quality teachers being drawn to the original schools, causing the cycle of decline to repeat and intensify unless it is interrupted. Toronto has experience both with this phenomenon of decline and with successful interventions to improve it, as seen in institutions such as the former Castle Frank High School (rebranded in the 1990s as Rosedale School of the Arts).

Education ministries in Britain, Germany and elsewhere have learned that this cycle of decline can be reversed with large-scale interventions, such as establishing 'magnet schools' in low-income immigrant neighbourhoods that have extra resources beyond those available to schools serving middle-class areas. These magnet schools then begin to attract students from better-off neighbourhoods, creating a more diverse social mix as well as a sense that second-generation students are competing to gain admission to their school rather than to leave it. Interventions on this scale are needed to prevent second-generation decline; they also carry educational benefits for the entire city.

Immigrants need to do business easily

For generations of Toronto immigrants, the pathway to inclusion and integration led not just through employment but alternately (and often also) through small businesses. The visible quilt of shops, markets, restaurants and services in the classic immigrant neighbourhood were instruments of success and investment, and often led to larger enterprises. Some of Canada's best-known corporations – e.g., the Sorbara Group, a major developer, or the auto-parts giant Linamar Inc. – began as new-immigrant ventures. The prospect of entrepreneurial success is even more important for twenty-first-century immigrants, who often don't have the access to the kind of permanent full-time blue-collar employment their predecessors enjoyed. So the small-business career path is often the preferred one, especially since many immigrant families come from small-business backgrounds in their countries of origin. But that option is becoming increasingly difficult in Toronto.

Starting a business, even a small one, is never simply a matter of hanging out a sign and waiting for customers. Entrepreneurs first need to obtain a commercial property lease, frequently a tax registration, often a business licence and sometimes a land-use variance from the municipal government.

These challenges can be onerous for established citizens seeking to go into business; for some new immigrants, often without full citizenship and frequently lacking in financial resources or existing connections to business networks, these bureaucratic hurdles can be very challenging at the best of times. Toronto's banks are comparatively enthusiastic about supporting new-immigrant businesses – the big banks often compete to get immigrant business even before families emigrate – and while government agencies and city hall are relatively accessible to small business ventures, the costs of and institutional barriers to starting a business have escalated.

Overly rigid planning rules introduced in recent decades prevent entrepreneurs from starting new businesses in many residential locations. Stringent building-code and public-health regulations often pose unnecessarily rigid obstacles to entrepreneurship (the ban on operating food trucks within a few hundred metres of restaurants, for example, or the requirement to purchase a ventilation system costing tens of thousands of dollars, present enormous barriers to the classic entry-level forms of immigrant food-service ventures). Officials should consider relaxing small-business regulations in immigrant-heavy districts in order to make these areas both more prosperous and more inviting to visitors and prospective entrepreneurs. Many of the most successful immigrant-launched corporations of the twentieth century would never have made it off the ground under today's stringent licencing codes.

Immigrants need non-segregated surroundings

The neighbourhood-level racial segregation that defined U.S. cities was largely absent from Canada in the late twentieth century. There were certainly exceptions: older Toronto neighbourhoods had been developed with restrictive covenants that prevented the sale of homes to non-whites or Jews, practices that continued to near the end of the century, and older Chinese-Canadian districts such as the Ward were products of racial exclusion as much as self-selected community building. Generally, though, while non-white Torontonians were generally poorer, it was because they were mainly recent immigrants to Canada from the Caribbean, Asia and Africa, as compared to African Americans, who were a historically subjugated population living in segregated conditions. Racial dividing lines, in Canadian cities, tended not to be defined by either strict geographic barriers or a history of slavery and institutionalized racism.

The new Toronto arrival city, however, is a far more racially and economically sorted place than it was two generations ago after Canada adopted a colour-blind immigration system. Increasingly, Toronto has evolved into a city with a largely white core and a racialized periphery. This shift is not the product of 'white flight' to the suburbs or the overt racial housing discrimination seen in U.S. cities, but rather of property-market conditions and the relative income levels of newcomers and established Canadians. The region's recent immigrants, who tend to be visible minorities with less income, often land initially in the arrival-city districts of the inner suburbs.

While this immigrant settlement pattern should be transitory, as for previous generations of newcomers regardless of race, it runs the risk of turning into a permanent form of racial segregation because residential housing markets have become inaccessible to many newcomers.

Is the Toronto region moving towards a permanent form of racial segregation according to income and neighbourhood? It's hard to say, because the formation of ethnic clusters is a traditional and successful part of immigrant establishment; it's when people are concentrated by race, ethnicity or class against their will that this becomes segregation. Unlike in cities with serious segregation problems, both education and employment in Greater Toronto tend to be very multi-racial and multi-ethnic. But there is plenty of evidence of discriminatory attitudes that could lead to dangerous forms of exclusion and isolation if combined with residential and economic barriers to success (the Toronto police 'carding' controversy of 2015 provided ample documented evidence that law enforcement officers disproportionately stopped and searched Black Torontonians). In other words, the effects of market-based housing segregation and immigration may be creating attitudes of active discrimination that could create permanent racial inequalities.

Racialized segregation represents a profound barrier to immigrant inclusion. The physical and institutional obstacles to integration cited in this chapter often arise, in other cities, as concrete manifestations of underlying discrimination. The social instability of a racially divided city must be acknowledged and then confronted directly; responses include the development of more affordable housing within established 'white' neighbourhoods and complexes; investing in transit infrastructure to prevent areas with high concentrations of newcomers and racialized minorities from becoming isolated from the city at large; and developing educational and institutional practices that actively foster inclusion. It's also worth considering practices employed in countries such as France to end 'postal-code racism,' in which neighbourhoods with racialized populations become subjects of discrimination; these measures include laws that forbid job-application forms from requiring applicants to provide addresses or photographs.

Immigrants need a clear and quick pathway to citizenship

Migrants who have some chance of becoming established and legal permanent residents, and eventually citizens, will focus their energies and investments on their communities. They will attempt to purchase housing, launch small businesses, pay taxes and save for the future. They will enroll their children in post-secondary education and attempt to secure other social and economic gains for their families in their new communities.

Conversely, the worst thing a country with immigrant-driven cities can do is to block the path to full legal citizenship. This outcome is repeatedly visible, for example, in the large-scale exclusion – and the lost opportunity for community investment – among Germany's two million 'guest worker' Turks, who had no citizenship option from the 1960s until 2000; or for the twelve million Americans of Latin American origin who lack documentation and therefore are considered 'illegal' and unable to invest. Canada's Temporary Foreign Worker Program, which accounted for half of all immigration during many of the years of Stephen Harper's Conservative government, also posed a real risk of creating permanently excluded immigrants. Torontonians without any citizenship option would not be able to follow the city's well-established, multigenerational path to inclusion. Canadian cities have long thrived on the entrepreneurial and social energy that immigrants bring; it makes no sense to take only their labour and then prevent temporary workers from aspiring to the benefits – for themselves as well as the country – of full citizenship.

Immigrants need to be part of the political system

When immigrants succeed, they become part of the economic, educational and cultural life of the city. But when newcomers establish businesses, find work, secure housing and pay taxes, they also need to be able to participate fully in the political institutions that govern all these activities. Political participation can have a transformative effect on the well-being and integration of immigrant communities; its absence poses a serious barrier to integration. In fact, the ability of immigrant neighbourhoods and communities to self-organize for improvement and acceptance hinges largely on their ability to fully participate in legal and democratic institutions.

Toronto city council's 2013 motion to give municipal voting rights to non-citizen residents was a crucial step and should be adopted by the Ontario government. Non-citizen voting has become standard practice in many European countries, including Britain and most of Scandinavia; it has had a tangible effect on immigrant communities whose members are often making the long transition to citizenship. A study of Sweden's shift to non-citizen voting found that 'the effect of enfranchising noncitizens was large, causing spending on education and social and family services to increase substantially in municipalities where noncitizens made up a non-negligible share of the electorate.'[1]

The next generation of immigrants to Greater Toronto will depend not just on good fortune and their own resources, but also on the broader region's capacity to create the conditions that lead to inclusion. If we want to have another century of immigrants as successful as their predecessors, we must begin by including them, fully and enthusiastically, in all of our institutions; singing the praises of diversity is important, but not sufficient. Almost all our families, at some point in recent history, confronted and then overcame the barriers that newcomers inevitably face. We owe it to coming generations of Torontonians to help them do the same.

Wasauksing–Vancouver–Toronto:
My Path Home
Rebeka Tabobondung

My path back home to the roots of my Anishinabek (Ojibway) ancestry in Toronto and southern Ontario began on a suffocating bus ride in Vancouver in 1999.

Thick rain clouds had filled me with an unrelenting nausea that didn't let up as I tried to navigate my daily activities. After spending ten years on B.C.'s west coast and ten years before that in Alberta, I felt my body was pulling me home. The sensation could no longer be ignored: it forced me off the bus and I gasped for fresh air, seeking clarity. I was left with a deep urge to head east to the Great Lakes.

I did not grow up within the traditional territories, culture or communities of my Anishinabek ancestry. My mother – a single parent who raised me, my older brother and my younger sister – was born in Holland and, at just a year old, immigrated to Canada with my grandparents. They settled in White Rock, B.C. My dad is Ojibway from Wasauksing First Nation on Georgian Bay, in Lake Huron.

As I grew up, my immediate family was disconnected from the extended family because of the large geographical distances between us. My mother did not instill in me cultural knowledge about my ancestry, and I grew up within a Western, Christian, working-class and Canadian identity. I believe her decision to exclude cultural knowledge from my upbringing was not a conscious one, but a result of her own experience of a colonial childhood and education. Being white afforded her privilege, so she never had to personally struggle or address issues of cultural identity and racism.

When we could afford it, I spent a few summers in Ontario on Parry Island and at Moose Deer Point with my dad. Looking back, I recall whimsical sojourns filled with swimming, frogs, bats and four-wheelers. One year, I danced at a powwow with other young girls my age and beamed with pride. I believed I could dance as well as any of them, but felt left out for not having a shawl or regalia for the dance.

As a teenager, I stopped visiting the reserve and began hearing negative stories about my father's struggles with alcoholism. I became distanced from him, and his lifestyle made it difficult for us to maintain contact. I arrived into adulthood angry and ashamed of my Native identity. Both my West Coast family and my teachers failed to offer any critical analysis about the socio-economic realities of Native communities, or their histories, cultures or contributions to humanity. At school, I heard only racist stereotypes about Native peoples.

Through these years, I lived in fifteen different towns and cities throughout Ontario, Alberta and B.C. From the time I entered kindergarten until I was expelled from high school in Grade 10, in fact, I attended nine different public schools. In elementary school, I was taught the history of the homesteaders of Alberta and about the slaughter of the buffalo for the fur trade and to make way for farming. I had already figured out that not being white was a disadvantage, but being Native meant you weren't a homesteader at all.

On one school trip to a replica homesteader village, I found it difficult to imagine myself in the past wearing a lacy bonnet with a long, floral-patterned dress and tall black boots. Rather, being Native meant this is what I was not – I should instead imagine myself as something wild, like the buffalo. Although I knew I was not from the Plains – my Ojibway family are water people from the Great Lakes – I still enjoyed this fantasy. But the photographs of buffalo skulls piled high on the prairie in my textbooks were a stark reminder that the Native way of life was long over, too.

These feelings of alienation were not new. Reflecting back on my experiences within the public school system, I see that my Native identity was completely severed from who I was. My mixed ancestry afforded me light-skin privilege, yet I felt isolated from both the white and local Native communities at my Vancouver Island high school. I convinced some of my classmates that I was Hawaiian or Spanish rather than admit my Native ancestry. I felt both pride and humiliation about my identity, but I shared that secret with no one.

In August of 1999, I bought a one-way plane ticket to Canada's biggest city. I didn't know a single person in Toronto, but I intended to make connections there with the Indigenous part of my ancestry.

It may seem paradoxical to seek these links in a giant metropolitan region, but finding a place within Toronto's Indigenous community was easy. I met people from a diversity of First Nations, and they welcomed me with familiar and familial arms. I felt at home for the first time in my life.

When I enrolled in the University of Toronto's Aboriginal Studies program, I brought with me with a heightened understanding of Native history. By then, I had travelled extensively throughout Central America, living with Indigenous peoples and learning about their histories and ways of life, as well as the thirty-six-year civil war and the murderous military repression of the Indigenous populations of Guatemala, atrocities that had ended only the year before I visited, in 1996. Those experiences fostered a deep skepticism of the mainstream media, corporate interests and dominant accounts of history. Upon returning, I'd sought out Aboriginal Elders, storytellers and activists, who taught me about the 'founding' of Canada from an Aboriginal perspective – a history also tainted by atrocities committed and justi-fied by settler society against Indigenous Peoples in Canada.[1]

At U of T, I was elected president of the Native Students' Association and met the late community visionary and leader Rodney Bobiwash, an Anishinabek man from the Mississauga First Nation who became a good friend and mentor. Director of the Centre for World Indigenous Studies in Toronto, Bobiwash was also the co-founder of the Toronto Native Community History Project (now called First Story and housed at the Native Canadian Centre of Toronto on Spadina Road, where I have volunteered for many years). I also became the librarian at the First Nations House Library at U of T, where I met my partner, an amateur historian and graphic designer from Rama First Nation.

Our son, Zeegwon, is a descendent of Chief William Yellowhead, Sr., who was mortally wounded during the War of 1812 and is buried at what is known as Sandhill Indian burial mound, located near Yonge and Bloor in the heart of downtown Toronto. As head chief, he kept the great wampum belt that recorded the final peace between the Ojibway and the Six Nations Iroquois (Haudenosaunee).

Before Zeegwon was born, I rented a house close to the Don River and went for many walks and bike rides along its shores, and made tobacco offerings for the water. One day, walking along the Don, I spontaneously began to breathe quietly and sing what felt like a traditional song. There was no explanation: the song just came, and it was beautiful.

The stories beneath the city continued to surface. As I explored the streets of Toronto with local Native historians, I could sense the power of the land under the concrete. This was our land: the bones of our ancestors were long buried here. The imprint of their power still meandered through the city's rivers and under its street grid.

Before contact, Spadina Avenue was known as Ishpadinaa, an Ojibway word that means 'going up the hill.' When I passed by Toronto's many homeless Native people, they'd give me a knowing 'Hey, sister' nod that left me feeling the power of their humanity. Though homeless, they belonged here more than anyone. It is ancestral power that reverberates through the land and our blood.

Long before local politicians began touting the city's ethnocultural diversity, Toronto had a deep history of traditional settlement from many First Nations. Today, the Anishinabek say the territory belongs to the Mississaugas of the New Credit because they had long-established territories and settlements in the area at the time of contact, and were the main signatories to the Toronto Purchase of 1787.

However, for my friends who claim Haudenosaunee ancestry, it is important for them to also acknowledge their connection and birthright to this land, and the presence of their Indigenous ancestors here. There are also many Haudenosaunee burial mounds throughout Toronto and Scarborough.

It's deeply poignant to me that Toronto was a 'Gathering Place' for many diverse Indigenous nations. Imagine an abundance of well-managed forest and agricultural land filled with food sources and vast networks of rivers that offered easy travel between portage narrows located along what are now known as Lake Ontario, Lake Huron,

Lake Simcoe and Lake Couchiching. Over the course of tens of thousands of years, Indigenous nations established flourishing settlements throughout the Greater Toronto Area.

Just as it was appealing to the first white settlers who walked upon its shorelines, the land offered Indigenous communities access to networking, trade routes and alliance-building. Multiple Anishinabek and Haudenosaunee First Nations established Toronto as a hub for trade, commerce and cultural exchange – a reflection, through time, of the identity of the culturally and ethnically diverse city of today.

The name 'Toronto' originates from the Kanien'kehé:ka word *tkaronto*, which means 'the place in the water where the trees are standing.' The reference is said to come from Haudenosaunee and Huron-Wendat fishers who posted stakes for fishing weirs in the narrows of the river systems, many of which are now paved over. Building fish weirs was an important gathering activity for the area's many Indigenous peoples. Yet as historian Heather Howard-Bobiwash points out, the name took on the broader metaphorical significance of a place where many diverse people come together to meet on positive terms.[2]

While strong local Indigenous presence and critical military alliances during the War of 1812 contributed to the founding of the City of Toronto, and Canada as a nation, Native history has been erased and replaced with a mythical colonial narrative justified by racist doctrines of discovery. The result is a great disconnect for settler Torontonians regarding the city's Indigenous roots and the subsequent perpetuation of negative stereotypes.

In the dominant histories, Indigenous peoples appear only when it is convenient for Canadians to build, justify and maintain their own imagined identity. For example, at the time of first contact, the land known as Canada is described as *terra nullius*, or 'empty land.' The phrase is a Latin expression and legal theory that derived from a 1095 papal bull, *Terra Nullius*, which allowed Christian European states to claim land occupied by non-Christians. Within this legal fiction, European powers asserted 'title' to the territories of what we now call Canada, disregarding the Indigenous nations that were already living there.[3]

As generations of schoolchildren were taught, First Peoples seemed to just appear and participate during the fur-trade era. Somehow, the Hudson Bay Company already held title to the vast expanse of Rupert's Land, which it sold to Britain to form the Dominion of Canada. When the fur-trade era ended, the Indigenous Peoples disappeared from history texts again, only to reappear two hundred years later in B.C. tourism advertisements, shoddy government inquiries and homeless, on the streets of a G-8 nation. There is no mention in the textbooks of the devastating cultural genocide of the Indian Act, which forced Indigenous Peoples into the reservation system and children into residential schools.

Cultural invisibility also characterizes the Native presence in Toronto. While the region is home to between 30,000 and 60,000 Aboriginal people, and thus represents one of the largest urban Aboriginal populations in Canada today, the local Aboriginal communities have been submerged in a city with millions of residents who know virtually nothing about them. There is no 'Little Indigenous Town,' no Indigenous-inspired architecture, few public displays of Indigenous culture and history, and only a handful of Indigenous-owned businesses with retail space. Sadly, Toronto's most visible Indigenous Peoples are the homeless and incarcerated populations. According to Andrea Chrisjohn, executive director of Toronto Council Fire Native Cultural Centre, 90 percent of Native homeless people in Toronto are survivors of the forced Indian residential schools.

The urbanized Canadian identity of today is shallow and stunted. While many Torontonians imagine their identities to include universal values of democracy, human rights, diversity and a form of environmentalism intimately connected with the pristine North, they must question the legitimacy of these claims after the historic attacks on Indigenous peoples and culture. There is still a lack of awareness, education and movement toward reconciliation, and of the forging of reciprocal relationships based on equality and respect. In this urban mosaic, Indigenous Canadians are too often regarded as just another cultural group in an immigrant city. But obviously, we have a completely different connection to place, and what's below the concrete. It's a cultural identity that includes concepts of nationhood, sovereignty and a worldview formed across millennia.

In 2014, Toronto city council adopted an historic protocol that for the first time formally recognized that Indigenous peoples were instrumental in the founding of urban places. For decades, Native people were said to have migrated to cities – a myth that served to isolate, stigmatize and reinforce racist tropes. The new protocol, sparked in part by the work of the grassroots Indigenous movement Idle No More, sought to correct the record. Following the singing of the Canadian national anthem, the council speaker now acknowledges that Toronto is the traditional Indigenous territory of the Mississaugas of the New Credit First Nation. The protocol invites citizens to address current power imbalances between Indigenous and non-Indigenous Canadians by honouring and generating awareness about pre-contact peace and friendship treaties that were based on equality and respect.

Such changes mark a larger shift in consciousness taking place across Turtle Island, and an attempt by some to understand and address the negative impacts of colonization. These developments create pathways for new conversations about cultural awareness and education that are connected to building a civic identity rooted in something far deeper than the shallow doctrines of discovery.

When discussion about the new protocol first emerged, Toronto councillor Mike Layton said that he and the other councillors consulted with the Equity and Human Rights Committee, the Aboriginal Affairs Committee and Mississaugas of New Credit Chief Bryan LaForme about the appropriate form for such an acknowledgement.

That conversation continues. Since the protocol was adopted, Idle No More Toronto consulted with Haudenosaunee clan mothers and made a subsequent presentation to the executive committee requesting that council also honour the diverse Indigenous history of Toronto when acknowledging traditional territory. Besides the Anishinabek and the Haudenosaunee, Toronto's Indigenous communities historically included the Wendat (Huron), the Neutrals and

Petun, and now Indigenous people from nations from all over Turtle Island who have come to the city seeking employment, education and new beginnings.

As they continue to build Indigenous spaces in the city, our leaders hold up those original peace and friendship treaties as a source of direction for protocol and governance models. In particular, they cite the One Dish, One Spoon treaty wampum as one of our best examples of respecting cultural diversity while ensuring that the land can take care of us all. Predating the Toronto Purchase, this wampum is an historic peace agreement between the Haudenosaunee and the Anishinabek nations to peaceably share the resources of their adjacent territories in vast regions of the Great Lakes. As the Well Living House Governance states:

> Described as 'one-dish alliances,' these treaties identified a specific area of territory to be held in common. Just as family members ate from 'one dish,' so too would nations eat from one common hunting ground … The concept of 'Dish with One Spoon' is still relevant in contemporary culture with all the nations across Turtle Island; First Nations continue to use a 'one-dish protocol' and request permission from their First Nations neighbors to hunt, fish and trap on their lands. The protocol also allows food and medicines to be harvested, and grants the right to travel across the lands.[5]

This inclusive agreement, which recognizes a deep connection to the land, is still acknowledged by both the Anishinabek and Haudenosaunee peoples. Such a framework could be a great starting point: why not acknowledge the land known today as Greater Toronto as a One Dish, One Spoon treaty territory?

Other cities and municipalities across the country are also looking to acknowledge the Indigenous histories in which they are rooted. Yet protocols aren't enough, and we must beware of tokenism. The protocol should bring about tough conversations, such as how we share the resources and power to construct a new Canadian and Torontonian identity grounded in the truth of Indigenous experience, as well as the values of equity and justice woven into the original peace and friendship treaties.

For Indigenous people living in large urban centres like Greater Toronto, these aren't abstract discussions. As a mixed-blood urban Anishinaabekwe mother with strong ties to my Wasauksing First Nation community three hours north of Toronto, I live and work in the city. I publish an Indigenous arts and culture magazine, *Muskrat*, which unearths traditional knowledge and smashes static and mythical representations of Indigenous peoples. I engage in a project of decolonization personally, politically and academically, and am motivated by my desire to promote positive cultural identity and nation-building. As a parent, I have a vested interest in ensuring that our traditional knowledge is preserved and available to future generations. It is my hope to be able to pass these teachings on to my son and family, giving them the sense of identity and community that I missed when I was growing up.

How We Welcome: Why Canada's Refugee Resettlement Program Undermines Place-making

Sarah Beamish and Sofia Ijaz

We meet for breakfast before work each week, at a café near Queen and Spadina in downtown Toronto.[1] We wake early; we set out; one inevitably forgives the other's late arrival; we hug; we share a plate of food and something hot to drink; we talk about our relationships, our work, our ideas, our plans, ourselves. For this offering of a place for one another in our crowded lives, we are thankful.

During the summer of 2015, our morning discussions often turned to the Syrian refugee crisis. Images of weary-looking Syrians in boats and at borders increasingly filled the news. This grim exodus had gripped us personally. One of us, Sofia, is a brown Muslim woman born to a migrant family and raised in Toronto. She had studied in Syria and ached for the people and places she knew there, growing ever more distressed at the swelling prejudice in public discussions that cast Muslims as dangerous outsiders. The other, Sarah, is a white and Maori woman born and raised in the Prairies. She had faced poverty, overcrowding, evictions and homelessness, and knew how it felt to take on worry and transience as a way of life. We carry these backgrounds with us into our work as young lawyers – Sofia in refugee law, and Sarah in social justice litigation.

It was during one of our breakfasts that we decided to privately sponsor a family of Syrian refugees[2] to resettle in Toronto. This family will be among an estimated 50,000 Syrians expected to arrive in Canada by the end of 2016 – one of the largest resettlement efforts in Canadian history. Most will be resettled in cities. Sponsored refugees, who make up the majority of refugees in Canada, can be brought in by the federal government, or privately by organizations or groups of individuals. Private sponsors commit to providing the refugee with financial, logistical and emotional support for one year, while government-assisted refugees without their own resources may receive income assistance for up to one year, and rely on service agencies for additional support.

Both private and government-assisted sponsorship programs are characterized by a charitable approach. We adopt refugee policy expert Tom Clark's description of charity as 'the giving of rights or benefits by a blend of the discretionary, the arbitrary and political convenience.'[3] The charitable approach emphasizes volunteerism and generosity by the giver (in this case, the sponsor) rather than the entitlements of the recipient (in this case, the refugee). It is true the surge in generosity in response to the Syrian refugee crisis has been exceptional. In particular, private sponsorship requires an extraordinary amount of effort and resources from sponsors and their networks. With our own sponsorship, we have been moved by support from over seventy-five people, sometimes given in honour of a loved one, in the midst of unemployment or from people we have never met.

Yet, as commendable as this generosity is, shortcomings of the charity model are apparent when we view resettlement outcomes from a place-making perspective. By place-making, we mean the creation of 'good places' – places of living, working, playing, learning and public engagement that create a foundation for lives of dignity, security and promise.

This perspective is especially relevant in the context of refugee resettlement, which is fundamentally about place: it is, in part, an attempt to heal the wounds caused by catastrophic losses of place through integration into and creation of new places. We believe the goal of sponsorship should be to help create the conditions in which refugees can feel a sense of 'good place' here. These include fair admission and integration policies, decent and affordable housing in comfortable neighbourhoods, welcoming communities, appropriate educational and job opportunities, economic security and socio-cultural integration.[4]

From a place-making perspective, some resettlement outcomes in Canada are very concerning, particularly when disaggregated by factors like gender, age and race.[5] While thousands of refugees have built stable lives and thriving communities here,[6] a large and growing number struggle in precarious and impoverished conditions that persist for years after their arrival. For example, since the early 1980s, refugees have faced greater challenges with economic integration, discrimination and poverty, with an increasing number living in substandard housing in racially segregated and poor neighbourhoods.[7] Some of the reasons for these declining outcomes are located outside the charity model of resettlement – reasons such as discrimination, growing income inequality and an eroding social safety net.[8] But others are tied to its key features. Two such features that constrain place-making are the concentration of control over key decisions in the hands of sponsors and the arbitrary and sometimes harsh limits on key resources that help refugees become rooted here.

Becoming engaged with the charity model as sponsors has challenged us ethically and practically, as we have reflected on its shortcomings in the context of resettlement. In this chapter we discuss these shortcomings, as well as some things we have done to improve our own sponsorship effort, and an alternative approach that would lead to better place-making possibilities for refugees.

The charity model offers sponsored refugees little control or choice.

For many refugees, resettlement prolongs their forced displacement, as they have little control over when or where they are resettled, and they can become isolated if members of their families and communities end up scattered around the world.[9] Accordingly, successful place-making requires that refugees be able to make choices that give them a sense of control over their lives.

The charity model undermines this process because it concentrates power in the hands of sponsors and other 'givers,' such as service agencies – power to make choices that have huge impacts on refugees' resettlement, with little accountability to the refugees themselves. With their well-being largely dependent on the emotions, biases, interests and preferences of their sponsors, refugees are left with little power over their own futures.

For government-assisted refugees, one of the most significant resettlement decisions made for them is their destination city. Refugees can request resettlement in cities where they have personal connections, but the final decisions are made by visa officers who also consider political interests such as municipal resettlement quotas. Some refugees are hesitant to advocate for their preferences too forcefully, lest they lose their resettlement opportunities altogether.[10] As a result, many refugees arrive in cities where they have no personal connections despite having close family elsewhere in Canada. A significant number[11] of these refugees take the drastic step of 'secondary migration,' moving to be closer to their social supports, such as family, friends or an ethnic community. In this effort to regain some control, these refugees must disrupt their lives yet again, sometimes expending scarce resources to do so. This is just one example of sponsor interests such as bureaucratic efficiency overriding critical needs of refugees.

Private sponsors, in turn, have the power to make decisions over very personal aspects of refugees' lives, from the neighbourhoods they live in to the pillows they sleep on. Unless refugees arrive with resources of their own, they may have little ability in the short or medium term to alter decisions they do not like.

While most private sponsors make sincere efforts to support refugees' comfort, some intervene or assert themselves in troubling ways. In one case, while at a meeting with other sponsors, we heard a woman insist that the children she sponsored should start school within the first week of their arrival – usurping the parents' role in assessing the best interests of their own children. Unfortunately, there is a history of such behaviour by private sponsors. For example, a study of Vietnamese, Laotian and Cambodian refugees who resettled in Canada between 1979 and 1981 (widely considered a success story in Canada's resettlement efforts) found that refugees considered the intrusiveness and insensitivity of private sponsors one of the program's key drawbacks.[12]

Stepping back from the decisions made in individual refugees' lives, we can also see how the dynamics of control, generosity and emotion operate within the parameters of the sponsorship program itself. We often hear of 'Canada's' generous policies toward refugees, implying that the Canadian public itself is a kind of charitable actor that gives refugees things like health care and permanent resident status. Because refugees have little ability to directly impact public policy at the moment they are most dependent on it, they are especially vulnerable to the public opinion that shapes it.

However, public understanding of refugee policy is generally low, and public opinion about refugees is often influenced by emotion. While some emotional responses can benefit refugees,[13] public indifference or hostility can just as easily harm them. One 2008 Canadian study of the impacts of public attitudes on refugees found that factors like inflammatory media coverage and misinformation lead to increased dehumanization and tolerance of poor living conditions for refugees, and decreased support for assistance.[14] Disturbingly, those more likely to be in positions to influence policy have a higher tendency to dehumanize refugees.[15]

The disempowerment of refugees is deepened by the perpetual gratitude they are often expected to feel. We have seen this dynamic in the media coverage of the resettlement of Syrian refugees, which, while relatively welcoming, has maintained an almost self-congratulatory focus on refugees' gratitude and indebtedness to Canada. While the gratitude is sincere, an overemphasis on such sentiments can be detrimental to refugees. In the short term, other emotions – including disappointment with their living situations and discomfort with their sponsors' expectations – are afforded less space and legitimacy. In the longer term, this sense of indebtedness can make it difficult for refugees to offer critiques or advance claims that could better their own lives. In some cases, it may even make their lives worse: another Canadian study found that a group of refugees who believed they should demonstrate gratitude by adopting their sponsors' religions were at increased risk of depression.[16]

Through its retention of control, at least initially, the charity model treats sponsored refugees as passive recipients rather than partners, and as occupiers of space rather than creators of place. Refugees know their own priorities, preferences and aspirations better than sponsors do, and a model that ignores this fact will impede refugees' place-making efforts here. Transferring greater control to refugees themselves will mean better use of resources, and more successful resettlement.

The charity model puts unreasonable limits on key resources.

In addition to having some control over their lives, refugees require resources to make homes for themselves here. In particular, they need the social resources essential for belonging and well-being; sufficient income to support an acceptable standard of life; and time to adapt and nurture a deep connection to a new place. However, many sponsored refugees face a range of poor outcomes by these measures, particularly around housing, income, employment and mental health.[17] Discrimination tends to both contribute to and worsen poor outcomes for certain marginalized refugees, with Black refugees faring especially poorly.[18] These outcomes provide strong evidence that the charity model limits key resources in harsh ways that bear little correspondence to actual needs.

The social resources typically offered through the charity model, such as language and job training programs, are often linked to service agencies. While such services are useful, other social resources, such as family and close community relationships, are frequently overlooked, despite the high value that refugees often place on them.[19] For example, resettlement policy greatly restricts who is considered to be the 'family' of sponsored refugees, and thus who can resettle with them. A Western-centric notion of the nuclear family dominates, and includes only a refugee's spouse or common-law partner and dependant children.[20] With few exceptions, everyone else is excluded. This definition is particularly unreasonable given the wide cultural diversity in conceptions of what constitutes close family. It strikes us that if we were refugees, this policy would force us to leave behind some of the most important people in our own lives.

Just as current resettlement policy values and devalues certain relationships, it also minimizes the importance of family itself as a resource. Family, both biological and chosen, can provide emotional support, stability and familiarity during a time of loss and tumultuous change.[21] Family can also meet practical needs that the sponsorship program does not, such as child care, translation and interpretation, as well as emergency expenses. Just as important, family honours and transfers personal and cultural history. Family members see the refugee as a whole person with capacity, individuality and value before and beyond the moment of displacement. Minimizing the significance of family by forcing refugees to leave behind important people and relationships can undermine their attachments to their new places, create unnecessary stress and trauma, and place them in the untenable position of neither being fully here nor there.

When social supports are limited, financial resources become more critical. We have been deeply concerned by how little financial support is guaranteed to refugees. Sponsored refugees with insufficient resources receive financial support for their first year in Canada at amounts approximating social assistance rates. For example, a family of four is guaranteed about $20,000, plus an additional $7,000 for start-up costs, like furniture, clothing and utility hookups. This amount is less than half of what such a family would need to afford a basic standard of living in Toronto.[22] These financial difficulties are compounded for the many refugees who must take out resettlement loans to pay for their travel and medical exams, which they must start repaying soon after they arrive. Over 50 percent of sponsored refugees reported that these repayments made it difficult to afford expenses like food and rent.[23]

The harsh reality is that, if not supplemented by other resources, this income provides only a precarious standard of living marked by indignity, insecurity and a preoccupation with just scraping by. Such a lifestyle, moreover, may go unnoticed by many Canadians because of the increasing prevalence and normalization of stark inequality and poverty in Canadian cities. Refugees are forced to live in neighbourhoods and dwellings that present a wide range of place-making challenges, including substandard housing conditions, exploitative landlords, over-policing, isolation and displacement due to gentrification. They may also have a difficult time lifting themselves out of this poverty because their professional and educational credentials are often not recognized;[24] they may lack the income necessary to invest in educational or business opportunities; they may have no credit history or connections to someone able or willing to co-sign loans; and they may face challenges finding employment that provides a living wage.

A related concern is the time period for which refugees are supported through the sponsorship program – just twelve months.[25] The program rarely looks past this point, and sponsors aren't accountable for what happens afterwards. Yet time is a critical resource in the resettlement process. It takes time to become familiar with a new language, city and culture; for children to adjust in schools and make friends; to find decent work; to cope with the loss of loved ones and of home; to begin to heal from trauma; and to re-establish a sense of connection to community. For some refugees, the twelve months of the sponsorship period may be enough. For others, especially those struggling financially, it will take much longer.[26] These people may be forced into longer-term poverty, and precarious dependence on other forms of charity.[27]

The limited resources offered through the sponsorship program are certainly better than nothing, especially given that many refugees may be fleeing from life-or-death situations. However, if our goal as a society is not merely to guarantee subsistence, but rather to support a process of restoration, we must provide refugees with the resources they need, a sense of agency and meaningful opportunities to address a complicated range of resettlement issues.

Conclusion

Whether or not the family we sponsor stays in Canada permanently, the way they feel about their place-making experience here in Toronto will be, as local cultural anthropologist David A. B. Murray puts it, 'a product of a complex interaction between space, location, social relations, security, intimacy, privacy, choice, and control.'[28] As sponsors acting within the charity model, we have reflected critically on how our approach will impact the sponsored family's ability to create good places here. We regularly ask ourselves two ethical questions. First, how can we best support the empowerment and autonomy of this family? Second, which decisions should be the family's to make, and which ones must we make?

These questions have shaped our choices about how to carry out our sponsorship. The two most important decisions we have faced concern fundraising and housing. Setting a fundraising target can be tricky: an amount too low would lead to an unacceptable standard of living, while an amount too high could establish one that is unsustainable, potentially forcing the family to move after the sponsorship ends. Accounting for expenses like a computer, internet and transit passes, which would facilitate place-making but are unaffordable within a $27,000 budget, we committed to raising $40,000 – almost 50 percent above the minimum required.[29] We also decided that the family – not us – should choose their new home, though this means we must find temporary housing for their initial time here.

We have been glad to see many private sponsors and service agencies taking a similar approach. But important problems remain. Thoughtful decisions by sponsors do not fundamentally transform the charity model. Control remains in the hands of sponsors with little accountability for how they exercise it, and the resources given remain a function of their potentially arbitrary decisions rather than of refugees' place-making needs.

Place-making concerns also illuminate the charity model's problematic indifference to a range of public policies and social and economic inequities that impact resettlement. These impacts cannot be managed by private citizens or through sponsorship alone. They require an approach that sees refugees not simply as recipients of aid, but as people whose presence here is interconnected and interactive with every part of our society.

While we are critical of the charity model of resettlement, we recognize what it means for refugees to resettle in Canada. There are tens of millions of refugees worldwide, and less than 1 percent of them are submitted for resettlement through official programs like Canada's.[30] Many more will spend years or even the rest of their lives in camps and cities with no formal status, few recognized rights and little stable ground on which to build anything lasting.

Many refugees who do make it here understandably feel fortunate and grateful, especially in a time of rising popular support for policies like racial and religious screening of refugees, the seizure of refugees' assets to finance their resettlement and the closing of national borders.

In this context, scrutinizing the inadequacies of Canada's sponsorship program may seem idealistic at best, and risky at worst. However, minimizing the weaknesses of Canada's sponsorship program has its own risks and costs – not only to those refugees whose ongoing hardships may be obscured, but also to the communities and cities in which they cannot fully participate.

To better ensure successful resettlement, we must take an approach that emphasizes human rights and states' obligations to uphold them. A rights approach acknowledges that certain things are foundational to the creation of dignified lives and must be guaranteed to everyone, even when it is inconvenient. This approach asks what we must do with and for one another to ensure that everyone enjoys a certain level of security, inclusion and choice. It does not consider reliance on charity as acceptable for refugees or anyone else. It scrutinizes irresponsibility and harm as readily as the charity model celebrates giving. Even as the rights approach aims to improve the lives of refugees, it also aims to prevent anyone from becoming a refugee, by targeting the rights violations that cause people to flee their homes.

A rights approach is not simple, cheap or magical. But it asks better questions and sets better priorities. It sees people as autonomous, diverse and embedded in community – as more than the sum of their survival needs. For these reasons, a rights-based model is far more compatible with robust place-making than the charity model could ever be. When we are considering people's lives, and the communities they aspire to build, better than bad is not good enough. We have to look beyond rescue toward renewal; past survival toward dignity; and past charity toward justice.

We dedicate our work to Mehdi, a young activist and friend who was killed by Syrian state forces in late 2011. May we all care about justice in our communities as he did.

Finding Space for Spirituality
Fatima Syed

The crowd that gathered outside the Mississauga City Hall committee room and in the corridors leading to it was eerily quiet. On one side stood the supporters of the Meadowvale Islamic Centre (MIC), a largely visible group of Muslim men and women petitioning for a permanent prayer space. Standing apart from them were the predominantly white Meadowvale residents who had turned out in even greater numbers to oppose the plan. There was an uncomfortable tension evident in the sarcasm and scorn present in whispered conversation and snide glances. There was no interaction between the two camps. No one could mistake the fact that the development application for 6508 Winston Churchill Boulevard had surfaced something deeply troubling in an affluent suburban community.

It was September 2015, and municipal councillors had organized a public forum to consider the proposal to build the mosque. In the run-up to the session, a lengthy process that involved many public hearings and hundreds of pages of complex planning documents, the MIC's plan had met with a reaction that was clearly different than the usual anti-development NIMBYism. A flyer had circulated, explicitly denouncing the mosque proposal and suggesting it would lead to increased violence and crime, and 'set women's rights back a century.' The flyer advertised an e-petition – available at stopthemosque.com – to halt the construction of 'another Canadian cultural hole.' At the bottom of the leaflet, two Canadian flags were placed next to each other. The first depicted the maple leaf; the other, a moon and star. 'We want this,' read the caption under the first; 'not this,' read the caption beneath the second.

As the city councillors on the planning and development committee began to debate the application, Mayor Bonnie Crombie took the time to condemn the flyer's author, one Kevin Johnston – a former mayoral candidate and founder of stopthemosque.com. She described his campaign as 'hate-mongering' in the presence of a council chamber filled beyond capacity – an overflow that had to be directed to adjacent committee rooms where people could watch the proceedings on television screens.

Crombie was lauded by the mainstream media and Muslim communities across Canada for what *Toronto Star* columnist Royson James called 'her principled, unflinching rejection.'[1] Despite those responses, reporters covering the conflict had already given Johnston serious journalistic attention and had aired the views of the local councillor, who opposed the mosque out of a stated concern for constituents, insisting their objections were only about planning issues such as traffic congestion.

All the mixed messages and steadfast rebuttals raised troubling issues. In settings such as these public meetings, it was easy to see the enormous forces stacked against new immigrant communities seeking to establish places of worship. And despite all the protestations to the contrary, the meeting had a distinctly racist overtone. There was simply no other word to describe what I'd heard.

'Toronto at one time, when it was a white Christian city, had a particularly high number of churches per capita,' says Jason Hackworth, professor of planning and geography at the University of Toronto. Churches were about ten minutes apart. Yet as the world's most ethnically diverse urban centre, the Greater Toronto Area struggles to reflect that demographic reality in its current spiritual landscape. The city has relatively few mosques or temples, considering the size of the non-Christian population; most operate in converted buildings, often unrecognizable as places of worship. Others are hidden behind the doors of churches no longer used by Christian congregations.

The GTA takes great pride in its multiculturalism: somewhere between 38 and 46 percent of Toronto's population is foreign-born. More importantly, the religious makeup of newcomer groups has diversified drastically: in 1971, those claiming to be Muslim, Hindu, Sikh and Buddhist comprised a mere 2.9 percent of immigrants to the region; by the 2000s, this number had shot up to 33 percent of newcomers. In 2016, 12 percent of the GTA's population is Muslim.

A city's built form should, in theory, reflect the multiplicity of faiths of newcomer groups, with a growth in the number of purpose-built, non-Judeo-Christian religious structures. But under the feel-good rhetoric about diversity lies a complicated, and oftentimes racist, conflict over space between established residents and newcomers. A 1999 study by the Joint Centre of Excellence for Research on Immigration and Settlement in Toronto found that seventeen of the thirty-five GTA municipalities had experienced at least one fight between immigrant communities and the municipal government over proposals for mosques or temples. 'Most compelling was the fact that in fourteen of these seventeen instances the conflicts involved zoning disputes over land use,' the authors note. 'Most typical were conflicts over attempts to establish or enlarge mosques which occurred in at least nine municipalities.'[2]

These clashes over public and spiritual space underscore some important notions about the nature of citizenship. Who belongs in the city? Who has a right to shape space, and on what terms?

Grand religious structures marked with domes, minarets, paintings and statues have always exerted a powerful emotional tug on urban communities and shaped the form of the cities in which they're located. But in periods of immigration, churches, mosques and temples have served as much more than just religious and spiritual centres. They become points of reference for newcomers, affirming their presence as they confront otherness. These places can provide a space of belonging and a reminder of the old on new streets. In the 1840s, for example, African-American refugees fleeing slavery founded a Methodist Episcopal church in a working-class Toronto enclave to serve not just as a spiritual and communal organization, but also a place to fight the injustice of slavery and help provide settlement services for those arriving on the Underground Railroad.

'New immigrants consider the church as a part of their homeland,' says Fr. Pishoy Wasfy of the Canadian Coptic Centre. The first step toward integration is to provide familiarity and settlement assistance, which is why the Coptic Centre also has a daycare, a gymnasium, a private school and banquet halls inside its grand, golden-domed building.

Such structures encapsulate years and generations of upbringing, tradition, community and language. 'We're a *centre*, not a church,' says Father Wasfy. 'You try and serve all the possible aspects of a person.' There was a time when the centre was just a school surrounded by farmland. Before that, founding members of the centre's community held Bible study in each other's dining rooms. Today, the centre is practically at capacity – a mark of its importance and relevance to the larger Egyptian Coptic Christian community in the GTA.

While newcomer faiths may differ in their specific beliefs and practices, all are rooted in this emotional attachment to a cultural community. Major Singh, architect of the Sikh Spiritual Centre in Toronto, wanted to design a structure that would be a visual representation of a traditional Sikh temple. 'But you have to marry the existing building with city codes and the views of everyone involved' – two vastly different perspectives that are difficult to unite. One is driven by practical policy; the other by emotion. Singh remembers when the centre was just a decrepit factory building in Rexdale, a 'Price Reduced' sign in its window. 'People came in the evening after work and stayed till midnight to convert the building,' he recalls. Some slept in the half-constructed structure at night.

Other groups with fewer resources are less concerned with building a temple or mosque than just finding a space to pray together, says Nazir Khan, founding member and president of Jam'e Masjid – the Islamic Propagation Centre of Ontario. Indeed, the stories of most newcomer spiritual spaces begin this way, with prayer services initially taking place in basements and school gyms. 'Halfway through a prayer service, a school caretaker knocked on the door and told us to go home,' says Singh. 'We knew then we needed our own place.' Khan, too, rented a storefront space in a plaza opposite his apartment at Dundas and Highway 10 before parking overflow became an issue for neighbouring store owners and forced the worshippers out.

But when one community claims space as its own, others may assert counterclaims, and the result is conflict infected with religious rivalry, or worse. Arpita Biswas, a Toronto-based psychologist who specializes in immigrant and settlement-related stress, suggests that opposition may derive from 'a prejudice that comes from the fear of the unknown and the fear of something changing in their familiar environment.' The clash occurs when one side demands assimilation while the other is trying to integrate on its own terms. In most cases, people integrate through a process of culture-shedding, where deep-rooted values are cast aside as the new culture is learned. Assimilation, on the other hand, occurs when cultural roots are abandoned completely.

Many people naturally perceive the world in stark us-and-them terms, says Biswas, and this instinctive dualism, manifest in most religions, has shaped and reshaped cities for as long as they have existed. Some early Christian popes built churches with material looted from ancient Rome's pagan temples. In the old city of Jerusalem, sacred Jewish, Christian and Muslim structures have existed for centuries in close proximity – a reflection of the three religions' common roots and historical rivalries.

Further west, Istanbul's skyline is unforgettably marked by the four minarets and imposing blue dome of the Hagia Sophia, a former Christian cathedral (the world's largest until 1520) later transformed into an imperial Ottoman mosque in 1453 (it is now a museum). Minarets were added by Ottoman rulers in the fifteenth century and the interior was changed – the altar was renovated to a mihrab, a semicircular niche in the wall that points to Mecca. Standing steps from the Turkish capital's defining Blue Mosque, the museum today captures the intimate, and sometimes uncomfortable, historical and spatial relationships between the generations of people who flow through cities over time.

In modern, culturally diverse cities like Toronto, places of worship pass from religion to religion as congregations build or dwindle, a process dictated by the specific needs of the flows of newcomer groups arriving and departing. How we negotiate those demographic transitions, and the emotionally fraught disputes over spiritual spaces, reveals much about the state of the region's diversity and its much-hyped tolerance. Questionable, in fact, is whether the planning-approvals process for structures such as the Meadowvale Islamic Centre is neutral, or if it detrimentally forces private religious congregations to venture into the public forum, where they encounter hostile – even racist – opposition.

In cities around the world, newcomer or minority religious institutions often face obstacles when they seek to insert themselves into urban spaces with dominant religions or cultures. These projects can become convoluted battles with both bureaucracy and human nature. In October 2015, for example, municipal officials in London, England, finally denied a proposal to build what would have been Britain's largest mosque, after a sixteen-year battle. The so-called 'mega-mosque,' with fifty-eight-metre minarets, would have boasted three times as much floor space as St. Paul's Cathedral, enough to accommodate 10,000 worshippers. The drawn-out application process was marred by accusations of racism on both sides, and the threat of terrorist links. Some observers blamed divisions within the Muslim community as a reason for the denial of the application. Other cities have experienced similar fights. In March 2016, municipal officials in Arhus, Denmark, halted plans to build a mega-mosque, while Muslim community members in a New Jersey suburb filed a lawsuit fighting the denial of a proposed mosque.

During the Mississauga council's 2015 public meeting to vet the Meadowvale Islamic Centre application, twenty-six deputants lined up to speak against the proposed mosque, all of them Caucasian. Two members of the MIC and their planning consultant were scheduled to speak in favour. As I watched the proceedings and took it all down in my notebook, every cheer and outburst of applause for the anti-mosque side felt like a brick in the dividing wall. One attendee, who sat next to me before the meeting began, recalls that walking into the committee room was an alarming experience. Clad in a light blue headscarf that day, she described how she'd felt like she was being watched, scrutinized and isolated by the crowd outside the doors. It was a deeply troubling sensation, difficult to shake.

For all that, Moid Mohammed, an MIC spokesperson, gamely refused to take offence at the negative sentiments directed at the project. 'Any change in the community will bring resistance and anxiety,' he said. His patient response contrasted sharply with the reaction of one woman who cried audibly as she insisted that, while everyone deserved a place to worship, the proposed site was not the right location.

Mohammed said such sessions necessarily dealt with technical and regulatory issues raised by comprehensive studies that only the experts and council could address. In fact, most residents directed their formal comments to such matters, saying the building was too big, or there was not enough parking space. Others said the traffic would endanger children attending nearby schools. A few claimed the minaret and dome were unnecessarily large and should be removed from the design entirely. These planning concerns had been raised over the past two years as the MIC moved through the application process. 'We worked hard to accommodate all the legitimate concerns of the residents,' said Mohammed. In fact, the MIC had significantly reduced the height of the minaret and the dome based on previous recommendations from the council's planning and development committee.

Across the GTA, the battle over the MIC was hardly unique. In 2012, a Markham mosque faced verbal attacks over a similar application, with some residents alleging that the minaret would be used to spy into their backyards. In nearby Thornhill, the Wong Dai Sin, a Taoist Tai Chi temple, had acquired a lot between two 1970s-era houses in 2007. In 2014, after seven years of community meetings, fights over the rezoning application and an appeal to the Ontario Municipal Board, council approved the application. Still, complaints about parking and traffic forced the temple to reconfigure the original two-storey structure into a raised one-storey building. As a result, the Taoist community had to forego planned space for Tai Chi gatherings. Today, the elevated Wong Dai Sin Temple stands on small steel columns painted red, blue and green, a lively rebuke to the mundane grey and brown suburban community that opposed its presence.

Theoretically, Ontario's Planning Act, which regulates places of worship, is designed to be a non-discriminatory decision-making framework for municipal planning. It governs how land may be used, not who may use it, and so does not set out any particular standards or policies regarding the users of land. The zoning provisions under the Planning Act in the last ten years have remained relatively unchanged, apart from amendments in 2006 that allowed for greater information, participation and consultation to take place early in the approvals process, giving local residents and community leaders more opportunity to play a part in the planning of communities. Jason Hackworth dismisses this policy framework as a 'banal expression of Toronto's new geography,' where planning favours the participation of established residents, and forces these conflicts to come out in the open.

Most planners, residents and local politicians deny that the approval framework is intentionally bigoted. Even immigrant communities involved in these battles refuse to use that label. 'As a society, certain words are not acceptable, certain things are not a legitimate thing to say in a multicultural setting,' says Myer Siemiatycki, a political science professor at Ryerson University.

Yet he has conducted many studies on the planning issues surrounding mosques and concludes that there is an underlying racist tone to what seems like a neutral process. 'The fear is that "those people" are taking over,' says Siemiatycki. 'Some instinctive unfounded fear gets triggered.' The public meetings and media coverage, too, are not impartial discussions on planning, but instead tense debates about who does or should belong, and where newcomers with different customs are allowed to worship.

'Ten years back, people were helping minorities,' says Major Singh. 'Now we aren't a minority, we're in the mainstream. So the question becomes "Why should we make concessions for them?"'

The crux of the problem is that while the region's demographics have shifted, the rules governing the use of urban space have not kept up. Where are the planning accommodations for the practices of different faiths with larger congregations? Where are the public education policies that close the knowledge and understanding gap between established and newcomer communities? Where are the buildings representing and preserving the cultural heritage of generations of immigrants?

At one of the public meetings held to vet the Meadowvale Islamic Centre's development application, Moid Mohammed stood to address concerns about the proposal. 'In the name of God, the most gracious and the most merciful … ' he began.

'Oh, not this again,' muttered the woman sitting next to me, shifting in her seat and shaking her head. A man seated in front of her, an MIC badge on his shirt, looked back at her and, just as quickly, looked away silently. Even after planning and council experts had explained thoroughly that the MIC met all the city's codes, residents continued to complain, before an uncomfortably divided audience, about traffic-related noise, the proximity to backyards and the shadow of the MIC's minaret.

A few weeks later, in mid-October 2015, the MIC rezoning application arrived at Mississauga city council for a final vote. As the session started, a petition was brought forth demanding a public apology from Mayor Crombie for accusing Kevin Johnston, founder of stopthemosque.com, of hate-mongering. 'We found the Mayor's remark to be inflammatory, leading to accusations that the residents of Meadowvale had a racist purpose or similar hidden agenda,' read the petition. Crombie refused to apologize, and all but one councillor backed her. When the vote was called, the MIC development plan won eleven to one. The councillor opposing in both instances was the same Meadowvale councillor concerned for her constituents. But the approval had a strange caveat: an amendment to ensure the MIC would not install external speakers for the call to prayer – something no mosque in Canada does.

What should we learn from such battles? Until municipal councils grant their approval, the members of faith communities who want to build religious centres find themselves facing an onslaught of audible and often illogical opposition. The underlying feature of these sessions, as well as many of the conversations I've had in their aftermath, is a strong feeling of otherness – ironic in a region that claims to value inclusivity and multiculturalism above all else. At some point, this contradiction must be recognized and reconciled so that the mosque and temple are no longer reminders of the outsiders among us, but rather the physical symbols of a tolerant and multicultural region that embraces diversity.

It shouldn't be hard to accomplish this shift in thinking. City planners and architects agree that while it's impossible to pass bylaws that suit everyone's needs, the approvals process can be made more flexible in its requirements, as well as in the way it engages with the public. Toronto is a dense city where space is an increasingly scarce resource, but newcomer communities should be able to secure places to practice their faiths. Municipal planners should be surveying the city to identify potential venues for new religious structures, and minimizing the red tape required to approve them. The entire process should become more accessible to immigrant communities, whose members often struggle to acclimatize. And councils ought to ensure that unreasonable and coded narratives over parking and minaret shadows don't get in the way of settlement.

As I researched this essay, an imam rhetorically asked me, 'Where is Canada's national mosque?' His point: there isn't one. His question suggests a desire on the part of communities struggling to raise enough funds to launch an application process, let alone find a space in downtown Toronto where such a structure might proudly stand. After all, Church Street is lined with tall, brick-walled structures with spires visible from great distances. But can we imagine Toronto with a Mosque Street or a Temple Street? Probably not. Yet the imam has hope that someday Toronto will be home to a visible mosque. 'There will be one,' he predicts.

His optimism, however, is unfounded. Despite the formal outcome, the emotionally strained council proceedings about the Meadowvale Islamic Centre mosque plan gave me a glimpse of a form of othering I hadn't thought existed in a hyper-diverse and apparently tolerant city like Greater Toronto. When those opposing the mosque claimed that Mississauga was *their* home and shouldn't include a mosque with a minaret because it would ruin the aesthetics of *their* streets, I felt speechless, my hands shaking as one deputant after another declared that a mosque didn't belong in *their* neighbourhood.

I had walked into that Mississauga city council chamber as a journalist. When I left, I felt like an unwelcome alien who'd been stripped of my right to belong in my city.

Navigating the City with an Invisible Illness: The Story of Dorothy
Denise DaCosta

'She's gone,' the friend she'd been staying with said, 'and she's taken her things.'

That's all we knew when Dorothy vanished. Over a period of two weeks in 2010, this middle-aged social worker and mother of two managed to fall off the grid. It was a deeply troubling ordeal for those who knew her. Her departure from the safety of her suburban Toronto home was the turning point in a staggered leave of self – the result of struggling in silence for years without the diagnosis of a debilitating mental illness.

In the months prior to her disappearance, Dorothy's progressively erratic behaviour coincided with a series of consecutive crises: separation, bankruptcy and, lastly, job loss. Some days after she vanished, an officer with the Toronto Police Service managed to track her vehicle to a location in the city. The car was being driven by an acquaintance and subsequently police found her unharmed in his apartment, where she had taken up residence. For the next three years, during which she had no source of income, means of communication or medical attention, her condition continued to deteriorate.

Dorothy hardly seemed like someone who would be afflicted by mental illness. She had emigrated from Jamaica during the 1970s at the age of seventeen with the goal of becoming a nurse. A disciplined high school student with a penchant for science, she was determined to thrive alongside her Canadian peers, even in the face of discrimination and poverty. However, high tuition fees forced her to defer her post-secondary education, and she found a job as a hotel housekeeper. She married and had two children, but when the relationship frayed, Dorothy and her husband divorced, and she moved into social housing.

By the early 1990s, she was a single mother living in a public housing complex, facing what would become a ten-year stint on welfare. During this time, the signs of her looming struggle with schizophrenia began to surface, but went unaddressed. She eventually returned to her studies and embarked on a career in social work.

Ironically, even an occupation in the health care field didn't prove to be an advantage when she became ill. How does an educated, middle-class health care professional slip through the cracks of our mental health care system? Very easily, her family and friends learned. They discovered that certain mental illnesses are incredibly difficult to treat when the sufferer is unaware or unwilling to accept that they are ill. When Dorothy finally received treatment in 2014, she had to be escorted to the hospital by police, and was administered medication by force after refusing it for weeks.

Helpless, bewildered and in a state of disbelief, Dorothy's friends and family watched a vibrant, independent woman transform into a recluse. With their friend just a decade away from retirement, the onset of mental illness had derailed years of hard work in a matter of a few years.

Beyond the personal tragedy, Dorothy's difficulty in accessing mental health care reveals some the complex issues facing the consumers of such services, especially those who belong to marginalized communities, including new immigrants, refugees and racialized groups. A growing body of research indicates that cultural stigma, the lack of proximity to services, cost and discrimination make it especially difficult for individuals like Dorothy to receive the treatment they desperately need.

Prior to her diagnosis, Dorothy had lived in a suburban area of Greater Toronto that is home to nearly half the region's population, yet has only three of the GTA's twenty-seven dedicated psychiatric facilities.[1] This disparity is a growing concern, underscoring the urgent need for a mental health strategy tailored to a city-region with so much ethnocultural diversity. Mental illness, according to the Centre for Addiction and Mental Health, is one of the leading causes of disability in Ontario. But the availability of mental health services hasn't kept up with the growth of the city and the settlement patterns of newcomers and marginalized groups.

The delay in Dorothy's diagnosis and treatment can also be attributed to cultural stigmas around mental health and a lack of awareness among those closest to her. Those within her support network couldn't agree on the root cause of her behaviour: younger family members almost unanimously warned that mental illness was the source of her decline, yet some of Dorothy's siblings and peers downplayed the severity of her paranoia or, worse, they believed her delusions.

The few who suspected mental illness kept quiet about it or simply avoided her and carried on with their lives. Shame undoubtedly impeded early intervention. Even Dorothy's intelligence and articulateness worked against her being treated, because of preconceived notions about those who suffer from mental health disorders.

After a voluntary admittance to hospital in 2011, she opted out of treatment and was soon released. Then, in 2014, her roommate moved out and Dorothy was finally admitted to a downtown hospital and treated for six weeks. After her release this time, she spent several months in a shelter and was later placed in a tiny bachelor apartment in Toronto, where, as of 2016, she lived alone on a small monthly stipend. She has refused to continue treatment, despite the resurgence of her symptoms.

For those suffering from mental illness, gender, ethnicity and socio-economic status play a role in accessing services. So does location: there's clearly a need for more mental health services in the suburbs. What's more, the success of these services are largely dependent on whether they are geared toward the specific needs of the intensely diverse communities in those parts of the region. Mental health awareness campaigns must be targeted, highly visible and delivered in a range of languages and through a variety of media so the information is widely accessible. By better educating both health practitioners and individuals from a broad range of backgrounds, we can dispel myths and encourage tolerance through language. Exploring our direction and the gaps in our current system is integral to the conversation of urban inclusivity.

The names and relationships in this essay have been changed to protect the subject's privacy.

Culture and Mental Illness
Karen Pitter

In 2010, Bell Canada launched what would become one of the most high-profile public advocacy campaigns in recent memory – the 'Bell Let's Talk' initiative, geared at fostering open discussion about mental illness. Each year Canadians are invited to tweet the hashtag #BellLetsTalk and work to end the stigma. Alberta Olympian Clara Hughes fronts the campaign, which has raised millions for research, by talking openly about her own struggle with depression.

Though laudable, the Bell campaign does not hold up a mirror to Canadian society: the spokespersons and the characters in the campaign's ads are mainly white and middle-class, and there is scant acknowledgement of the nature and extent of mental illness among the many ethno-cultural communities that make up Canada's largest city-regions.

The Mental Health Commission of Canada has gone further in probing the intersection between diversity and mental health. According to its 2015 report on mental health indicators, the MHCC found that immigrants report lower levels of diagnosed stress and anxiety than the general population, but the study notes that these individuals may also face more barriers in accessing care.[1] In addition, the report found a troubling upward trend in the past decade among Canadians who have faced discrimination, an experience that can result in psychological distress. The picture is not all bad news, however. The study cites surveys showing that two-thirds of all immigrants say they feel a somewhat or very strong sense of belonging to their local communities – a figure that now exceeds Canadian-born residents.

In my own graduate work and professional practice in working with individuals in the Caribbean community, I have seen evidence of a disparity in racialized and refugee communities' mental health experiences, based on intersecting social identities related to race and culture. While anyone is susceptible to mental illness, researchers have found that interrelated economic, social and systemic factors make racialized, Aboriginal and refugee communities more vulnerable. Furthermore, place also plays a role.

On a per capita basis, mental health issues are more pronounced in global cities where urban migrants, immigrants and refugees experience multiple stressors, such as long-term poverty, discrimination, the lingering effects of torture, disconnection from supportive community networks and the alienation sometimes associated with being a visible religious minority. The problem is that the current mainstream model of mental health service provision has not kept pace with the hyper-diversity of urban regions like Greater Toronto.

Mental health and well-being are determined by various external factors, many of which are not within our control. According to a 2010 study by York University researchers Juha Mikkonen and Dennis Raphael, the determinants of mental health are linked to the way we locate ourselves, in terms of culture, race, Aboriginal status, gender, immigrant status and disability.[2] Mental health determinants are also a function of early childhood development, education, income, unemployment and job security, employment and working conditions, housing, food insecurity, social safety network, social exclusion and access to health services, including mental health services.

Race is not only experienced at the individual level, but also structurally, with pervasive discrimination in the legal and educational systems, in government policies such as immigration, through the media and in the workforce. Racialized people, then, have a higher probability of experiencing social exclusion, unemployment and or precarious, low-paid employment. According to research conducted by the Colour of Poverty campaign in 2007, racialized communities also have a higher probability of residing in housing with poor living conditions and in neighbourhoods with increased poverty rates.[3]

Income insecurity leads to health disparities and hardships. Someone who belongs to a racialized group is not necessarily more at risk than anyone else: people from both mainstream and marginalized communities face significant mental health vulnerabilities when they feel out of place, lose their social networks or struggle to meet basic needs. Still, social identity can significantly impact mental health. The reality is that in daily life, our social identity can determine whether we get the job or get pulled over by the police.

Cultural Nuances

Culture is understood as the values, beliefs and traditions shared within a community. Increasingly, culture has also come to incorporate place, online connections and social networks. Mental well-being, then, is clearly related to our cultural environment, and our capacity to manage our own lives.

Culturally diverse groups bring varied understandings of what constitutes mental health. For instance, in some marginalized communities, mental health problems tend to be more stigmatized and less well understood. The decision to seek help is often deferred, and problems may instead be addressed within the family or through consultation with trusted authority figures, such as spiritual leaders.

Furthermore, while the *Diagnostic and Statistical Manual of Mental Disorders* offers the medical consensus around what constitutes mental illness, different cultural communities may have very different perspectives on the causes of certain behaviours.

Every culture, in fact, has unspoken rules about what is 'normal.' As an insider in the Caribbean community, my experience is that there is a pact of silence around mental health issues. People rarely speak about these conditions; when they do make comments, they are often negative and reveal the stigma attached to mental illness in my community.

Likewise, South Asian communities tend to stigmatize or fall silent on this subject. In a 2015 feature in the *New Republic*, Boston lawyer Priya-Alika Elias wrote about the unexpected onset of mental illness among women who had recently immigrated to Canada, citing 2004 research into the impact of migration on Hindi women.[4] Elias reported that, for the first time, these women found themselves dealing with the symptoms of depression. She also noted a Toronto study that concluded that South Asian women dealing with family violence avoid seeking support outside their community because of shame, cultural stigma and family responsibility. Consequently, they often suffer in silence.

Other immigrant groups bring similar outlooks. According to a 2013 study by scientist Mary Amuyunzu-Nyamongo, executive director of the African Institute for Health and Development, many African nations have failed to place a focus on the importance of mental well-being, which is not surprising given the preponderance of civil conflict and natural disaster throughout the continent.[5] According to Amuyunzu-Nyamongo's research, reported mental health problems have been found to double following emergencies. Furthermore, the social breakdown that occurs during and after famines, epidemics and forced migrations contributes to the increased risk of mental health problems within communities dealing with such crises.

Amuyunzu-Nyamongo cites studies that revealed that, in Uganda, the notion of being 'depressed' is culturally frowned upon, and deemed to be an unwarranted condition. In Nigeria, meanwhile, study participants overwhelmingly reacted with alarm and anger toward people living with mental illness; they cited a range of reasons for their response, including inadequate information, drug abuse, God's will and witchcraft.

In many parts of Africa, family members provide primary care for people with mental illness, with help from traditional healers or religious leaders. In Ethiopia, 85 percent of people with mental health issues turn to healers instead of professionals for support.

Among Asian communities, mental health concepts are heavily determined by perceptions of health and disease rooted in traditional Chinese medicine and religion. According to 2011 research from the National Alliance on Mental Illness, an American advocacy network, traditional Asian medicine regards mental illness as rooted in a range of causes, including an imbalance between the Taoist conception of yin and yang (contrary forces combined to create the whole), disrupted chi (energy) flow, punishment by God for neglecting ancestral ceremonies, fate, genetic susceptibility, physical or emotional pressure, biological disorders and deficiency in character.[6] Compared to Western societies, Asian communities tend to view mind and body as being more interrelated. Traditional medical practitioners may view physical symptoms as clues revealing emotional discord (a view that has become more mainstream in Western medicine with a growing understanding of the links between physical and mental stress symptoms).

Research published in the *British Journal of Psychiatry* in 2007 shows that traditional Chinese medicine has been used to treat mental health issues such as schizophrenia for thousands of years.[7] While antipsychotic drugs are used widely in mental health treatment in the West, they may have harmful and unpleasant side effects and have proven to be ineffective for a small percentage of the population.

Many Aboriginal communities, in turn, approach mental health using a community-based holistic approach that takes into consideration an individual's physical, spiritual and psychological condition. According to a 2011 document subtitled *Guide to Mental Health Resources for First Nations, Métis and Inuit People in Winnipeg*, traditional healing approaches include natural herbs, spiritual ceremonies, singing and dancing, vision quest (a rite of passage used in Aboriginal cultures), prayer, meditation and self-reflection to gain a better understanding of self.[8] Some communities make use of sweat lodges for prayer, purging and the cleansing of the spirit, mind and body.

Healers, elders or spiritualists use traditional teachings to analyze an individual's experiences so he or she may gain self-knowledge and reclaim a sense of spiritual well-being. Spiritualists prescribe lifestyle alternatives for those seeking support and make offerings on their behalf to spirits considered to be generous, while herbalists prepare plants for medicinal purposes. Some Aboriginal communities also have diagnostic specialists or seers who commune with the spiritual world for support in identifying the problem.

Finally, while experiences such as grief, loss and trauma are part of the human experience, mental health issues may be passed on from generation to generation within communities whose members have been deeply impacted by tragedy, poverty, war, political instability, colonization or other forms of upheaval.

The psychosocial geography of a hyper-diverse metropolis like Greater Toronto includes all of these complicated cultural variations. What is less clear is whether the region has the capacity to respond.

The Refugee Experience

In significant ways, refugees arrive to cities like Toronto with experiences of dislocation and flight that are distinctly different from those of more traditional immigrants, including those who leave impoverished countries.

Refugees come to Canada from all over the world, and have been arriving at a rate of about 11,000 people per year since 2000, according to McMaster University researchers Marie McKeary and Bruce Newbold. In the past decade, federal data shows that the main source countries have been Afghanistan, Colombia, Ethiopia, Myanmar (formerly Burma) and Syria.[9]

Having been exposed to persecution, violence or the denial of basic human rights in their home countries, refugees arrive with immense vulnerabilities. They may have been victims of torture. They must deal with the reality of being torn away from their families and possessions. Also, because many endure extended periods of flight or deeply stressful stays in refugee camps, refugees typically have poorer physical and mental health than immigrants and the general population.

A 2015 study in the *Canadian Medical Association Journal* found that the migration experience increases the risk of psychotic disorders for both immigrants and refugees.[10] The study concluded that, compared to the general population, Caribbean immigrants and refugees who resettled from East Africa and South Asia are 1.5 to 2 percent more likely to suffer from mental health conditions such as schizophrenia and schizoaffective disorders. The researcher also found that, in contrast to other immigrants, refugees faced a 25 percent greater risk of experiencing psychotic disorders, as well as other conditions, such as post-traumatic stress disorder. These problems are often further compounded by racism, extended unemployment or other issues these immigrants encounter during the resettlement process.

Barriers to Culturally Competent Care

Due to cultural nuances and limited resources in the mental health sector, racially diverse and First Nations communities face significant barriers to what can be described as 'culturally competent care.' This concept describes how people from diverse backgrounds reach across those differences. For mental health practitioners in particular, cultural competence refers to the importance of being mindful of the unique needs and challenges facing consumers, and the need to respond in culturally sensitive ways. In urban regions as diverse as Greater Toronto, mental health providers must be acutely aware of the political, social and cultural backstories of the people they serve.

Much depends on whether practitioners can establish trust and collaboration with mental health consumers, and the degree of understanding these professionals possess about the broad range of cultural and historical experiences that accompany the people who turn up in their waiting rooms.

Those who deal with individuals from First Nations communities, for example, must understand the impact of residential schools and cultural genocide. If they are treating racialized people of African descent, they must take into account the residual impact of the slave trade and daily discriminations. Additionally, when treating refugees, practitioners must be mindful not to lump their experiences of migration in with those of voluntary migrants.

Mental health practitioners must also design treatment plans to address barriers to culturally competent care, such as gender, unemployment, stigmas or other forms of discrimination. A plan of action is essential for trust-building with First Nations and racialized individuals who often avoid seeking support due to a lack of trust in the health care system. In a 2013 feature of the *Windspeaker,* Canada's national Aboriginal news source, journalist Shari Narine wrote about this lack of trust in the Aboriginal community.[11] She concluded that many Aboriginals do not use the health care system because of discrimination and encounters with preconceived ideas about their culture. Members of the community, Narine wrote, often feel afraid or vulnerable in accessing health care services and some even forego seeking support when they are unwell.

Research conducted in 2001 by the U.S. Department of Health and Human Services found that racialized communities' lack of trust was a significant obstacle in their seeking mental health support.[12] Reasons for skepticism of the health care system by racialized groups varied, and included past transgressions in these communities and present encounters with discrimination.

Cities as a Treatment Site

For many big-city police services, a growing proportion of emergency calls involve responding to individuals in crisis. While law enforcement officers have only nominal training for such encounters, they've increasingly become front-line mental health responders. The question is, why are we criminalizing health problems?

We should turn the question around: what if we reimagined the city as a site of treatment instead of a punitive and emotionally harsh place, especially for members of marginalized communities? Such a shift requires neighbourhood networks and support systems, ongoing professional development services for mental health providers, safe green and healthy public spaces, and supportive workplaces.

Our cities contain community gardens, urban hiking clubs, squares and parks, art gallery classes and film festivals, among other amenities. Public spaces that are safe and foster a sense of mutual respect and collective belonging are psychologically crucial because they connect people and potentially reduce feelings of isolation. Research has shown that urban green spaces – parks, forests, gardens, etc. – improve mental health and help manage stress or mood disorders. Furthermore, social networks and informal community activities or resources – child-care swapping, street potlucks or barbecues and familiar neighbourhood businesses, for example – also provide emotional support that can mitigate the sources of stress.

The presence in big cities of a broad range of ethnocultural and faith-based organizations, as well as progressive workplaces, allows service providers an opportunity to forge partnerships and gain a deeper understanding of the specific psychological concerns facing individual communities, especially those susceptible to increased incidence of mental illness due to dislocation, poverty or other factors. Practitioners, in fact, can draw on the city's diversity, incorporating cultural healing practices such as Ayurveda, natural herbs, spiritual ceremonies, meditation, prayer, sweat lodge, sharing/talking circles and progressive faith-based interventions.

Racialized communities, however, must work internally to break silences around mental illness. Such a dialogue begins with family members and friends, and extends to faith leaders, ethnic newspapers, educational institutions and community leaders. Diverse groups can also use cultural celebrations, such as Black History Month or National Aboriginal Day, to bring awareness to mental health issues.

So while the increased attention to mental health through high-profile public advocacy campaigns is encouraging, they must become more representative of diverse urban communities by acknowledging specific cultural nuances and social barriers. Such efforts will not only reduce the stigma surrounding mental health within cultural communities, they could foster more co-operative and inclusive neighbourhoods that allow individuals and families to live, love, share and care about one another.

Neighbourhood Watch:
Racial Profiling and Virtual Gated Communities
Asmaa Malik

My new east-end neighbourhood borders Thorncliffe Park, one of Toronto's most densely populated immigrant communities and home to some of the best Pakistani supermarkets around. We're steps from Danforth East and its Ethiopian, Moroccan and Greek social clubs. The elementary school down the road has one of the most diverse student populations in the city. Residents of public housing homes and high-rises share the parks with new homeowners who've just dropped $1 million to live in a detached house close to the subway line.

This is what my corner of the city looks like on the street level. But its digital reflection, especially as seen on local social networks, reveals a very different picture.

Old-school citizen-patrolled 'neighbourhood watch' programs, advertised by their iconic street signs featuring houses with big, watchful eyes, are meant to be, by their very nature, conspicuous. Would-be thieves and criminals are supposedly alerted and thereby deterred when they know they are under collective surveillance. But what happens in a diverse city like Toronto when a self-selected group of residents takes to the internet to share this kind of intelligence behind the presumably closed walls of a secret social network? These virtual gated communities, which exist in every corner of the city, from Liberty Village to Kingston Road Village, have the troubling potential to split neighbourhoods – especially those still in early stages of gentrification – along the digital divide while raising tensions across the fault lines of race, class and privilege.

Before I moved to the east end, I joined two east-end Facebook groups. One was public and the other was not. From the invitation-only 'Pocket' community group, I hoped to learn more about the area and the people who share my streets, my grocery store and my subway station. The neighbourhood borders my own and is defined by its closed-loop streets, which end at the TTC streetcar yard. It is located within the economically and ethnically diverse Blake-Jones corridor, and in 2012 *Toronto Life* listed the Pocket as one of the city's ten hottest real-estate neighbourhoods. The volunteer-run community group is known for its work to beautify the local park and to rename an alley after the late street musician and long-time mayoral candidate Ben Kerr. It organizes several events for residents, including movie nights for charity and block parties.

When I first joined the Pocket group, I was pleased to get useful insider information about local daycares and eavestrough-repair services. The tone of the comments on the Facebook group seemed friendly and appeared to come from well-meaning neighbours who took pride in their community.

But soon a particular post gave me pause. At first glance, it seemed innocuous enough. It was from someone who wished to visit a local mosque to learn about Muslim culture and wanted to know if others in the group were interested in coming along. Clearly, the poster's intentions were good-natured, and even liberal-minded. But what troubled me was the assumption, evident in the tone, that Muslims could only be found in a religious centre. Not next door and surely not in the same Facebook group. A few weeks earlier, another poster had written about how they were offended because Muslim children in the nearby park didn't want to pet their dog and, in fact, ran away.

In both cases, the assumption appeared clear. Muslims may reside in the area, but they live apart from 'us.' Their customs and beliefs aren't 'ours.' Therefore, a special trip needs to be made to visit 'them.' Separate and equal, perhaps, but certainly not neighbours in the Facebook-group sense of the word. Defined in this way, a Muslim is a person to be viewed as a devoutly religious figure, divorced of individual spiritual outlook, culture, class and social context.

But then again, maybe I was reading too much between the lines. After all, it was just a friendly Facebook post, right? As a journalist and a racialized Canadian, born of Pakistani parents in the U.S., who has also lived for extended periods in South Asia and the Middle East, I am acutely aware of these kinds of racial undercurrents. Maybe even too acutely.

Who was I to question a well-intentioned neighbour's desire to reach out?

In 2014, I'd just returned to Toronto after almost ten years in Montreal. When I'd first moved to Quebec, I was struck by how conspicuous I felt. My mildly passable French and brown skin often prompted questions about my origin, as well as my assumed religion. ('Tell people you're American,' a friend once suggested, because then they would be far more forgiving of my shortcomings.) Even within the city's youthful Anglo enclaves, which have a small-town, everybody-knows-everybody vibe, there were few faces similar to mine.

In the rest of Canada, Quebec has often been singled out for the blunt nature of its debates over minority rights. The province's proud history of upholding its status as a nation within a country and the roiling tensions between its *pure laine* stalwarts and new immigrants have long been considered by many Canadian as anomalies in our national 'mosaic.'

I lived in Quebec when the mayor of rural Hérouxville published his own anti-multiculturalism charter, targeting Muslim women by saying, 'The only time you may mask or cover your face [in our town] is on Halloween.' The newsroom I worked in covered extensively the 'reasonable accommodation' hearings that yielded a toothless report calling for Quebecers to take a more evolved approach toward integration. For years, as an educated, worldly person, I felt I could comfortably handle the outsider status I would always bear, no matter how long I lived in the city.

And then I gave birth to my son. Soon after, in the summer of 2013, the Parti Québécois introduced its Charter of Values. Most significantly, it forbade public servants from wearing religious symbols – such as the turban, hijab, niqab and yarmulke – with the exception of small, 'inconspicuous' crosses. During the hearings, led by the newly appointed provincial minister for citizenship and democratic institutions, the atmosphere in the media and on the streets was tense. The minister even banned the use of the word *racist* by people testifying during the hearings, saying it was 'unpleasant.'

Mercifully, the Charter soon appeared destined for the ash heap of history, along with the PQ and its historic rout, the following year. But when the newly elected provincial Liberals announced they might revive the popular push for the Charter, with some modifications, I knew it was time to move. I could handle the blatant double standards and the uncomfortable conversations, but I did not want my son to grow up in a province that would, at first glance, consider him a second-class citizen. With its vaunted diversity and multicultural backbone, this kind of systemic racism, I strongly believed, would never be tolerated in Toronto.

Months after our move back, however, I was startled to find myself in the middle of one of the most heated and upsetting discussions about race I'd ever witnessed. And it occurred, of all places, on that seemingly innocuous neighbourhood Facebook group.

On a sun-dappled summer afternoon, a member of the Pocket Facebook group posted photos of Black teenagers biking on a residential street. She meant it as a warning, saying she had seen them 'snooping' into private laneways and pegging them as potential suspects for a recent bike theft. As I read the comments below the pictures, I was alarmed to find that a majority of Facebook group members appreciated her alert.

Again, the assumptions about the membership of the Facebook group were evident. The poster and her supporters were not concerned about the potential consequences of uploading photos of teenagers without parental consent. Implicitly, the move presupposed that the parents couldn't possibly have been members of the group. These teenagers were Black and allegedly up to no good – never mind that they were not guilty of doing anything but being teenagers. What was worse, the Pocket group membership included a local community police officer, who now had access to images of these targeted teens.

My earlier misgivings about the nature of the neighbourhood group quickly returned. Under the neighbourly chatter, the local recommendations and friendly swaps there existed a layer of racial assumptions, coded messaging and micro-aggressions ready to be expressed but later vehemently denied at the first provocation.

Indeed, it was only a matter of minutes before that first defensive comment was posted.

Lauren Simmons, a high school teacher and often-outspoken member of the Pocket group, pointed out that this was the same group that just weeks earlier had 'liked' the link to writer Desmond Cole's recent *Toronto Life* cover story about being a persistent target of police harassment. But now, within the confines of this group, people were racially profiling minors and identifying them as potential criminals. Simmons, who is white, quickly found herself on the defensive against accusations of political correctness and incivility. Fellow residents failed to see her point.

'Racial profiling is not a Toronto thing,' wrote one poster responding to Simmons. 'It might be a popular stance currently but a country that prides itself to have been the freedom of the Underground Railroad … we do not share similarities with our great neighbours to the south.

'We don't segregate people of colour in Toronto and we do not tend to be a racist set of people. To assume your neighbour would be racially profiling is to assume she is part of the systemic racism she would have been raised in. And I am pretty sure that isn't a position most Torontonians are [in].'

Fellow neighbourhood commenters did not take kindly to be being labelled racists, yet they saw no issue labelling those racialized teens as potential criminals. It was startling, especially as I had thought I had left these kinds of vocal, intolerant arguments behind. It had quickly become clear, however, that the smugly favourable comparisons of Ontario to Quebec, and now Canada to the U.S., were far from sound. Toronto's reputation as one of the most diverse cities in the world leaves its citizens with little inclination or incentive to examine the more discreet prejudice in our own backyards.

One after another, new comments kept popping up under the photos. Most were in defence of the original poster. Though some people did step up and support Simmons's point of view, the attacks against her soon became personal.

To me, it was clear that the parameters of the discussion didn't allow for a few simple truths: everyone has their prejudices and perhaps we should take time to examine ours, especially because we're neighbours – and especially because we live in Toronto, which prides itself on its diversity and tolerance.

Social networks promise a free exchange of ideas, open to all and for all. The prevailing perception is that through collective movements like #BlackLivesMatter and awareness-raising blogs such as Humans of New York, we can transcend traditional power dynamics, leaving discrimination with no place to hide. But in the real world, traditional power structures can be remarkably resilient in the face of this kind of change. And in this sense, it was only a matter of time before this new model of neighbourhood civility revealed itself to be nothing more than a virtual gated community.

At this point in the increasingly heated Facebook thread, you might ask why, as a brown person, I didn't speak up.

The commenters appeared to be predominantly white and more concerned with how they felt personally offended than with how their actions may have hurt the teenagers or the community. In that moment, I felt the crushing weight that all outsiders carry when they realize they have to be the one to draw attention to themselves, and to bear the burden placed upon them when they are assumed to be speaking for an entire race or religion.

If that was the price I had to pay to learn more about my community, I wasn't interested. I had learned enough already and, in a quiet instant of anger and hopelessness, I quit the group.

Toronto is far from the only place where these kinds of racial tensions find their expressions on social-network groups. Suburban Fear is a Tumblr launched last year dedicated to reporting on online neighbourhood-watch groups in South Africa that, it says, are 'the bastion of white middle-class fear.' In a country still reeling from a painful legacy of murderous race relations twenty years after the end of apartheid, the problem is very real and very dangerous. 'The page was inspired in reaction to a spate of racist incidents stemming from the southern suburbs in Cape Town,' the creator, who asked not to be named, told South Africa's *Times Live*.[1] His or her self-imposed anonymity clearly speaks to the risks involved in sharing these incendiary and deeply racist posts.

In several of the screenshots of Facebook group posts collected on the site, white residents use racial codes to describe unwelcome non-white visitors passing through their pristine enclaves. *Bravo* is used for a Black person and the word *Charlie* connotes a 'coloured' person. In several cases, photos of individuals accompany vague accusations – for example, a photo of four Black men on the sidewalk captioned, '4 very suspicious "bravo" individuals, spotted walking slowly.' These kinds of racial descriptions 'really wouldn't help identify a possible perpetrator. It would be like saying "a white male in Norway,"' said William Bird, of human rights group Media Monitoring Africa, in an interview with *Times Live*. The coded language and surveillance-style images are testament to the fact that the ghosts of apartheid are alive and well – and in the machine.

Suburban Fear has tapped into another trend taking over neighbourhoods from South Africa to North America: the private social-network neighbourhood group. On its website, which features idyllic photos of Black and white people sharing suburban pleasures like backyard barbecues and trips to the playground, OurHood calls itself 'a digital networking platform that connects communities to strengthen neighbourhoods and build a stronger, safer South Africa.' As of September 2015, more than 1,000 communities have created groups on the platform. These groups are not connected to existing social networks and members have to be vouched for by their neighbours, almost guaranteeing a like-minded group.

Nextdoor is a similar private social network based in San Francisco. Earlier this year, an investigative piece in *East Bay Express*, a Bay-area alternative weekly, told how white residents of Oakland, California's neighbourhoods are using the 'Crime and Safety' section of the site to report on what they call 'suspicious activity' by Black residents. Reporter Sam Levin spent months talking to residents who shared posts from private groups and described an environment where Black residents felt unsafe walking on their own streets.[2]

In the story, the parents of two mixed-race teenagers expressed the very real fears they had about their children in a time of trigger-happy policing. 'This looks like a good neighbourhood until you get on the Internet and see some of the craziness,' said father Mitsu Fisher. His wife, Ann Nomura, added, 'I have no assurance that police would not grab my kid for no good reason.'

According to Levin's story, 'White residents have used Nextdoor to complain and organize calls to police about Black neighbours being too noisy in public parks and bars – raising concerns that the site amplifies the harmful impacts of gentrification.' As in the Toronto and South African groups, men of colour have been called out as being suspicious for walking down the street, hanging around bus stops and wearing hoodies. One Black resident said he stopped jogging in his neighbourhood because he feared being pegged as a criminal suspect, and another woman said she was profiled in her own neighbourhood when a resident thought she was breaking into her own home.

Levin recalls an incident where multiple Nextdoor posters complained about a Black boy who was apparently not picking up after his dog. After a woman asked for suggestions on how to get him to collect his dog's waste, a commenter suggested she call the police: 'Not picking up poop from your dog is against the law – it's a health violation.' Another person posted an image of the boy and wrote, 'Here's his photo. [The Oakland Police Department] might find this handy.'

'This,' said one African-American resident quoted in the story, 'is how little Black boys end up getting shot.'

With the spectre of police carding and racial profiling looming large over Toronto, Black teens in the city may not fare much better. Although no one can predict when such a tragedy will occur, we have unfortunately become all too familiar with the narrative of a Black person killed by police under questionable circumstances. Looking at the pictures of the Black teens riding through the Pocket's streets doesn't tell you much. Perhaps they are mischief-makers. Others had reported them for mouthing off when they were confronted for snooping around. But the question is, does any of that matter when the stakes are so high for racialized teens in the city? Criminalizing a young person not only carries heavy psychological and emotional implications, but, especially now, it poses life-threatening danger as well.

To object, in this case, is not, as many would have you believe, a form of censorship. It is a plea to think twice about casting suspicion on anyone, especially people whose very existence is under constant scrutiny. The deeper question is, how do we define neighbourhood? Who gets to be in? Who is assumed to be out? Who matters?

Challenging prevailing assumptions, even about unruly teenagers who may look and even act suspicious, is the starting point for broadening our notions of community. The problem with our virtual gated communities is they shut down powerful tools in social media that could help us grow and strengthen our connections.

Homogenous groups, whether they are on Nextdoor or on Facebook, are not known for suffering detractors gladly. The hive mind can easily turn defensive and hostile when confronted with criticism. In one reported case that made it to the South African courts, a Johannesburg-area woman who called out her Facebook group members for their racist remarks was verbally threatened by a neighbour who said he 'would take her down.'

There is a false sense of security that comes from neighbours posting on a presumably private social network. The presumption is that others in the group share the same goals – i.e., 'improving' the neighbourhood – and that the comments and photos posted are visible only to like-minded neighbours. These privileged discussions in secret Facebook groups, of which Toronto has many, do not give non-members who may share the streets a voice to express alternative views on serious issues such as policing, for example. In most cases, racial issues in these closed networks are brought to light only if someone speaks up outside of the group.

Psychologist and University of California Berkeley public policy professor Jack Glaser says racial profiling on social media is a reflection of what happens in real life, but with a significant difference. 'This is definitely a social media story,' he says. 'In terms of the perceptual processes, that's largely happening in real terms – seeing people and perceiving them to be suspicious. But on social media, they can share that information with a large group of people with lower stakes than calling 911. That creates a norm. When we see someone suspicious, we tell someone about it.'

Glaser, whose book *Suspect Race: Causes and Consequences of Racial Profiling* examines the significance of racial profiling by police forces, says several studies have found that implicit racial bias influences decision-making. For example, if a certain group, such as Black men, is associated with criminality, then non-consciously, race activates thoughts of crime-related events. 'Social media is a catalyst more than anything else,' says Glaser. 'It's changing the nature of this kind of thing. Before that, people had to pick up the phone and call 911 and stick their necks out. The stakes are lower in a way. Psychologically that creates a more uncertain, ambiguous decision space. More likely to see stereotypical judgments. More accountability in real life, but none of that is present.'

It is a double-edged sword, Glaser adds. 'The anonymity of the internet allows people from stigmatized groups greater access to things,' so people can speak up against racism and others can be held accountable for their harmful words. 'But on the other hand, that same anonymity gives people a fair amount of cover to say racist things.'

In the wake of the *East Bay Express* investigation, which caused considerable waves in social media and in several Bay Area neighbourhoods, Nextdoor executives met with Oakland's Neighbors for Social Justice and unveiled a new 'racial profiling' button that lets members flag stories directly to the social network. In the past, residents complained that neighbourhood moderators would simply delete posts that accused people of racial profiling. This way, these kinds of posts would be sent higher up the chain. Proposals that Neighbors for Social Justice members made and that were not adopted included banning the use of descriptors such as 'AA' for African-American and banning posts that are based on 'suspicions.'

In the tony Washington, D.C., neighbourhood of Georgetown, a coalition of local shopkeepers, police officers and community members use the same kinds of coded language to keep track of suspicious customers from store to store. The network, which uses the popular messaging app GroupMe, 'has attracted nearly 380 users who surreptitiously report on – and photograph – shoppers in an attempt to deter crime,' reported Terrence McCoy in the *Washington Post*.[3]

McCoy's investigation into Operation GroupMe messages found that African-Americans were primarily targeted and their movements were reported to local businesses. He found that, since March 2014, more than 90 percent of the 230 photos uploaded to the group have been of African-Americans. If Black people are systematically being closely watched while shopping, it follows that store owners are more likely to find more Black shoplifters. This is the same dynamic playing out in social media neighbourhood groups.

'Necessarily, if police are focusing on one group, they're going to catch more people from that group,' says psychologist Glaser. Ironically, while those in the targeted population may be getting disproportionately punished, those not targeted may be offending more. Glaser recalled a lab experiment in which white students in an exam situation were told that Black students were going to be observed more closely for cheating. The result? The white students cheated more than the Black students.

Days after I left the Pocket Facebook group, I felt frustrated with my own inaction. How could I let people get away with overt racism? I didn't want to go back into the fray, so I decided to write a story about the incident for the *Toronto Star*.[4] As a long-time journalist who used to work at the newspaper, I'm aware of the privileged position I enjoy. Most people don't have access to publishing in such a broadly disseminated publication, and that may be one reason they feel the need to express themselves so stridently in private social-network forums.

I'm familiar enough with the internet and comment threads on news sites to have anticipated a frustrating reaction to my story, which was headlined, 'Do I Really Belong in "Inclusive" Toronto?' and appeared online with a giant full-width photo of me. When the link was shared on Facebook, readers saw my big head and the question right below. The comments under the post on the *Star*'s Facebook were almost universally negative. 'Stop whining about inclusiveness. Are you an adult or an insecure child clinging to your mommy's apron?' wrote one poster.

A day or two after the article ran, a friend I used to work with in Montreal shouted my name after spotting me on the sidewalk. She just wanted to say hi. I was startled, because after reading the comments on my story, I felt kind of paranoid about walking around the neighbourhood. The response on Twitter was more constructive and supportive than on Facebook. Simmons had posted screenshots from the neighbourhood Facebook exchange a few days earlier and had reached out to local activists. She retweeted the article and identified herself as the person who had challenged the group.

Because I had left the Pocket group, I wasn't able to follow members' reaction to the column, so I decided to lurk around a neighbouring group to get a sense of what people were saying in their own communities. I Am a Leslievillian! is a public Facebook group, meaning anyone can read comments posted on the site, which serves as a forum for residents of a rapidly gentrifying east-end neighbourhood south of the Pocket. This site has a reputation for strident and outspoken members who aren't afraid to voice their opinions. Ironically, in the angry back-and-forth about racial profiling on the Pocket page, one tone-policing poster chastised their critical neighbours for being 'very aggressive, very Leslievillianesque.'

Yet what I found on the Leslieville group was a significantly different discussion than the one I had been expecting – though it didn't start out that way. Someone had posted the column on the page, and commenters quickly started discrediting it by questioning the ethics of posting unattributed quotes from the Pocket discussion thread. 'Not okay to take someone's picture but it's okay to print someone's words without their permission … double standard, no?' wrote one poster. (I would argue, by the way, that the Pocket commenters were presented anonymously in my story. I didn't post their names or profile photos.)

However, off the Leslieville page, another discussion was taking place, recalls Karima-Catherine Goundiam, who runs a Toronto digital agency. She was receiving messages from members of the group who were reluctant to post in the comment thread. 'A lot of minorities were there,' Goundiam recalls, 'but they weren't saying anything. We were having a back-channel conversation.'

It was a conversation Goundiam passionately believed should be made public. So she rolled up her sleeves and jumped into the Facebook thread. 'I think I spent half a day trying to respond to people,' she says. 'I'm wasting my time with it because I want to make a better world for my kids. I cannot fathom that 2015 is here and we're having the same stupid conversation. When they're thirty, they'll say, "Why did you do this to us?"'

People on the Facebook page 'will bitch about anything,' she says. So Goundiam was used to rowdy debates. In fact, she welcomed them. Neighbours should speak their minds, even if what they say comes across as offensive. 'If you don't say something, it's worse,' says Goundiam, who self-identifies as Black. 'You're going to have your own conversation in your head and no one is going to tell you the truth.'

What followed was a very heated, but mostly civil, discussion in which Goundiam and other posters, including Simmons – also a member of this group – explained the concept of white privilege and the importance of listening to the views of minority neighbours. The exchanges weren't always pleasant, but they resulted in the creation of an online community diversity group with the mandate of staging an off-line event so people could talk about these issues face to face.

Goundiam, who spearheaded the formation of the new forty-person group, says she wants her neighbours to echo their objections in person just as loudly as they did on Facebook. 'Be consistent,' she says. 'Be a jerk on-line and be a jerk off-line.'

The Pocket borders community-housing complexes and also includes some public housing. But few, if any, residents of those units are members of the private, invitation-only Facebook group. Moreover, a shared park is a particularly controversial space on the forum, with socially networked neighbours worried about teenagers playing basketball and making noise after the sun goes down. Apparently, with the help of their local councillor, concerned residents were able to get the City of Toronto to dismantle the nets every evening in the summer from sundown to sunrise, limiting court time for youths looking for an athletic outlet.

I contacted Lauren Simmons a few months after the photos of the Black teenagers were posted on the Pocket group, wanting to hear about what happened after I made my impulsive decision to leave. She said the discussion on the page rapidly became personal and she found herself under attack not only for her comments about racial profiling, but also about something she had said when she first joined the group four years ago.

Simmons recalls that she started speaking out when group members posted queries looking for free items. 'If you live in the [neighbourhood],' she responded to those requests, 'you can probably afford to buy your rain boots.' Continues Simmons, 'It's kind of self-serving ... sharing clothing items amongst each other while not looking at the people around them who might need them.' Although not everyone who lives in the Pocket is rich, she says, people in the group seemed more willing to help each other than those on 'the other side of the tracks,' including residents of the adjacent public-housing properties.

After the pile-on over the photos of the Black teenagers, Simmons was blocked and removed from the group. 'I share community space with people whose views seem so archaic and exclusionary and danger-ous,' she says. 'They're more scared of being called racist than not being racist.'

Blocking residents with opposing views has implications beyond social media. Neighbours still have to share the same streets, bus stops and parks with each other in the real world. So how do you stop virtual tensions from escalating on community Facebook pages?

After watching this complex digital battle play out, I have a few suggestions:

• *Be hyper-aware that the members of the group do not reflect the entire neighbourhood.* Social networks are selective by their very nature. I'm not just talking about private Facebook pages, but about who gets left behind across the digital divide. Internet access and smartphone data plans aren't as ubiquitous as we'd like to believe. Your neighbourhood group is only a subset of your community and your city. Make connections at the street level.

• *Understand that people have different experiences.* There are no guarantees that the photos and information you post on a private social network will stay private. Similarly, there is no law protecting content in a closed Facebook page. Also, remember that many neighbourhood groups, including several in Toronto's east end, allow community police officers to post updates. Their virtual presence may have a chilling effect for some members who are part of groups that have been targeted by the police.

• *Consider whether your neighbourhood group needs to be private.* Keeping your neighbourhood Facebook page public may be the best defence against inflammatory and incriminating discussions. Ask why you want to keep your posts secret and your group invitation-only. Are you comfortable with excluding fellow community members and posting content that may target other groups? Probably not.

By the fall, the *Toronto Star* piece I had written was behind me, and I was starting to feel more settled in our corner of the city. Then I saw a tweet from another outspoken member of the Pocket Facebook group.

'My neighbours have formed a FB group to post photos of alleged criminals,' wrote Katy Pedersen. 'There will be no comm to community about this.'

The new secret Facebook group is called Pocket Watch. It will no doubt have photos of Black teens on bikes and unshaven types walking too close to parked cars. But who will be featured next? Young Muslim kids who run from dogs? Will there be any photos of suspicious people who look like the posters?

'Most people are a little more willing to say things in the Facebook groups that they wouldn't necessarily say to you when they met you on the street,' says Pedersen, who works in the non-profit sector. 'It's like, "I'm gonna post it and let it fly."'

But the consequences are real and tear at the fabric of urban communities. Social networks, and Facebook in particular, are not known for sterling privacy policies. No matter how private or secret the group, photos can be easily downloaded and shared. Do they ever even disappear? In our post-surveillance era, who can we reasonably assume is monitoring our internet activity, sifting and sorting through people's radicalized suspicions?

I moved from Montreal hoping my son would find a warmer welcome in this stridently multicultural metropolis. Based on our in-person experiences with people and places in Toronto, it still feels like a good decision. But my fears about his future have not diminished so long as those around him – whether they're in Ontario or in Quebec – quietly, and perhaps secretly, harbour racialized assumptions and won't hesitate to snap and disseminate his picture for the 'greater good.'

The impulse to watch and post is what propels Karima-Catherine Goundiam to take these discussions out of the virtual world. She hopes that emerging from the shadows of social media and into the broad daylight of her neighbourhood will have a positive and lasting impact. 'People see me outside with my kids and say, "They're so cute,"' Goundiam says. 'But in ten years … they'll be teenagers and you'll see them again. What are you going to do? Call the police?'

Accessing Education: An Immigrant's Story
Nicholas Davis

In September of 1970, American songwriter Bobby Bloom's 'Montego Bay' was a Top 10 hit in the U.K., Canada and the U.S. The track extolls the virtues of Montego Bay, with images of vacationers lying on the beach, drinking rum and partying. The Jamaican Tourist Board couldn't have asked for a better advertisement to attract visitors to Jamaica's north coast and its burgeoning tourist industry. Montego Bay, Bloom often said when introducing his song, 'has a certain peacefulness that really sticks in your mind.'

The peacefulness tourists found in Montego Bay was elusive for the locals, however, especially in the fall of 1971. Violent crime was soaring and Jamaica was experiencing tough economic times, with high unemployment and high taxes – factors that led to a mass migration from Jamaica in the seventies.[1]

Over 325,000 Jamaicans immigrated to the U.S., Britain and Canada – ironically, the three places where Bloom's song topped the charts.[2] Linda Yarde's family was part of that exodus. In 1971 her father decided to move his wife and three children to Canada. 'I was only seven at the time,' remembers Yarde. 'My father told us he came to Canada for a better life.'

I met Linda, a single mother of three, at a high school basketball tournament at St. Michael's College, on the corner of Bathurst and St. Clair in midtown Toronto. Her oldest son is a teacher and basketball coach at a school playing in the tournament, and she was there to cheer on his team. She shared with me the story of how her father's decision to move his family from Jamaica to Canada enabled her to help her children reach their academic potential. It's a story of parenting, community and advocacy.

Linda's parents' story is similar to that of many immigrants who leave family and friends to start a new life. When they arrive in their new country, they have to find a job and a place to live, and figure out how to survive in an unfamiliar world. Many immigrants say they make the sacrifice for the sake of their children.

I once encountered a taxi driver from the Middle East who told me he was an engineer back home, but came to Toronto in 2010 to find a better life for himself and his family. When we spoke, he was living in Lawrence Heights and couldn't find a job as an engineer because his credentials weren't accepted here. He ended up driving a cab twelve to sixteen hours a day to make enough money to look after his family. He was living paycheque to paycheque.

Though he said life was hard for him, he was optimistic it would be better for his children. They were going to get a good education, he said, which was the key to their future success. My parents felt the same way. My father always told my brothers and me that 'nothing in life is guaranteed, but if you have a good education it increases the odds for success.'

The challenge for many people, especially new immigrants and the poor, is that access to a good education in highly polarized city-regions like Greater Toronto is no longer a given. Much has been written about the GTA's income divide and the impact this social polarization has on the quality of education. In 2013, the *Globe and Mail* ran an article entitled 'A Tale of Two Schools: The Correlation Between Income and Education in Toronto.' It told the story of two families who lived in different postal codes in the GTA, and how very different the educational experience was for their respective children.[3]

Other analysts have come to similar conclusions: David Hulchanski's report *The Three Cities Within Toronto* shows that in 2006, 61 percent of residents twenty-five years and older in predominantly high-income areas in the city had a university certificate, diploma or degree, compared to 31 percent in low-income areas.[4]

This is not unique to Toronto. It's a big-city problem across North America. In the U.S., they call it the urban-suburban gap. A 2009 article in the *New York Times* revealed that the average graduation rate in the fifty largest cities in America was 53 percent, compared with 71 percent in the suburbs. The gap was even more pronounced in places like Cleveland, with a 38 percent graduation rate in the city compared to 83 percent from suburban high schools. In Baltimore, only 41 percent of students graduated from city schools, whereas 81 percent came through suburban ones.[5]

The divide is really about poor neighbourhoods versus affluent neighbourhoods. Those who live in so-called 'good' areas are perceived to have better schools than those who live in so-called 'bad' neighbourhoods.[6] The divide, moreover, has a measurable impact on people of colour who live in poor neighbourhoods. The GTA's affluent areas were 82 percent white, whereas only 34 percent of the residents of the region's poorest neighbourhoods are white.[7] Toronto's poorest communities are overwhelmingly racialized.[8]

Over the past twenty-five years, the yearly income of newcomers to Canada has declined in relationship to the native population.[9] With the cost of housing so high in Toronto, many new immigrants end up in poor neighbourhoods. Attending a school in such a neighbourhood doesn't mean a student can't get a quality education. But with the current provincial funding model for GTA boards of education, many schools rely on fundraising to improve the quality of education they offer. Across the GTA, school-generated funds in 2008–2009 topped $240 million, according to a *Toronto Star* investigation, based on data collected through Freedom of Information requests. Critics say the money was being used to help fill the gap between what the province provides to school boards and the real cost of educating kids.[10]

On the elementary school side in Toronto, the top twenty fundraising schools were mostly from wealthy neighbourhoods, while the bottom twenty were from mostly needy neighbourhoods. At the high school level, the top four schools raised over a $1 million each. They were all from affluent neighbourhoods.[11]

'For schools that can raise a lot of money,' observes Annie Kidder, spokesperson for People for Education, an advocacy group, 'it ends up becoming a private school in the public system. And it puts poor kids at a "double disadvantage," because they may miss out on enrichment opportunities at school as well as at home.'[12]

Increasingly, it seems as if the best way to ensure your child gets a good education is to make sure he or she goes to one of the so-called better schools in the GTA. That means living in the catchment areas of those desirable schools. But the cost of living in a neighbourhood with these apparently better schools is steep. On average, a Toronto family must pay a $317,000 premium to raise their children in a good-school zone.[13]

The Red Pin, a real estate firm, collects data and information so people can make decisions on residential properties. In their report 'Toronto's Most Affordable Top School Neighbourhoods,' the company cites the annual results of province-wide Education Quality and Accountability Office tests to identify 'top schools.'[14] Many Toronto real estate brokerages, in fact, use neighbourhood-level EQAO test results when they set house prices and market properties to buyers.

For those who can afford to move into one of these affluent neighbourhoods, the likelihood of attending a 'top school' is high. Conversely, for those who can only afford poorer neighbourhoods, the local school may further disadvantage their children when it comes to getting a quality education.

The stakes for a hyper-diverse region like Greater Toronto couldn't be higher. According to a 2009 report by higher-education experts Joseph Berger and Andrew Parkin, someone with a bachelor's degree will earn $745,800 more than a high school graduate over a career, and someone with a postgraduate degree will earn over $1 million more. Drawing on Statistics Canada data, Berger and Parkin concluded that access to education is one of the most important ways in which individuals can improve their circumstances and ensure a high quality of life for themselves, their families and their communities.[15]

In a metropolitan area with what appears to be a two-tier education system – a Cadillac for those who can afford to live in affluent areas, and a beater for everyone else – Berger and Parkin's conclusions should force us all to think hard about the opportunities that await the next generations of Torontonians.

The Yarde family settled in the northwest end of the city in a culturally diverse neighbourhood on the border of York West and Rexdale. The area had a history of strong community spirit, but as in Montego Bay, its residents wrestled with many socio-economic issues related to poverty, unemployment, affordable housing and education.[16]

Not quite the promised land Linda's father was looking for, but if the Yarde family had any questions about the opportunities for success for Black families in their new country, they needed look no further than the office of the local MPP, which was inhabited by Leonard Braithwaite – the first Black elected to Parliament and a provincial legislature in Canada.[17]

Braithwaite was born in 1923 in Toronto to Caribbean parents who highly valued education. After graduating from high school, he spent three years in the Royal Canadian Air Force before attending the University of Toronto and earning a bachelor's degree in commerce. Braithwaite then went to Harvard and earned his MBA before returning to Osgoode Hall Law School, where he graduated with honours. Two years after opening a small law practice in Etobicoke, Braithwaite was elected as an Etobicoke school trustee. The year was 1960, and it was the beginning of a lifelong political career for Braithwaite.[18]

During his term as an MPP (1963–1975), Braithwaite fought against an injustice that made him an iconic figure for West Indians in Etobicoke, as well as for Blacks across Ontario. In his first speech to the Ontario Legislature in 1964, he spoke out against the fact that some Ontario schools were still legally segregating Black children from whites.

After his speech, the then–Progressive Conservative government abolished a 114-year-old law that allowed for separate, segregated schools for children of colour. 'That was perhaps my greatest accomplishment,' Braithwaite said in an interview for the Ontario Black History Society. (Braithwaite also fought for gender equality. In 1966, he spoke in favour of the addition of female pages in the House at Queen's Park.[19])

While those reforms removed a legal barrier, the cultural obstacles remained. In 1979, a group of parents in Toronto, under the name Organization of Parents of Black Children, set out to convince the Toronto Board of Education that the school system was failing their children. Keren Braithwaite (no relation to Leonard) was one of the co-directors of the group. She had come to Toronto from Antigua in 1967 to attend graduate school at the University of Toronto.

The OPBC presented school officials with a range of their concerns: the high dropout rate of Black students, the dearth of Black teachers, culturally biased IQ tests, low expectations for Black students, and teachers' lack of knowledge about Black culture and the history of Blacks in Canada.[20]

'I found out that access to education was dismal, especially to university education and to graduate education,' Keren Braithwaite observed in the *International Journal of Multicultural Education*. 'That would be my first point of knowledge because I could see it. But in moving out into the community, and mixing with African Canadians who had been here, I began to be exposed to the weight and the depth of the lack of access in the public school system, employment, etc. The whole question of racism loomed.'[21]

Linda Yarde and her siblings went to the local elementary school near their home, but when it came time for high school, Linda's mom sought out schools with better reputations. She lived in a low-income area, and was keenly aware of the shortcomings of the education system in her neighbourhood just by talking with other local parents. While middle-class parents in gentrifying working-class neighbourhoods make a virtue of sending their kids to the local school, low-income families or newcomers may be less inclined to take the risk.

Linda's brother went to De La Salle College, a private Catholic high school in the Deer Park neighbourhood of Toronto, near Yonge and St. Clair, while Linda and her sister attended Loretto Abbey, an all-girls Catholic high school in Hoggs Hollow, one of the most affluent neighbourhoods in the city. Both schools were arguably the best academic schools the Yarde family could afford, and both were far away from their neighbourhood.

For Linda, it was the beginning of a contemptuous relationship with Ontario's education system. Her resentment began with the hour-long bus ride to her new school. Linda hated getting up early every morning and having to leave the comfort of her neighbourhood and friends to go to a place where she felt unwanted.

'I just remember going to school with a bunch of rich kids,' says Linda. 'I stood out like a sore thumb ... I felt totally out of my environment. No one really came to my aid to make me feel welcome. It was all business there.'

With no real friends and only a cordial locker partner, Linda struggled socially and academically. 'I had no one to study with,' she recalls, 'no one to have fun with. I always felt so alone there. At some point I didn't bother to put in the work I needed to get grades that were acceptable to my parents.'

One day she came home with what she thought was a decent mark in mathematics. 'I struggled in math with my marks hovering around the sixties' she says. 'So when I got a 72 on a test I was so proud I decided to share the mark with my parents. When my father saw what I got, he threw the paper on the floor and walked out of the room. At that moment I felt like I could never do enough in school to make my dad happy.'

It was after that year, in Grade 10, that Linda decided she'd had enough – enough of the commuting, enough of the uniforms and enough of the loneliness. 'I was so unhappy, I told my parents I wasn't going back, no matter what,' she says. 'We argued a lot that summer, but my mom finally agreed that I could go to a public school – of her choosing, of course.'

I empathize with Linda's school experience. I was six when I realized I hated school. It was my first day of Grade 1 at a public school in LaSalle, a Montreal suburb. As I waited in the schoolyard for the bell to ring, I noticed on the wall in big white letters a racial epithet urging me, the only Black student at the school, to go home.

That wasn't the first time I had seen those words or heard them uttered toward me. My family had immigrated to Canada from Kingston, Jamaica, in 1966 – Mom, Dad and four boys. Initially, we lived on a farm near Hamilton, and knew of only one other Black family in the area. Although we could probably have shared stories about the racism our families faced when we went into the town, we hardly saw each other as we often stayed locked in our homes.

My father died of pneumonia three years after we came to Canada, and we moved to Montreal to be near my mom's family. At the time,

Montreal was rife with anti-English, anti-immigrant sentiment. Our neighbours treated us disparagingly, like outsiders. I wasn't surprised to see racist graffiti in the schoolyard, but there was something about this particular message that frightened me to my core. At first I didn't know what it was, but then it dawned on me. The writing was so high up on the wall that it couldn't possibly have been written by a student. In the playground, I informed an adult whom I assumed to be a teacher, and she told me how sorry she was that I had to see such things. She comforted me until the bell rang, then told me to go to class, and she would take care of it. I trusted her. But later that morning, when I came out for recess, the hateful message was still on the wall.

After that incident, I disengaged from school for a long time. The only thing that made me go to school every day was the fear of disappointing my mother, who demanded that my brothers and I not only attend school but also do well. She was convinced that a good education would lead to a bright future, devoid of the struggles she faced as a single mom raising four boys in a foreign country.

When I was eight, she moved my brothers and me from a poor neighbourhood in Montreal to a poor neighbourhood in the Toronto suburb of Mississauga. During my school years, we had to move another thirteen times; I went to three different public schools and three different high schools. And because we lived in mostly poor communities, the schools I attended didn't have great academic reputations.

I never felt like I belonged: I was often the only Black student in the advanced classes my mother made me take, and what we were learning in school never spoke to the reality I experienced as a poor Black boy from a single-parent West Indian family, living in government housing with three siblings.

Despite the statistics that implied I was less likely to get a good education growing up as a poor Black male in low-income neighbourhoods, I survived school. My mother never skipped a parent-teacher meeting, despite the fact that she was often working two or three jobs to support us. She told my Grade 8 guidance counsellor, who recommended that I take basic classes in Grade 9, that I would be attending advanced classes. She also denied me extracurricular activities for a year when I brought home a 78 percent average in Grade 11 math. In fact, if my mother hadn't advocated for my brothers and me – as well as many of my brothers' friends – we would have never finished high school, much less gone on to university, which we all did.

Linda Yarde wanted to go to one of the two local high schools in her area. 'I would see these Black kids get on and off the bus wearing regular clothes and they appeared to be having so much fun,' she recalls. 'I wanted to feel what it was like to wear regular clothes to school and look like my Black brothers and sisters.'

Her mom, however, refused. 'She felt those schools were too 'ghetto.' She told me there were too many kids underachieving at those schools. How my mom knew this I will never know. I guess the parent grapevine was very strong in my neighbourhood.'

Rexdale's parent grapevine led Linda's mom to pick C. W. Jefferys, considered a good academic public school at the time. For Linda it was a dream come true. She found friends, good times and a feeling of belonging. 'Those were the best school years of my life. Maybe they were too good. I loved the whole cafeteria liming. The benches at the back were reserved for the Black kids playing dominoes and cards. You had the Italians, the stoners ... Everyone had their sections. There were basketball games, and then of course there were boys.'

In her last year, Linda got pregnant. 'My mom encouraged me to finish high school, which I did,' she says. 'It was the best decision I ever made and I thank my mom and dad every day for supporting me through my last year of high school.'

Linda's parents wanted her to go to university when her son was born, but Linda felt she had to finish school as quickly as possible so she could take care of her child. So she enrolled in Seneca College where she earned a two-year diploma in business administration.

'My parents were proud of me, but I felt like I let them down a little. So I encouraged my younger sister and brother to make sure they went to university to make our parents proud, which they both did.'

Linda has some regrets about not getting a university degree, she says. 'Things could have been better if I had gone to university, if I waited to have children. Time keeps running and next thing you know you're twenty-five and have two kids and are in a dead-end job. Things weren't disastrous, but when you put the horse before the cart, you end up playing catch-up.'

As a parent, Linda is faced with the same dilemma her parents confronted. By the time Linda had her third child, she was living in a poor neighbourhood in Mississauga. Her son was entering high school and her first daughter was beginning middle school. Linda was already preoccupied with putting her children in the best possible position to be successful academically.

'I lived in a government housing complex where I could look out my apartment window and see the front of the local high school,' she remembers. 'I can't tell you the number of times I looked out that window and saw police cars at that school. I was pretty sure I did not want to send my children there.'

Before she completely wrote off the school, Linda talked with other parents in the neighbourhood and read through the Fraser Institute School Report Card – a Canadian public policy think tank that issues a yearly report on the best high schools in Ontario. The neighbours told her the school was full of 'thugs,' and the Fraser Report had the school in the lower end of its best high school rankings. Both sources confirmed Linda's fears.

Finding academic success for her children would not be an easy task. All three had unique educational needs. Her son was an elite athlete who wanted to focus on basketball as much as academics. Her oldest daughter wanted to be around her friends. And Linda's youngest was an elite athlete and a gifted student.

Linda decided to send her son to a school out of the area that offered an Extended French program and he later transferred to an alternative school catering to elite athletes. Her son and a friend travelled to that school every morning. 'It was good that the two of them went together every day,' she says. 'If I had a travel companion when I was going to the all-girls school, I might have finished school there like my sister did.' Linda's son ended up graduating from high school and attended Wilfrid Laurier University, where he played varsity basketball and graduated with a BA in geography and a minor in French. He received a teaching certificate in Australia.

Linda's oldest daughter went to the same Extended French program where her brother started high school. Unlike her brother, she loved French and studied hard. She also made great friendships. 'She gave me grief with the friend business, boys, the party life and the social life,' Linda recall. 'But she was always an excellent student.'

Linda credits her older sister with keeping her daughter focused on her academics. Linda's sister was an excellent student and a high achiever. She was very close to all of Linda's children, but had a special bond with the oldest daughter. After graduating high school, Linda's daughter went to York University, where she earned both a bachelor's degree and a master's degree in social work.

By the time Linda's youngest daughter was fourteen, her other children had already finished university and were working – one as a teacher and the other as a social worker. 'My youngest daughter saw first-hand what a good education could do for you just by watching her siblings,' Linda says. 'I didn't really have to push her to do well. She was easily the best student of all my children.'

When her youngest was ready for high school, Linda moved so she'd be within the school boundaries of the best high school in Mississauga. As she explains, 'I knew other parents who had moved to certain parts of the city to make sure their child attended a "good" school. I was planning on moving anyways, so I hired a real estate agent to help me find an affordable home in the school's boundaries. It was a bit out of my price range, but I made it work.'

As it turned out, Linda's daughter, who'd attended a French camp before enrolling in an Extended French program, was way ahead of the curve. On top of getting straight A's in school, she was heavily courted by U.S. schools for a soccer scholarship. She graduated with honours from high school and accepted a Division One soccer scholarship to Texas Christian University, where she is currently studying biology with hopes of becoming a doctor.

Like her own parents, Linda made sacrifices so her children could have a better life, dedicating herself to advocating for her children, finding the best schools for them, helping with homework and involving them in the decisions about schooling. 'I didn't work three jobs like some of the other parents in the neighbourhood,' she says. 'I wanted to be there for them when they needed me so they could land on their feet and take the world by storm. I learned quickly along the way that money isn't everything; it's about the family time we spend together.'

But what about children who do not have parents able to advocate for them in our two-tier system? School boards should play a part in helping increase the odds of academic success for students in poor neighbourhoods. Finding better funding models for schools, sharing fundraised money from the affluent schools with schools in need and paying teachers better wages to work in disadvantaged-area schools are just a few ideas that may help.

Boards need to be innovative and find new ways to deliver curriculum. The Toronto District School Board, for example, opened an Afrocentric alternative school in September 2009[22] and in 2014 launched the first Afrocentric high school program, which is named after Leonard Braithwaite and located in Scarborough. The classes are de-streamed and taught by an all-Black faculty.

There are systematic changes that can help as well, such as revamping curriculum to reflect a diverse student population, providing incentives for educators to adopt new tools to help children succeed in poor neighbourhoods and holding them accountable when the system fails students.

People have been grappling with these ideas, but none of them are easy to accomplish, especially without the political will needed to turn them into reality. Some of the ideas (merit pay for teachers, new curriculums, magnet schools) have been implemented across Canada and in the U.S. with some degree of success. But in hyper-diverse places like Toronto, there is no one-size-fits-all solution. School boards, governments and families need to find solutions that best suit the needs of the students who live in low-income areas, where the chances of academic success are troublingly low.

We must ask, in fact, why it is so difficult for children in poor neighbourhoods to have access to high-quality education. In a 2008 paper for the Cambridge, MA-based National Bureau of Economic Research, education analysts Brian Jacob and Jens Ludwig argue that there is a compelling moral justification for educational interventions that help impoverished young people find success in school: 'Disadvantaged children should not be punished for the circumstances into which they are born, and improved education policy is one of the best ways to prevent this from happening.'[23]

The academic success of the Yarde family shouldn't be an anomaly; it should be the norm, and accomplished without all the hurdles.

Policing and Trust in the Hyper-Diverse City
Nana Yanful

'In a democratic society, the police serve to protect, rather than impede, freedoms ... A democratic police force is not concerned with people's beliefs or associates, their movements or conformity to state ideology... Instead, the police force of a democracy is concerned strictly with the preservation of safe communities and the application of criminal law equally to all people, without fear or favour.'
— *United Nations International Police Task Force 1996*

Kendrick Lamar's song 'Alright,' an impassioned reminder of resilience and light in these dark times, hit hard and right on time during 2015's summer of protest, with activist groups, led mostly by the Black Lives Matter movement, chanting the song's lyrics to highlight police brutality against Black bodies, and providing a sense of hope driven by despair. Lamar also performed this song at the 2015 Black Entertainment Television awards on top of a police car, a poignant and provocative image from one of our generation's new critical voices. While the image and lyrics crystallize the frustration, anger and sadness over police brutality and the lack of action by police services, prosecutors and courts to be accountable and enact punishment, they also signify yet another example of my generation's negative perceptions and severe distrust of the police.

Modern policing in North America is rooted in Sir Robert Peel's nine principles of policing, including his famous notion that the police are the public and the public are the police. But in practice, in cities that are increasingly racially and ethnically diverse, racialized people have always been over-policed. In Toronto, for example, in the late nineteenth and early twentieth centuries, police were tasked with regulating citizens along income and class lines – which meant ethnic lines, as the majority of immigrants came from Italy, Eastern Europe and China. Into the early twentieth century, policing took the form of moral regulation, when a series of provincial laws, commercial bylaws and licensing regulations designed to uphold social order were enforced by the police; most of the folks affected were racialized, low-income citizens.[1]

Despite the intervening decades of immigration, multicultural and anti-racist policies, as well as evolving human and civil rights laws, old habits die hard. As former Ontario chief justice R. Roy McMurtry and the Honourable Alvin Curling noted in the 2008 Roots of Youth Violence Report, the long-standing belief held by many members of racialized communities is that overly aggressive police tactics and the use of racial profiling cause young people to 'become alienated, lose self-esteem and feel that they have less hope or opportunity in this society.'

The Trust Deficit

The persistent over-policing of members of racialized or marginalized communities has a cascading impact on cities and neighbourhoods, creating deep and far-reaching divisions that result from the institutionalization of distrust directed at particular groups. Social cohesion exists only when individuals in a community enjoy high levels of mutual trust. We all have trust-based personal relationships. But at a societal level, much depends on our ability to trust in those who provide essential services, such as teachers, transit operators, pilots and engineers. The architecture of trust is baked into the governance, training and accountability frameworks surrounding many professions. If we cannot trust the pilot to land the plane or the engineer to design a structurally sound bridge, society cannot function.

Similarly, for society to function and for all citizens to feel they belong, we must trust that law enforcement agencies will act democratically and be accountable to those whom they serve. One wonders whether there was ever a time when the police were a proxy for trust and safety. Those whose daily interactions with officers may be mundane or almost non-existent may have always viewed the police in this fashion. They may celebrate the images of police culture on television shows or in movies, or feel comfortable calling the police when they are in trouble. By virtue of their own experience, they trust the police to uphold the peace and protect citizens.

However, many individuals and families view the police as being at the forefront of a system that maintains injustice in our society. Policing, in fact, is the one public-facing profession where trust is so often found wanting. Whether this is due to implicit and explicit biases, a lack of anti-racism and anti-oppression training or a failure to understand that police work must first and foremost serve communities, the police have lost the trust of many of the same citizens they have sworn to serve.

There are many reasons for this distrust. First, aggressive police tactics are much more frequently directed at racialized communities, especially the African-Canadian community. Eric Morgan is one example. The Brampton man was acquitted of second-degree murder in 2013 after the Hon. Justice Fletcher Dawson, of the Ontario Superior Court of Justice, instructed the jury in Morgan's case to find him not guilty. Dawson found that the police used abusive and threatening tactics against key witnesses and manufactured incriminating evidence against Morgan. Such aggressive techniques can improperly shape witness statements and lead to wrongful convictions. Yet in November 2015, the Office of the Independent Police Review Director decided it would not lay charges against the Peel Regional Police detectives involved in Morgan's case, concluding that the officers' tactics were consistent with the Peel detectives' training. Since then, Morgan has filed a $25 million civil suit against the Region of Peel Police Services Board, the former police chief and five Peel homicide detectives. In their statement of defence, Peel law enforcement officials claimed that Morgan 'was entirely the author of his own misfortune.' When it comes to building trust in communities, such denial of misconduct and the institutional approval of coercive and improper techniques is the complete opposite of what police forces should be doing.

Ontario's Special Investigations Unit is a body tasked to investigate when serious injuries and deaths may have resulted from criminal offences committed by police officers. When complaints reported to the SIU do not involve serious injury or death, the unit refers the incident for internal investigation, or to other non-police agencies, such as the Ontario Civilian Police Commission. However, the SIU lays few criminal charges against police, and most of the cases that do go to trial end in acquittals. That track record has caused many to question whether the SIU truly acts as an accountability mechanism to increase trust and reduce the incidents of police violence against the citizenry.[2] Further, African-Canadians and Aboriginal people are highly overrepresented as civilians involved in SIU investigations.[3]

Many in Toronto's racialized communities are skeptical that these accountability measures have an impact on police organizations and officer behaviour. And who could blame them, given the SIU's record when it comes to laying charges? Take the 2014 case of the Peel police officer who shot and killed Jermaine Carby. Despite a year-long investigation that found the police tampered with evidence at the scene, the SIU didn't charge the officer. Or the more recent killing of Andrew Loku by Toronto police, which also did not result in charges following SIU review. Rather than building trust, social cohesion and accountability, the SIU seems to have accomplished precisely the opposite in its almost three decades of operation.

As a criminal defence lawyer, I have many clients who are racialized, mentally ill and/or homeless. The majority of their interactions with police are negative: multiple traffic stops, searches, raids, arrests and over-surveillance. As a result, their sense of trust, belonging and citizenship has been drastically eroded. Police services have been grappling with the problem of how to repair this breakdown, and have sought to apply different techniques, programs and models to address it. However, these efforts have often been either misguided or are deployed within an already toxic system. It's true that overall confidence in the police is high in Canada as compared to its international counterparts, but when we break down those findings based on various indicators, the data tells a different story.[4]

For instance, a 2007 article by Jeffrey Reitz and Rupa Banerjee entitled 'Racial Inequality, Social Cohesion, and Policy Issues in Canada' showed the disconnect between how recent immigrants, immigrants with longer experience in Canada and the children of immigrants (second-generation children) felt about their Canadian identity, voting behaviours and sense of trust and belonging.[5] The results were surprising: the parents felt more Canadian, held more positive views about voting and demonstrated more trust and a greater sense of belonging than did their children. Further, these results were impacted by race, demonstrating that white, second-generation children felt a greater sense of belonging and trust toward institutions than did their racialized counterparts. Why is this?[6]

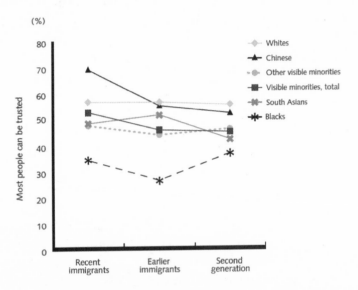

Some researchers argue that despite being born in Canada, second-generation young people, particularly those from racialized backgrounds, may experience higher levels of discrimination and racism than their parents, which in turn may affect their sense of belonging, cultural identity and/or self-esteem, group behaviour and involvement in activities such as voting and volunteerism.[7] Some argue that second-generation children may also have higher expectations than their parents of social acceptance, economic opportunity and equal participation.

This research is important for many reasons, including the implementation of policies for policing and the administration of justice. Policy-makers must be keenly aware that any actions they take that further a sense of distrust or of not belonging among racialized groups has a ripple effect on other aspects of Canadian life, such as voting.

An awareness of being distrusted also has a direct impact on one's sense of identity, equity and justice as a Canadian citizen. The consequences of systemic mistrust and alienation, in other words, are not to be taken lightly – they deserve special attention instead of denial. As some of the discourse around the recent carding and street-checks practice in Toronto and across the province has shown, those who are made to feel like second-class citizens in their own neighbourhoods have little incentive to place their confidence in the police and perhaps other public institutions. If anything, the multi-sectoral outcry for amendments and stronger repercussions for police services that continue to engage in discriminatory practices such as carding reminded politicians that carding or raids on specific communities doesn't increase safety or trust.

The False Promise of Community Policing

The crusade for community-based policing began in the 1980s, and this approach is often seen as an innovative way to curb crime and increase feelings of personal safety. 'Community policing,' however, is a broad concept that means different things to different people. Some view it as a philosophy, while others see it as an actual set of policing techniques. Northwestern University crime policy expert Wesley G. Skogan argues that most police services that adopted a community framework have three core strategic components: decentralization, citizen involvement and problem-solving.[8] Here in Ontario, police services are mandated under Section 1 (1) of the Adequacy and Effectiveness of Police Services Regulation to provide community-based crime-prevention initiatives, such as Neighbourhood Watch. I would argue, however, that community policing has been ineffective in increasing trust in Toronto police. Instead, police have deployed inappropriate and discriminatory practices while publicly promoting a belief in community policing.

In theory, community policing requires engagement meant to develop trust between the police and members of high-density neighbourhoods. Police must readjust their focus from traditionally reactive law enforcement to becoming an integral part of the community and making space for residents to assist them in determining priorities and allocation of resources in these neighbourhoods. Community members must also have a willingness to identify problems and then develop strategies to address those problems in partnership with the police.

Don't get me wrong: this kind of community crime control, in the form of block watches or citizen foot patrols, has occurred for decades, in part due to the public's eroding confidence in the police. However, to mobilize citizens, trust must be at the centre of the community-police partnership. The viability of such partnerships depends on the ability and willingness of the police to learn from community members, to hear critiques and implement changes, and to create an organizational climate that meaningfully investigates misconduct as a means of holding officers accountable to the public.

One of the myths around community policing is that the presence of officers in a neighbourhood is sufficient for citizens to feel comfortable enough with the police to approach them, share information with them or seek their assistance. Yet genuine community policing is more than just transactional encounters. Police must learn to treat each citizen with respect. There's been a noticeable, ongoing presence of police officers under the guise of community policing, but without the sharing of power and the buy-in from community, can result in negative interactions between citizens and the police; it does little to repair the deep-rooted ambivalence some citizens hold toward law enforcement.

Further, community policing has the potential to be misused as a form of zero-tolerance policing. Take, for example, the so-called 'broken windows' school of policing, introduced in the 1980s by sociologists James Q. Wilson and George Kelling. The broken-windows philosophy is that any evidence of disorder in a neighbourhood, such as broken windows, litter, graffiti or loitering, is a signal that no one cares. The evidence of neglect, according to the theory, prompts residents to be fearful and use the streets or other public spaces less often. As such, proponents of the broken-windows theory believe neighbourhoods with such evidence of neglect are more vulnerable to criminal invasion; therefore, policing low-level offences will prevent the occurrence of more serious crimes. This theory was the foundation for many controversial reforms in policing practice, including stop-and-frisks in New York City. It has been criticized for targeting marginalized groups by pushing more people who are mentally ill, homeless and/or racialized into the criminal justice system.

Community policing, in many ways, is a logical consequence of the broken-windows theory. Many police forces in recent years, moreover, have used the term 'community policing' to describe and recast their over-policing practices.

Critics of community policing suggest the term is misleading. For example, U.S. sociologist Peter Manning, who has written extensively about law enforcement, describes community policing as the 'rhetorical giant' and a 'creature of nostalgia ... full of the necessary ambiguities and contradictions that can draw together diverse people and unite them behind an idea.' He argues that community-based policing is undermined by conflicting objectives and, at best, serves to prompt police services to reflect on their work and possibly introduce some reforms.[9]

Osgoode Hall Law School professor Margaret E. Beare suggests that the contradictions in community policing are many. First, which 'communities' are we talking about? The generic use of the term is dangerous and perpetuates stereotypes. Second, where does community policing actually occur? In affluent neighbourhoods or only in low-income, racialized neighbourhoods? Third, who is the 'leader' in the community policing relationship? The imbalance of power and resources results in the police being the only 'partner' with the resources. As a result, the police end up leading the initiative or partnership. Fourth, is community policing really a priority? Police services may claim it is, but no systemic changes occur. Lastly, is community policing viewed as 'real' policing within police services? When officers are encouraged to engage in or are tasked with community policing, it is not valued in the same way as an officer engaged in a big drug bust or a high-profile sting. Redefining police culture means that work that encourages trust-building and equality is seen as valuable within police services.

The case of the Toronto Anti-Violence Intervention Strategy (TAVIS) offers another perspective on how community policing has been used to deliver other agendas. Toronto police established TAVIS in 2006 after homicides involving guns doubled the year before. The strategy is intended to reduce crime and increase safety in particular Toronto neighbourhoods, and involves extra plainclothes officers being placed in neighbourhoods and schools. But this heavy police presence has resulted in over-surveillance and high rates of carding of racialized people – mostly young, African-Canadian men. There have also been incidents of aggressive actions by TAVIS officers who were unfamiliar with those communities and acted on stereotypes of the area and its residents. While viewed by some as a community policing strategy, TAVIS – more than any other policing tactic in Toronto in the last decade – has shattered trust in the name of curbing gun violence, with little observable effect or verifiable data on what the strategy has accomplished.[10]

The Case for Democratic Policing

What, then, is a good crime-prevention philosophy that does little to no harm and also allows trust and belonging to develop, especially among people from marginalized communities?

It begins with a system of policing that is subject to rigorous democratic processes and accountability mechanisms that compel police services to repair and rebuild the relationships with those they have been entrusted to serve and protect. I believe that implementing 'democratic policing' is a good start.

Democratic policing is sometimes viewed as a process, rooted in the rule of law, whereby all actions by law enforcement are subject to public accountability, involve respect for the dignity of the citizenry and place limits on the power of the state to intrude on individual and collective liberties. Democratic policing was dispersed throughout the nineteenth century, and adopted in Canada and North America more generally, with some modifications in places like Quebec with the influence of civil law. Many scholars have examined democratic policing, including Peter Manning, who, in his book *Democratic Policing in a Changing World*, suggests a working notion of democratic policing within the context of Western democratic societies. He argues that this framework should not be studied as a 'system' of abstract principles, but rather should form the basis for 'an ideologically derived policy of imposed social change from "above."' According to Manning, democratic policing is an 'ensemble' of practices based on a set of general principles.[11]

Democratic policing requires police organizations to be accountable to the law rather than to government. At the centre of democratic policing is a 'do no harm' principle, based on the belief that nothing should be done by the state that increases existing inequalities on the basis of policy or practice. While the police chief in a city like Toronto answers to the Police Services Board, which includes the mayor or a designate as well as city councillors, the institution should not be seen as a replacement or proxy for public rule-making and citizen input. Many citizens are unaware of policing tactics and strategies until an event occurs that sheds light on those practices. Studies have shown that individuals are more likely to comply with the law and cooperate with law enforcement when they perceive the officers' actions as legitimate. Legitimacy, then, is the key to improving police effectiveness. However, to view the police and their actions as legitimate, citizens must perceive that the police are responsive to community demands.[12]

Democratic accountability ensures that policy choices are vetted in the public arena, and the rule of law requires that those choices be constitutional. Informed public discourse is central, given the rise of securitization over the last couple of decades, such as increased reliance on private security officers in shopping malls, stores, banks, office buildings and schools. This change unfolded with little public consultation, yet it marks a significant expansion of the policing and surveillance of urban spaces. As another example, Torontonians recently learned that the Toronto Police Service would soon be purchasing semi-automatic assault rifles, to be used in the city's seventeen divisions beginning in spring 2016. The rifles are similar to those carried by Canadian Forces soldiers and specialized tactical units. The decision to purchase these rifles was not publicly debated. In fact, when it comes to the regulation of policing, we are typically left to rely on court challenges and judicial reviews to ensure that policing practices are constitutional. Proper public scrutiny of police practices, such as the use of Tasers, often occurs only in the wake of tragedies, such as the death of Robert Dziekański at the hands of RCMP officers in the Vancouver airport in 2007.

All levels of government, including territorial and Aboriginal governments, should be directly responsible for regulating police activity to ensure it is conducted in line with equitable values. The police routinely trumpet initiatives such as gang and neighbourhood targeting of 'priority neighbourhoods,' or sweeps of those individuals living on the street, as effective crime-prevention strategies. But these practices violate the shared rights we as citizens all have, and they increase the inequalities that exist within neighbourhoods. Policing, rather, should operate as a kind of restructuring mechanism, with notions of trust, equality and legitimacy at its foundation.[13]

Examples of Democratic Policing Strategies

Can democratic policing practices reduce current inequalities, or at least do no harm? And how does one build a city where the most vulnerable and marginalized members of that community *trust* the police? And what role do the police play in shaping equality and justice? While Toronto is a unique city with its own challenges, it is beneficial to look at how other municipalities have implemented alternative or democratic-type policing strategies.

The Prince Albert Model

Community Mobilization Prince Albert, also known as the Hub model, was introduced under former police chief Dale McFee in Prince Albert, Saskatchewan, and inspired by a model used in Glasgow, Scotland.[14] Prince Albert struggled, like many communities, with growing social issues and increasing arrest rates – the city's crime and violence levels exceeded national and provincial averages. Front-line personnel in the human services sector were frustrated by the lack of buy-in from community members and those in power. With the costs of policing and arrest rates set to double within a decade, stakeholders came together in 2011 to find a new approach to community safety, with a focus on addressing the root causes of crime, including poverty, unemployment, poor housing and mental health issues.[15]

Fifteen agencies comprise the Hub, including the police, the fire department, the city, social services, the RCMP and various government ministries. The members meet twice weekly to discuss high-risk situations, and immediate responses aimed at reducing various risks that cross multiple sectors of the human service. These gatherings identify the complex risks confronting some individuals or families that cannot be addressed by a single agency alone. When situations are brought to the table, the appropriate service provider engages in a discussion, which results in a collaborative intervention to connect services and offer supports where they were not already in place.

The Hub is supported by the Centre of Responsibility, which provides full-time 'research, analysis, and long-term solutions to systemic issues, and root causes of social problems.'[16] It is critical for police officials to engage with civilian service providers in a setting such as the Hub, where the focus is not on arrests and incarceration, but on a public health model for reducing crime and violence in a particular community. As a result, service providers, including the police, can mitigate risks within a day or two and connect individuals and families to much-needed services. For example, instead of the police repeatedly arresting an individual who is regularly intoxicated and disorderly, the Hub can connect that person to a treatment facility. Before Prince Albert adopted the Hub approach, that person may have been arrested, and later released from jail without any treatment for their addiction or possible mental health issues, only to reoffend and go through the cycle again. The Hub, which in 2012–2013 took on 307 cases, aims to address the underlying issues quickly, so that such individuals are more likely to reduce their contact with police and the criminal justice system. Since the launch of the Hub in February 2011, Prince Albert has seen a drop in its violent crime severity index, which tracks the change in the volume of a particular crime, as well as the relative seriousness of that crime in comparison to other crimes.[17]

Through a recent evaluation conducted by the University of Saskatchewan, stakeholders, including human service professionals, provided feedback on their experiences in the Hub. One of their criticisms is the perception that the Hub is yet another tool for police, instead of a forum for multi-agency collaboration. As the Hub was originally a police initiative, officers are still commonly involved in front-line collaborative interventions, which may include 'door knocking,' trying to locate the individual at risk or connecting and communicating with that individual's family or friends. The reliance on the police as first responders concerns some stakeholders, specifically in situations involving mental health or addiction issues. Despite these concerns, the Hub has provided a Canadian model of a collaborative risk-driven intervention strategy that has contributed to a reduction of harm and improved client outcomes of human service professionals.

The Los Angeles Model[18]

In 2011, the Los Angeles Police Department (LAPD) partnered with the Advancement Project's Urban Peace program and the city's housing authority to form the Community Safety Partnership (CSP) in L.A.'s public housing developments of Watts. CSP was formed through a memorandum of understanding between the three partners. They describe their work as 'relationship-based policing,' because the police focus not just on crime statistics, but on building their legitimacy within the community through the use of procedural justice, authentic relationships with individuals and sustained commitment to improving the health and well-being of the community.

The LAPD hardly seems like an obvious candidate for this kind of project. The agency has a long history of racist practices, and pioneered the deployment of military-style SWAT teams in low-income and racialized neighbourhoods. Its abuses have incited civil unrest, including the riot that swept through parts of the city after several officers were acquitted in the videotaped beating of Rodney King.

Some L.A. communities, however, have faced severe problems with rampant crime. Residents in the Watts neighbourhood experienced high levels of gang activity and violence, as multi-generational gangs operated openly in its three largest housing developments, whose residents also contend with poorly performing schools, high unemployment, lack of green space, poverty and a shortage of prevention resources. In 2010 alone, Watts housing residents reported 1,604 property crimes, 288 gang crimes and over eight hundred violent crimes. It is also a place of historically heightened tension between the community and law enforcement, a dynamic that persisted for decades.[19]

CSP provided for the deployment of forty-five LAPD officers to the housing developments as a special unit with an independent chain of command. All of the selected officers received a promotion for participating and committing themselves to being deployed to the unit for five years. LAPD assumed the cost of the officers' salaries, and the housing authority provided the funds to pay for the officer promotions and overtime, the evaluation of the project and a pool of funds to support community-based prevention and intervention programs. One of the community partners, the Advancement Project, supported the project by conducting ongoing officer trainings (e.g., collaboration, mediation skills, understanding of youth development), technical assistance for program implementation and strategic partnership development.

In addition to the long-term deployment of officers to a particular community, CSP also designed an incentive structure to reward officer behaviours that prioritize relationship-building. For example, officers are rewarded for diversion of youth offenders, ensuring the safe travel of students to and from school, and partnering with community stakeholders to solve safety issues. The program has fostered closer ties between the police and the residents of the Watts housing developments, and has also helped to reduce both violent crime and arrests by 50 percent during the program's first three years.

Moving Forward

Ontario has the highest policing costs in the country, despite the fact that the severity of police-reported crime in the province is the lowest in the country.[20] In November 2015, the Toronto Police Services Board approved a 2.76 percent increase in a Toronto Police Service (TPS) budget that now exceeds $1 billion annually, making it the City of

Toronto's largest single expenditure. That budget, moreover, is approved every year, even though the spending plans are not made public or debated before the decision is made. Citizens can't even view the approved budget, making financial accountability of TPS impossible. Given the steadily increasing costs of policing, the lack of transparency around these outlays and the recognition that such expenditures are not sustainable, more communities are seeking to improve community safety in ways that involve less policing and more innovative collaborative practices with both civilian service providers and community members. Not only are these initiatives cost-effective, they have been shown to reduce interpersonal crime. In fact, there is a growing body of evidence that suggests that police involvement in certain situations – for instance, incidents involving emotionally distressed individuals – can actually make things worse.

In 2012, the TPS partnered with the United Way of Toronto and the City of Toronto to launch FOCUS Rexdale (Furthering Our Communities and Uniting Services), an innovative community safety strategy modelled directly on the Prince Albert Hub. Once a week, human-service agency workers convene to identify and intervene in situations involving someone who is at risk of emotional or physical harm to self or to the community at large due to addictions, child welfare issues, criminality, domestic issues or poor mental and/or physical health. Participating agencies that have signed an agreement with FOCUS Rexdale include Albion Neighbourhood Services, Breaking the Cycle, Toronto Community Housing and the Toronto District School Board.

The purpose of FOCUS Rexdale is to first identify an individual, family or group at high risk of gang activity, violence, criminal involvement, homelessness or suicide. Once the person or persons have been identified, participants determine which member agencies should take the lead and which should provide support. Through coordinated and integrated intervention, agencies assigned to a situation are expected to collectively address it within forty-eight hours of the meeting and report back at the next meeting on the action taken and its results. As with the Prince Albert Hub model, interventions often consist of joint home visits or 'door knocks.' Cases are closed when one of three things happen: the individual, family or group concerned is connected with and accepts service; the individual, family or group is connected with and refuses service; or the individual, family or group cannot be reached.[21]

Regular evaluation and reporting of these and other models is critical given the value placed on statistics versus qualitative measurements, especially for preventative programs. While it may be difficult to measure what didn't happen, the Prince Albert Hub model, for example, has done well in measuring what does happen, in terms of the reduction of crime and arrests in their community. However, more evaluations and assessments of community members' perceptions of risk and their relationship with the police are necessary as part of the democratic policing model.

Whatever framework or name is chosen as a city-wide alternative to the current policing doctrine, it must start from an understanding that police brutality and racist and discriminatory police practices have fractured the relationship between law enforcement agencies and many communities in Toronto. To build public trust in Toronto, many systems must revolutionize the way they operate.

For example, a democratic policing model would require serious and sustained commitment from governments and the leadership of police services (including the chief of police, the Canadian Association of Chiefs of Police, the Ontario Association of Chiefs of Police), as well as community members with a real seat at the decision-making table. Those communities that have endured over-policing and aggressive tactics must see real sanctions for police violations. In other words, when officers act outside the 'do no harm' framework, transparent and effective accountability structures must exist to provide redress for complainants, restore public trust in the police and deter future abuse of police powers.[22] Some have suggested that the use of body cameras would increase public confidence in the police and accountability. While not sufficient on its own, the use of these cameras is a step toward rooting out excessive use of force and promoting transparency. However, as the American journalist Ta-Nehisi Coates and other scholars and activists have noted, it's not enough to look at police reform without investigating the wider public's attitudes around race, justice and police practices.

The mainstream attempts to discredit or derail the urgency and significance of the Black Lives Matter movement, for example, paired with widespread silence and inaction by the broader public, tends to suggest that there is implicit support for the status quo as it relates to discriminatory police tactics and the justice system as a whole. In his 2015 book, *Between the World and Me*, Coates writes: 'The truth is that the police reflect America in all of its will and fear, and whatever we might make of this country's criminal justice policy, it cannot be said that it was imposed by a repressive minority… And so to challenge the police is to challenge the American people who send them into the ghettos armed with the same self-generated fears that compelled the people who think they are white to flee the cities and into the Dream.'[23]

While Coates is referring to the rampant and highly visible nature of police violence in the U.S. against Black bodies, it is important to remember Canada is not exempt from this kind of institutionalized racism. We have a long history of it. However, racism in Canada – from the individual to the institutional level – tends to be perpetrated more covertly. This doesn't make the issue any less real for those who experience it on an everyday basis.

It all comes back to trust. We are approaching a point when the majority of Torontonians will have come from elsewhere. In such a diverse city, fewer of us will have a shared history, culture or language. How do we build and sustain trust among neighbours, co-workers and classmates, let alone with law enforcement? Is it enough for police services to continually tell the public that they are hiring more women, university graduates or people from various backgrounds? Or that they have hired a racialized police chief and increased diversity on the police services board? Do these symbolic gestures obscure the need for deeper reform?

I believe more is needed. We need a permanent, ongoing process that requires our elected representatives to methodically examine law enforcement activity to ensure that the democratic ideals of fairness, transparency and accountability are reflected in police behaviour. We also need to better understand what the police do. Our elected representatives should require the SIU, civilian oversight bodies and police services themselves to collect and disseminate disaggregated race-based data on arrests, police violence and the use of force.

This data would assist police services in their efforts to unearth patterns of undemocratic policing. The requirement to collect such data would mean officers document – in the context of a traffic stop, for example – the reasons for the stop, driver information, outcome of the stop and the officer's perception of race. But most importantly, in terms of developing trust between law enforcement and the citizenry, this data would assist citizens in supporting their lived experiences of racial profiling at the hands of the police.

Democratic policing reforms, in my view, can truly gauge the behaviour of the police and the quality of law enforcement, and is thus vital for the health of our hyper-diverse city-region, our province and indeed our country. We should not only be evaluating whether our police are enforcing the law. We should also monitor the quality of police-citizen interactions and track perceptions of police behaviour and legitimacy on the part of those who are subject to over-policing.

Only then can we begin to rebuild trust.

Three Questions about Carding
Idil Burale

'People don't resist change. They resist being changed.'
– Systems scientist Peter M. Senge

In 1829, Sir Robert Peel, the British statesman who established London's Metropolitan Police Force, drew up a list of ethical principles for policing by consent, which became the foundation of modern law enforcement. Often referred to as the Peelian Principles, these value statements reinforced a central tenet of his philosophy: 'the police are the public and the public are the police.' Today, in Toronto, an estimated 80 percent of police officers do not live in the city whose residents they have sworn to serve and protect, according to an analysis by the *Toronto Star*.[1] In a metropolitan area struggling with tensions between the police and marginalized communities, but especially young Black males, the housing location choices of all those officers offers an important clue about how law enforcement indirectly contributes to the rifts within an increasingly divided city.

In recent years, this tension has come to focus on the long-standing practice of carding, more formally known as 'street checks' – a hot-topic issue that has dominated media coverage of policing, invited provincial intervention and generated national attention. Law enforcement regards street checks as proactive policing. Black and Indigenous communities see the practice as racial profiling, and for good reason. Carding describes the process of being stopped, questioned, asked for identification and documented, all for non-detention and non-arrest purposes. These stops, in theory, are supposed to be voluntary; the individual has the right to walk away. But psychologically – and even physically sometimes – they feel like arbitrary detention. When officers conduct a street check, they see themselves as fulfilling their main duty: to preserve the peace and prevent crimes or other offences. But members of communities that face intensive street-check activity feel targeted. They leave these engagements often without knowing why they were stopped or what becomes of their personal information.

These are important questions.

When it comes to the lack of trust between law enforcement and marginalized communities, decades of aggressive police strategies have left the residents of so-called crime hot spots or 'priority neighbourhoods' stranded between the gun violence they fear and a police service that often seems to treat entire communities as suspect. The practice of carding and the Toronto Anti-Violence Intervention Strategy (TAVIS) have significantly diminished police legitimacy and trust in certain neighbourhoods. Daily life, already a struggle for the many law-abiding, low-income residents of these communities, has become increasingly oppressive under the special police scrutiny. The perverse result is that these areas may have actually become even less safe and more isolated from the life of the rest of the city.

These tensions are not unique to Toronto. The debate over the racialization of police street checks has spread to cities as far away as Edmonton and Halifax. While most Canadian police chiefs have distanced themselves from this issue, two formal efforts have sought to confront the implications of a long-standing policing technique: the Toronto Police Service's Police and Community Engagement Review (PACER) project, and Ontario's 2015 reforms, which will govern the future of policing in Ontario in general, and the nature of big-city police-community interactions more specifically.

The extended debate around carding taught us that future relations between police and the members of marginalized or racialized communities revolve around three crucial questions:

- *Why did you stop me?*
- *What did you write down about me?*
- *How will that information be used and retained?*

Provincial regulations introduced in 2015 attempted to answer those questions by setting up a 'rights-based' framework to govern the way police engage with members of the public during non-investigative stops. The PACER process – which involved an internal organizational analysis of all aspects of TPS's engagement with the public, a literature review, a legal evaluation and consultation with service members and the community-at-large on police-community interactions – sought to go a step further by launching the first comprehensive overhaul of the systemic nature of biased policing. Its aim was to reshape the fundamental social compact between citizens and this institution.

During the 2012 Chief Internal Organizational Review process, senior TPS officials began an evaluation of the use of Field Information Reports (FIR, a.k.a. carding) in an attempt to respond to growing public scrutiny around street checks. In the wake of intensive policing and anti-gang enforcement activity initiated after the so-called Summer of the Gun in 2005, the *Toronto Star* regularly featured disturbing revelations about carding in its 'Race Matters' and 'Known To Police' series. While the TPS, at the time, faced political pressure to cut costs, senior progressive police officials knew they also had to deal with the allegations of racial profiling. This is how PACER was born. In charge of the review was a veteran cop named Peter Sloly, who served as the deputy chief responsible for the Community Safety command (the unit responsible for all front-line officers).

In 2013, I was consulted on how TPS could improve police-community relations in the northwest corner of the city. Having grown up in Rexdale after immigrating from Somalia as a young child, I knew first-hand what the social consequences of seemingly well-intentioned police policies could do to trust. I knew how barriers to communication could affect a police division whose members didn't reflect the ethnic diversity of the zones they patrolled. And I recognized what long-held and unchallenged stereotypes could do to the way we understood ourselves, internally as a community, and how we viewed the police as an external occupying force. At the same time, I'd seen what good policing – by officers who were sensitive, and attentive, to the community's needs – could do to reduce crime while also restoring police legitimacy.

At the time, I had been working closely with the Dixon community and 23 Division on a community safety pilot called the Somali Liaison Unit, whose goal was to improve relations in order to increase safety (the more trusting people are of the police, the more likely they are to report crime). I was also collaborating with a group of young advocates on a public education campaign called the Policing Literacy Initiative, which sought to influence policy around policing and neighbourhood safety. I was a rare breed – a young person from Rexdale who actually *wanted* to engage with the police.

Given my experiences, the TPS asked me in 2014 to participate with other community members as external advisors to the PACER team, with a mandate to oversee the proposed three-year implementation of their thirty-one recommendations for changing the culture, training and practice of policing. This was the first time the TPS had gone beyond consultation to truly partner with the community to bring about reform.

We decided to focus on carding, a practice symptomatic of the broader systemic failures around how police officers do their work, what they feel they can get away with, and how they are held accountable. The PACER team aspired to tackle issues like poor training, spotty supervision and weak accountability measures, all of which contribute to what goes wrong when police become overly reliant on street checks. While the PACER team initially focused on carding, its members expanded their scope to look at eleven key areas of policing: service governance, public accountability, community consultation, professional standards, human resources, performance management, information management, operational improvements, intelligence-led policing, corporate communications and project management.

But, as I learned, the TPS went through the motions of implementing PACER's proposed changes without changing the culture. Herewith, three scenes from the reform campaign that wasn't.

Why did you stop me?

Recommendation 6: Professional Standards Unit (PRS) Develop New Risk Thresholds

'That the *Professional Standards Unit develop new risk thresholds specifically designed and implemented with respect to bias and racial profiling and create a new dimension with respect to an early detection and intervention alert system to support Officers working in high-risk assignments.*'

Officers notice many things, including race. But how should the TPS track racial bias? Recommendation 6 aspired to tackle that precise problem. Currently, the Professional Standards unit, which is part of central command, monitors officer conduct using various measures, but none that account for racial bias. However, when a citizen launches a complaint against an officer, it is handled only within his or her division.

In other words, when officers are applying for promotions or assignment changes, the centralized PRS does not have access to citizen complaints, including those alleging racial bias. PACER proposed that the PRS assume responsibility for all internal and external complaints against officers, including those involving racial bias, so they can track patterns over time and tailor training programs in response to the feedback. Because of the TPS's internal structure, critical information about the behaviours of individual cops didn't flow to the right places.

What did you write down about me?

Recommendation 2: Procedural Revisions – Community Safety Note
   'That Procedure 04-14 be revised to reflect new terminology concerning Community Safety Notes (CSN) and that the Procedure be rewritten to include and define: the operational purpose of ensuring public safety, a legal and human rights framework, information management and retention requirements, new quality control processes and introduces heightened supervision standards.'

Policing is situational. When officers patrol communities, they actively look for 'antisocial' behaviour because they are trained to recognize anomalies and determine whether or not those activities pose a risk to public safety. This is the basis of street checks: to conduct informal community inquiries based on hunches. Until the practice was put on hold in January 2015, Procedure 04-14 (street checks) was the most frequently used discretionary procedure to document police-community interactions.

The TPS also used the volume of street checks as a means of evaluating an officer's performance: in other words, Toronto cops had a personal incentive to engage in carding. The number of cards they produced had more importance than the quality of the information they gathered. This practice has since changed. As Recommendation 19 in the PACER report stipulated, officers would now be evaluated on the quality of their 'community safety notes' (the rebranded 'field information report,' as carding documents are known), which would mean having a valid public-safety concern to initiate the stop, and then clearly describing the usefulness of this intel to an ongoing case or for crime prevention purposes. Recommendation 19 sought to get officers out of the numbers-based rut and to start being more intentional and cognizant of why they were asking for information and how they thought it could be used to solve a specific public-safety concern.

How will that information be used and retained?

Recommendation 21: Information Management
'That the Service retain all Community Safety Note submissions for a maximum of seven years while continuing to explore industry best practices for information management, retention, privacy and access.'

Police officers record a lot of information in the course of a day's work. According to TPS, various provincial laws allowed them to hold on to information collected during a street check indefinitely. The public's primary concern is why this information is collected in a database when the individuals involved are not suspected of a crime or connected to an incident. On the other hand, officers, especially those investigating cold cases, are concerned about losing potentially useful information that could help crack a case later on. For them, intel never expires, and the more you collect, the better.

PACER had to balance those two concerns and come up with a compromise that would enable officers to do their job while also reassuring members of the public that the information would not remain in a large police database and come up during background checks down the road. The solution: keep contact cards for seven years and prompt the service to implement a four-tiered data retrieval system based on rank (e.g., a constable would have less access than a detective). PACER also suggested establishing software that could isolate personal identifiers from the aggregated data.

While the TPS has often touted the value of street-check information in investigations, the data suggests the benefit is limited. As the PACER report noted, 'Analysis indicated from 2009 to 2011, there were 1,104,561 persons entered into the [field information report] database ... [F]ewer than one in ten FIR cards collected since 2009 had been assigned a nature of contact which flagged the card as being directly related to an intelligence led policing strategy.' In other words, less than 10 percent of all those street checks were tied to an active criminal investigation. Personal information on the other 90 percent – over 900,000 people – still resides in police databases, as a kind of hedge against future criminality.

Accountability: Still an elusive goal for TPS

The goal of PACER was to establish a new social contract between police and the community, with changes to organizational structure that would have reformed both the front end and back end of why police do what they do. Unfortunately, this seemingly high-minded objective was derailed by police board politics. While the TPS can claim that it has implemented the thirty-one recommendations in the PACER report, many of the fixes seem like half-measures. For example, the TPS talks about the need for public education so individuals understand their rights when stopped, but the reality is that we haven't seen a full-blown 'know your rights' campaign in schools and community centres proactively explaining to people what the police do and what citizens' rights are. All the TPS opted to do was post a 'Know Your Rights' document on its website. The reluctance to broadly disseminate this information is revealing.

In fact, the evidence of the TPS's reluctance to change – or its intransigence – left me wondering: how can ordinary citizens bring about meaningful organizational change in an institution like the Toronto Police Service? There are stacks of outside reports with sensible, important recommendations by experts like criminal lawyer Frank Addario (on the community contacts policy) or former Supreme Court justice Frank Iacobucci (on police encounters with people in crisis). Yet there's little evidence of reform. Even when an internal leader, like former deputy chief Sloly, advances an agenda for improvement based on an open dialogue about biased policing, genuine change depends on who, if anyone, is willing to make it happen.

The report of the PACER task force aspired to transform the way in which Toronto's police force engages with the residents of a hyper-diverse city. It came as close as the TPS will ever come to admitting any wrongdoing, by setting out a framework to improve police-community relations and eliminate racial profiling with a range of reforms, such as better training or the use of body-worn cameras. Beyond the specifics, however, PACER was all about the social compact, and why building trust with the public ought to be of primary concern to front-line officers.

These aren't new insights. As Sir Robert Peel observed almost two centuries ago: 'The ability of the police to fulfill their duties is dependent on *public approval* of their existence, actions, behavior, and the ability of police to secure and maintain *public respect*.' If nothing else, Toronto's difficult debate over carding, TAVIS and the handling of security at the 2010 G-20 summit has re-emphasized the need for Canada's largest police service to work toward reinstating the Peelian principles of trust and legitimacy.

An Overburdened Promise:
Arts Funding for Social Development
Ian Kamau, Paul Nguyen and Ryan Paterson, with John Lorinc

On Boxing Day 2006, a barrage of gunfire broke out on Yonge Street, near Toronto Eaton Centre. In the chaos, a teenager named Jane Creba, who'd been out shopping with friends, was struck and killed by a stray bullet. Her death unleashed a public and media outpouring, prompting calls for tough action on gun violence.

Creba's death occurred in the aftermath of the so-called Summer of the Gun, and a record-setting number of gun-related homicides for 2005 for the City of Toronto. Most of the victims were racialized youth living in inner-city neighbourhoods, yet their deaths hadn't elicited the same degree of attention. This single incident served to amplify the ways in which age, gender, race, place and economics trigger political action.

At the time of the shooting, forty-five-year-old David Miller, a lawyer with a Harvard economics degree, was entering the second year of his first mayoral term. With support from urbanist Jane Jacobs, Miller espoused the vision of the 'creative city,' which emphasized creativity as a driver for economic growth, diversity and social equity. In 2002, this framework had entered popular culture when urban geographer Richard Florida published *The Rise of the Creative Class*. Florida's theory, built on Jacobs's work, outlined what he saw as the defining role of a growing 'class' of creative people he believed were key to shaping a competitive global city.

A few months after Creba's death, Miller unveiled his Community Safety Plan. 'Pockets of poverty have sprung up in Toronto,' the document stated. 'Certain neighbourhoods are in danger of being left behind. Not only is poverty itself fundamentally unacceptable, it can also lead to increased violence and other criminal activity.'

Poverty, of course, had not simply 'sprung up.' It was the result of market forces, spurred on by decades of devaluation, disinvestment, marginalization and deskilling. Miller's plan, which focused on 'vulnerable' neighbourhoods, outlined the need for prevention and enforcement, investment in neighbourhood-building, programs in recreation, culture, health, employment and civic engagement.

The combination of the creative-city vision, a place-based neighbourhood strategy and urgent cries for safety opened the floodgates for new funding pools in the creative and non-profit sectors, much of it focused on arts initiatives largely geared toward the marginalized youth considered by politicians and the police to be 'at risk' for gang involvement and gun violence. But what did these funds practically mean for these young people and their communities? Could the creative-city agenda, with its focus on the spinoff benefits of cultural activity, turn the page?

We all confronted these slippery questions in the years since: Ian Kamau as an artist, Ryan Paterson as co-founder of Manifesto and Paul Nguyen as editor-in-chief of the local news site Jane-Finch.com. Here is some of what we've observed.

Ryan Paterson

In 2007, artists and collaborators Ryan Paterson and Che Kothari brought together dozens of artists, promoters and youth interested in creating a platform for hip hop and other urban art forms absent from the mainstream cultural landscape. They founded what is now known as the Manifesto Festival of Community & Culture, a multidisciplinary celebration of youth arts and culture. Given that hip hop emerged in the midst of 'white flight' to the suburbs, reduced government services and the Black community's desire to eliminate gang violence, Manifesto's mandate was both social and creative. The festival's founders also wanted to create space for emerging and established artists to showcase and develop their talents, and to bring together artists and young people from across the city to foster greater connection and civic pride. To deliver on this vision, Paterson and Kothari established Manifesto as a non-profit in order to access grants for arts development, some of which had social-impact requirements.

Over the course of a decade, Manifesto grew into a scrappy, ambitious youth arts organization. It has produced over a hundred events reaching thousands of people. More than a thousand local artists in various disciplines have performed, exhibited or hosted workshops, panels and lectures. The organization has paid over $1 million in fees and salaries to artists and young people, creating some 1,200 volunteer, internship or employment opportunities.

Amid this success, Manifesto faced challenges intrinsic to the non-profit youth arts sector, and learned a lot of lessons. Some critics pointed out that Manifesto's efforts to engage with young people in underserved neighbourhoods didn't go far enough. The festival's very existence raised expectations, especially in communities where many young people were seeking artistic or professional opportunities. In too many cases, Manifesto had to say no because it didn't have the resources to accommodate the demand.

These experiences reveal deeper systemic issues about the ways in which arts funding and youth engagement have become troublingly conflated. In some ways, the grants to youth arts represent a response to poverty, unemployment and lack of safety. Yet this funding can amount to an offloading of social services onto non-profit arts-based organizations, where young people hungry to make a difference in their cities create a vulnerable pool of inexpensive labour. Further, the overemphasis on the arts for engaging racialized youth can perpetuate stereotypes much like midnight basketball programs, because it reinforces the perception that arts and sports are their primary paths to success.

Freighted with high expectations, Manifesto came face-to-face with another major hurdle: financial sustainability. Lacking experience, mentors and a pipeline to corporate or wealthy donors, Manifesto – and other upstart youth arts groups – struggled with a cumbersome and competitive arts-granting system that privileges those with education, influence and risk tolerance. Despite being relatively well-positioned to navigate those challenges, it was still difficult, and the system can actually exclude many of the youth these programs were designed to serve.

Manifesto also had to confront the problem of the passage of time. Like everyone, young artists, and their grass roots arts groups, grow older. And as they age out of eligibility for or attractiveness to funding opportunities, usually around the seventh year of funding, years of hard work and accumulated experience can be lost, and some of these young people are thrown back into a precarious labour market. Even for a relatively resilient organization like Manifesto, creating long-term sustainability is a daily challenge, and one heightened by the awareness that what the organization wants to achieve goes far beyond the work of producing cultural activities for diverse audiences.

Paul Nguyen

Across Toronto, the Jane-Finch community has come to be synonymous with street crime and poverty. News reports have dubbed the area 'the gun crime capital' and 'the most dangerous place to be a kid.' It is our very own Compton.

Long before that reputation took hold, rapid building in the area in the 1970s provided affordable housing for waves of new immigrants from around the world, many living in high-rises. Yet inadequate planning and infrastructure created socio-economic challenges. High unemployment, low voter turnout and many single-parent families gave Jane-Finch a reputation for being unstable and undesirable.

In 2004, Paul Nguyen created Jane-Finch.com to counter the negative stereotypes. He had grown up in the area and witnessed the discrimination, labels and challenges so-called marginalized kids faced. Jane-Finch.com began as a modest one-page website showcasing local homegrown rap videos and listings of local services and businesses. There was nothing else like it.

Within a few years, the site took on a new role. Nguyen trained local residents and youth volunteers in basic journalism and gave them broadcast equipment to report on life in the community. The idea was to allow residents to become authors of their stories rather than letting the news media impose labels.

Jane-Finch.com soon expanded into a multimedia news service providing local video coverage of positive community events ignored by the mainstream media. It also provided an unfiltered platform for local residents, covering controversial topics in authentic voices. Over time, the contributors became active and visible participants in the neighbourhood's socio-political discourse, and some went on to careers as award-winning journalists, media personalities and local artists. Their work is read and viewed by reporters, teachers and students, creating a link between marginalized local residents and the larger city.

Throughout, Nguyen chose not to apply for the growing supply of youth and arts grants or corporate backing, in part to maintain editorial independence. He saw Jane-Finch.com as a labour of love and wanted to use the site to create opportunities for other young people in the neighbourhood.

Nguyen has also seen the cynical side of such funding streams, which swelled into a tidal wave after Jane Creba's murder. He's been told that when there's a homicide in the area, that's an optimal time to apply for grants. He's seen opportunists scrambling to develop new programs and services, many of them duplicated. Indeed, in communities like Jane-Finch, youth-violence prevention has become something of a cottage industry. A community program might only service a dozen youth 'clients,' but its staff – often from outside the area – can easily be paid double or triple the minimum wage, from administrative staff to managers to executive directors who can be making a relatively high income. Outsiders work in vulnerable communities during the day but return in the evenings to their two-car garage homes in the city's more affluent parts. There's quite a difference between delivering programs and then leaving the area at the end of the business day, and bumping into clients at the local mall or on the streets.

The process of securing grants can give rise to the strategic use of the 'victim narrative.' Residents are forced to repeat a common story to secure funding, with some inflating their narratives to ensure support. Nguyen has talked to many young people in the area who were encouraged to exaggerate their own stories as a means of helping non-profits secure more funding or media attention.

By freeing Jane-Finch.com from the grant treadmill and the associated risk of offending an important funder, Nguyen could react swiftly to new or emerging issues and use the site to tackle sensitive subjects, like voting, local elections, race relations and other hot-button topics in the community. The website, for instance, has given voice to the victims of local gun crime, allowing grieving parents to speak at length rather than be restricted to the typical TV sound bite.

As well, at-risk youth in need of social programs and supports are often well outside the margins. They have criminal records and behavioural problems – their stories tend not to appear in a non-profit's annual report, but Nguyen reached out to them and gave them a platform.

After more than a decade, he feels that improving the community must not depend solely on the availability of funding, and it's a calling that cannot be limited to business hours. As a community, Nguyen says, Jane-Finch residents can't rely only on a system of outsiders to fix its problems. They must encourage each other to be good neighbours. This begins in the heart, and money shouldn't be the driving force.

Ian Kamau

In 2006, Toronto artist Ian Kamau heard about a high-profile national arts organization that was developing a progressive program. The organization, which had previously run DJ workshops in schools around the city, wanted to deliver music classes for youth living in low-income neighbourhoods. It was casting around for younger artists who could run fifteen-week after-school courses from a community centre in northwest Toronto. Kamau decided to apply.

The son of Canada's first Black filmmakers Claire Prieto and Roger McTair, who founded the Black Film & Video Network, Kamau was building a career in the arts, but he knew first-hand the challenges facing aspiring artists and creators of colour.

Kamau, then twenty-six, and a colleague put together a program that focused on the history of Black music, and the connection between traditional forms and hip hop. The course was geared toward building technical, studio and performance skills, and would culminate with the youth recording a CD and shooting a video – in other words, something the participants could use if they wanted to continue in music.

When Kamau and his colleague launched the course, it initially attracted a small core group of youth, most of them between the ages of fourteen and seventeen. But as word spread in the area, more local teens began inquiring about the course, and wanted to know when the next phase would begin.

But after that initial course ended, the downtown organization decided – with no warning or explanation – not to renew the funding, despite the increasing number of inquiries from local young people who'd heard about it from friends and wanted to participate.

Not wanting to disappoint the kids who'd expressed interest, Kamau and a few artist friends – including a photographer, a graphic designer and a writer – decided to run a modified version of their course on a volunteer basis, this time including a monthly open-mic session. Although three times as many youths turned out for those sessions, the arts organization didn't renew the funding.

In the end, Kamau and his friends couldn't continue to operate the program for free, and so an evidently successful youth-engagement effort petered out because the art organization's financial priorities had inexplicably shifted.

Kamau came away from that experience with a jaded view of the non-profit sector, and the way that large and seemingly well-intentioned institutions with no connections to marginalized communities can raise and then dash local expectations. He also realized that serious community development in racialized or immigrant enclaves must involve far more than a few arts programs that merely raise hopes. When residents are dealing with housing, transportation and employment issues, successful community development turns on partnerships between residents and groups prepared to invest for the long term.

Outside organizations, he says, can't just jump in and out.

Discussion

In December 2015, we met to discuss the nuanced politics of the youth-oriented arts and cultural funding that had flowed into priority neighbourhoods following the surge of gang-related gun violence that culminated in the murder of Jane Creba.

JOHN: After the Summer of the Gun in Toronto in 2005, millions of dollars flowed into youth arts programs for music, graffiti murals and so on. The idea was to see if cultural activity could help sort out some of the social problems seen to be at the root of the violence. Ten years on, has the funding achieved that goal?

IAN: I think it's slightly unfair to ask for youth arts funding and the programming that comes from it to be the thing that solves such large problems.

JOHN: Were the expectations placed on the potential of arts careers too great?

RYAN: There was a disproportionate expectation placed on the arts and culture sector. That created a host of challenges that are surfacing many years later. In effect, it created a bit of a downloading of social services. There was a saturation of these sorts of programs, which reinforced a message that this was the most viable path to success or solving some of these social issues.

JOHN: Paul, you didn't apply for arts funding for JaneFinch.com. Why not?

PAUL: Arts funding is just one tool to give youth an opportunity. Especially in the Jane-Finch area, not everyone is into doing art or playing ball. They have all kinds of interests. When I did my website, we didn't just do the music and rap videos. Make opportunities for young people to get employment, be heard, to matter and say something to society. It's not just always about doing the mural.

JOHN: Can you unpack some of the assumptions and stereotypes embedded in this torrent of arts funding?

IAN: There were racial assumptions and also assumptions about the economic standing of people in areas such as Jane and Finch, Malvern and all the other priority neighbourhoods. Those assumptions go back to stereotypes about a connection between poverty and violence, which I'm not actually sure is true.

JOHN: Ryan, what was the implicit agenda in this arts funding?

RYAN: I'm not sure there was a conscious agenda so much as a stop-the-bleeding response. In a way, arts and culture and youth engagement created an inexpensive labour force. It was a quick action, and relatively easy to mobilize.

JOHN: What about this idea of the need for a quick fix? How should we get past the idea that there are quick and easy solutions fuelled by money?

PAUL: Money doesn't solve the problems, although it helps, certainly. We've been running my website for ten years, but with no money. It's all by sheer will and passion and a lot of people who want to do something – either change their own lives or the lives of other people. With the arts stuff, I think the youth weren't consulted as much. There's a tangible result you can see: 'He makes a mural. He makes a song. He makes an art piece.' You can see it, but you have to go beyond that and make investments in people. But you don't necessarily see those results.

JOHN: Ian, how do we change the thinking that there's some quick-and-easy solution, both among young people and also among politicians?

IAN: It's about changing the way the policy-makers think. It's dangerous to say that because young people think a certain way, they are then responsible for the outcome of whatever happens in their life, ignoring the systemic disinvestment in housing, food, transportation. You can't change those problems by changing the way a fifteen-year-old thinks. At the same time, it is the thinking of people like David Miller, Jane Jacobs and Richard Florida, who are behind the neighbourhood initiatives, the creative-city initiatives. It was their thinking that made all of this stuff happen.

RYAN: There's still value in that arts and culture investment, and it has a role to play. But we need to be clear on that message and not create false expectations. It's not necessarily going to be able to address everything. It's one piece of what has to be a very comprehensive strategy that goes far beyond arts and culture and starts to ask other questions about what systemic issues exist in cities like Toronto.

PAUL: A lot of the youth I talk to, they're not even aware these programs exist. They don't know how the city is run and how decisions are made. They don't know jack, and for them to help themselves is nearly an impossibility. If you filter some of these people through a specific arts program and some sort of training, they still need the life skills. And you can't just help someone during business hours. It's all hours of the day. My message has always been, we need more big brothers, big sisters, more mentors. You can't always rely on external programs.

JOHN: What are the key lessons from these past ten years? What do you know now that you didn't know then?

IAN: You can do a lot of things, sometimes superficially, that seem like you're doing good for the city. But if you can't identify the specific impact of the program on people's lives – not in a feel-good way, but in a very practical, economical, social, political way – I don't know what any of those programs are really doing.

PAUL: What I learned: doing it on your own is difficult, but not impossible. I think all worlds have to come together – resiliency and self-help, along with whatever supports exist out in the community. It all has to come together. Most importantly, it's up to the individual. They have to care about themselves, and their own futures. If they don't, you can stuff them in a program, but when they graduate, they're not going to make it. With young kids who are at risk, what they want is to be heard and to matter, and that what they say or do is valuable.

JOHN: When you've applied for arts grants, have you had to shape your applications to meet some political objective, like youth poverty or exclusion?

IAN: I've always had a social imperative to everything I was doing. I have had the privilege to just do what I want to do, even in my work as an artist. But I have seen organizations pulling in things they may not be best at.

JOHN: For instance?

IAN: There are many organizations in competition for arts and community funding. These social and political imperatives come through policy from politics, depending on whatever the direction of the city is at the time. Those priorities will shift every five, seven, ten years. That means, every five to seven years, these organizations will have to shift whatever they're doing. Some will actually have no background in whatever that trend happens to be – disability, race, arts and culture, youth. But to survive, they'll have to find the funding, even though that's not the work that they do. That's inherently problematic.

JOHN: Was this outpouring of arts funding another way for residents of predominantly white downtown neighbourhoods to feel like they're doing something good for young people living in areas where there are no jobs? Was that the impulse underneath this big push on arts funding?

PAUL: When there's a funding announcement, Jane and Finch kids don't say, 'Hey, that's great.' Instead, it's the same old folks who are going to get paid and profit off the misery in the community. That's the general feeling.

RYAN: With Richard Florida, the commodification of culture is itself a big ingredient here that really complicates things. Yes, there's a social agenda, but there's also an economic agenda. It's 'How do we make the city more marketable, and have healthy neighbourhoods so we can have more condos?' Again, investing in young people is still very important, and arts and culture is an undeniably powerful point of entry with young people still exploring who they are. Even if it can't solve systemic issues on its own, the incremental impact in shaping consciousness, identity and pride should not be discounted. But how this work is undertaken and how competing interests and expectations are managed is a delicate balance.

IAN: The 'creative city' is fundamentally about developing the economy. It's very specific. When David Miller comes in and says, 'This is the framework we will be following,' then gets everybody on-board with that framework, there is a political and economic impetus to his actions.

That political and economic imperative makes assumptions about the way investment should be made, where it should be made and when it should be made. It benefitted some and didn't benefit others. The resulting arts funding was good for some people who had the ability to execute on some idea, and I'm sure it helped with things like self-esteem and confidence. But if we can't eat, self-esteem isn't going to put food on the table. That's not to say that arts programming is not good. It's just to say that there is a systemic issue we are not addressing.

Designing Dignified Social Housing
Jay Pitter

The Summer of Endings

As a kid, I lived in a tower at the end of a dreamless street. Each summer, the bushes out back bore sweet raspberries as a reprieve from the unyielding sun and oppressive poverty. But when 'Mikey the Pimp' moved into my neighbourhood in the early 1980s, that tiny bit of grace was lost. From afar, I watched him seduce Kate, a stocky blonde who was barely a teen, with a skittish gaze and an uncomfortable giggle. Soon, he also won over her welfare-dependent single mother and moved into their fourth-floor apartment. Having established a base for his 'business,' he recruited neighbourhood girls, many of whom were the older sisters of my friends. All of them had intersecting vulnerabilities – poverty, low performance in school, prior sexual violation and/or the lack of a male caregiver. Mikey's two cohorts, and a couple of 'clients' clearly from more affluent neighbourhoods, followed. Not yet thirteen, I didn't fully comprehend what was happening, but I knew enough to mistrust men who wore red snakeskin shoes and shiny shirts.

It wasn't that I was afraid: in my building, I'd regularly navigated blown-out hallway lights, perpetually broken elevators, shattered beer bottles from last night's fight and women brawling over washing machines. But with Mikey the Pimp's arrival, I sensed an unfamiliar foreboding. Sadly, my instincts were right. One evening, while I was regaling my mother with the details of my day, a news report on TV caught my attention. The remains of a violated girl, identifiable only through dental records, had been found by a group of Boy Scouts. And not just any girl: the victim was Britney, the older sister of one of my friends. She had been working for Mikey the Pimp.

Although I'm many miles and years beyond that tragedy, my inner twelve-year-old self compels me to search for Britney. I recently found an online article focused on the man who murdered her. She is a mere footnote – an insignificant girl from an insignificant neighbourhood.

Through tears brought on by the raw injustice of it all, I contemplate how the absence of dignity – defined as human worth – in the design and provision of social housing were complicit in the underage sex trade in my building and ultimately in Britney's death. I interrogate social housing's paternalistic beginnings, its poorly designed neighbourhoods, the implications of place-based identity and stigma, and the violence against women and girls. But I also create space for guarded optimism, imagining that it's possible to transform social housing residents from clients of the state to citizens of the city.

I embark on a work of blood, memory and critique.

It isn't that we haven't been talking about social housing. Most everyone knows of the repair backlogs, safety issues, wait lists, funding models, concentrated poverty and the despair of the residents, and also that these problems have been deemed a crisis for global cities like Toronto. The problem is that we haven't been talking about it in the right way.

Although Canadian social housing neighbourhoods are considered substantively more livable than their American counterparts, a task force appointed by Mayor John Tory to provide recommendations for improving properties managed by the Toronto Community Housing Corporation (TCHC) has conceded defeat. Led by Senator Art Eggleton[1], this group surmised the obvious – the city's social housing provider, the same one that managed the building I grew up in, was an ineffectual landlord. The 'Transformative Change for TCHC' report, released in January 2016, characterized the organization as 'unsustainable financially, socially and with respect to operations and governance.' While many of the recommendations, such as increasing support to vulnerable residents and transitioning to a new public-private funding model, are valid, what's missing from this report – and current social housing conversations generally – is the centralization of dignity as a frame of reference for both understanding and addressing multiple issues, all of which pose significant barriers for sustainable social housing redevelopment.

Design conversations are commonly centred on principles of aesthetics, usability, economics, technology and, more recently, environmental resilience. The notion of human dignity is certainly of concern to *some* designers. But it is rarely, if ever, explicitly stated as a guiding principle or outcome in policy development and professional practice.

Yet when it comes to human dignity, design is anything but neutral. Architect and scholar Richard Buchanan points out that while designers grapple with their ethical and political responsibilities, all design, intended or unintended, either supports or undermines human dignity.[2]

Buildings Born of Crisis

If human dignity is indeed a fundamental design principle, social housing is one of the largest failed experiments of the twentieth century. North American social housing schemes dating back to the 1930s had three aims: to initiate systematic clearance of slums; to resolve and prevent significant public health risks emerging from slums; and to squelch public unrest and insolvency resulting from both the Depression and the postwar era. In fairness, some early social housing advocates had good intentions. Progressive-minded social housing pioneers hoped that state-run initiatives would provide stable housing for low-income and working-class families, and provide homes for returning veterans. However, the design approach was primarily based on problem-solving, not respectful and collaborative place-making.

In the early 1970s, my mother, like so many immigrants, set out to find better places to raise a family – places with strong democracies, humane social policies, safety and opportunity. She travelled from the Caribbean to Canada to join my grandmother, who had impressed immigration officials with a glowing referral letter from a judge, a commendable work record and, as family folklore has it, striking good looks. Soon after, my mother sent for my sister and me. We arrived in mid-winter, around my fourth birthday, and moved into a large, multi-unit house on a residential street purchased with the fruits of my grandmother's courage and sacrifice.

But even the high ceilings and winding hallways were not vast enough for the huge personalities of these two women. My mother was a free-spirited newcomer intent on integrating. My grandmother was a traditional Pentecostal who loved the Lord, wrestling, and judging women who wore miniskirts. They fought incessantly. Before long, my sister and I found ourselves living in the public housing community that would become my mother's greatest shame and the barrier to her dream of becoming a 'respectable' Canadian.

Social housing as a conceptual and physical barrier is neither imagined nor accidental. Like most postwar social housing complexes, the design of our community was influenced by the now widely contested 'towers in the park' ideal, pioneered by Swiss-French architect Le Corbusier and then propagated by Robert Moses, a powerful and polarizing New York City planner. The confluence of Moses's control over hundreds of millions of dollars through numerous public authorities, and the complete dearth of citizen oversight or input, enabled him to bulldoze large parts of the city in service of his vision or, depending on whom you ask, ego. One of his earliest housing projects, Stuyvesant Town, was built atop the debris of an entire community complete with family homes, local businesses, places of worship, schools and cultural spaces. Before the dust settled, a number of cities across North America, Toronto among them, obliterated existing neighbourhoods in the name of urban renewal and replaced them with sky-molesting towers for the poor.

Just as my mother and most social housing residents couldn't articulate the correlation between design and their sense of despair and disconnection, they were also unaware of the larger system of housing inequality that contributed to the conditions within their communities. While the disparities we're struggling to rectify today are largely a result of flawed design, we mustn't oversimplify the situation and place the fault entirely on designers. Social housing was, and still is, developed within a complex system of housing inequality.

Last year, Columbia University's Temple Hoyne Buell Center for the Study of American Architecture published a report called *The Art of Inequality: Architecture, Housing, and Real Estate*, in which the editors articulate a clear definition of this particular inequality:

> By 'inequality' we mean not only the measurable socio-economic gap that separates the very wealthy from the very poor, but also

a seemingly endless chain of inequalities around which both individuals and social groups hold conflicting interests ... with a close eye on how they link with others: structural racism, gender discrimination, and other exclusions or expulsions that are internal (that is, *built-in*) to the American housing system.[3]

A system with disparities that, they assert, cannot be attributed to 'mysterious' economic forces. Rather, as the authors note, 'Insurmountable housing disparities are not a historical accident, nor are they merely the unintended side effect of well-meaning policies and practices. They are designed, built into the system by which housing is produced and maintained in the first place.'[4]

From Indigenous reservations to elite gated communities, housing has intentionally been used to sort groups of people by class, race and perceived worth. All of this is governed within a real estate environment biased toward the profit-generating private market. So in spite of perceptions that Canadian social housing is 'fancier' or more socially progressive than those of our American counterparts, there are remarkable similarities in terms of design, history and intent.

A number of Canadian housing scholars and advocates have made these connections and unpacked the disparities that exist here. At its simplest, social housing was never intended to provide its residents with beautiful homes connected to the larger city. Even a housing moderate like the scholar and author John C. Bacher, who champions the baby boomers' efforts to create accessible and high-quality affordable housing, acknowledges that 'social housing in Canada was visually designed to affirm that it was inferior accommodation intended to serve a low-income group.'[5] The scheme to provide the poor with inferior accommodation and its disastrous outcomes are far too grand to pin on any particular designer or even a single-minded city-builder like Robert Moses. The principles underpinning the development of social housing are part of a larger system fuelled by capital and human casualties, to which we have, to varying degrees, consented.

Social housing has aptly been referred to as a form of colonialization due to its paternalistic beginnings, privileging capital over human lives, and our collective consent. The vision for these communities was forged by a socially affluent class of people who imposed their ideas and intentions on the poor and working classes, for economic and political reasons. There was little, if any, consideration for the capacity and eventual ascent of newcomers like my mother, or the vulnerability of children like Britney.

Place and Identity

While observing public housing, *New York Post* reporter Emily Badger wrote that 'the stigma that would become attached to the residents was, in many ways, built into the buildings themselves.'[6] Place and identity theories can help us to understand this bold indictment and, more broadly, the connection between people and places.

Consider place identification: it's common for people to identity themselves with a place – we're New Yorkers, Torontonians or Angelenos. It's a natural and, in many ways, healthy expression of place-based pride and connection.

That said, place-based identity is not neutral. People who live in social housing communities are often perceived by the outside world in a derogatory manner and may even identify themselves that way. For example, the Lawrence Heights social housing community, located in northwest Toronto, has long been referred to as 'the Jungle' by police officers, taxi drivers, residents and even media outlets. This moniker has been attributed to its high crime rate, 'wild' social structure and/or the race of many of its local residents. In all instances, the term, regardless of who it's used by, is deeply problematic.

In the case of my social housing community, there wasn't a specific name ascribed to our neighbourhood, but there were nonetheless strong place-based identity associations. Outsiders wielded pejorative terms like 'gangster,' 'ghetto' and 'baby mama' to describe residents. It's a phenomenon that occurs in other stigmatized places: prisoners may be reduced to their cellblock number, just as people living in trailer-park communities are disparaged as 'white trash.' As in the case of the 'Jungle,' residents living in stigmatized places often embrace these labels.

Our relationship with place extends much more deeply than just identification. City University of New York environmental psychologist

Harold Proshansky, who developed the theory of 'place-identity,' described a substructure of self-identity that explained the profound ways in which physical settings can define our daily experiences. Proshansky and others have found that, whether good or bad, the experiences emerging from our physical settings shape our memories, ideas, feelings, values and other cognitions. As such, places, spaces and their properties play an integral role in satisfying or neglecting our biological, psychological, social and cultural needs. Design thought-leader Clare Christine Cooper builds on these ideas by revealing our fascination with the places where we reside, noting that 'the home is perhaps the most fully researched with regard to its contribution to identity.'[7]

It's no wonder we've delineated the home as being distinct from other types of places. Second only to our name, our address is our principal identifier. The problem is that mainstream conceptualizations of home, and resulting research, are narrowly defined within the frame of a Norman Rockwell painting or postwar suburban 'oasis.' These iconic images situate the home as a refuge – a prized possession and bastion of belonging inhabited by a thriving nuclear family. This image is clearly out of step with the increasingly diverse population of global cities, the economic realities of the labour market, dwelling types and today's complicated family and community arrangements.

People living in social housing are one of the groups most impacted by these factors. The location of these homes has a profound role in determining the residents' quality of education, physical and mental health, exposure to beauty and culture, ability to access nutritious food, interactions with law enforcement and development of a healthy sense of belonging. For those in the social housing community where I grew up, our address and postal code were the equivalent of a scarlet letter – a place-based mark branding us as second-class citizens.

I learned this in first grade. My teacher, Miss Norman, would smirk when asking children from my community if their parent(s) worked, or when she asked why they did not have the same last name as their siblings. To this day, I'm pained when recalling the shame that overtook the tiny bodies of my classmates. I was shielded from much of her vitriol because, while my older sister and I had different fathers, mine had adopted her and granted her his last name before we left the Caribbean. Additionally, my mother showed up to every parent-teacher night wearing a paper-thin blazer and as much pride as she could summon. I recall her telling me that Miss Norman – and all teachers, for that matter – worked for *us* and that as long as I was respectful, I should settle for nothing short of respect in return, regardless of my neighbourhood, skin colour, gender or any other silly premise people used to minimize others. I didn't fully understand the depth of what she was telling me, but her words emboldened me to look Miss Norman – and all the adults I encountered – in the eye.

But all of the sass and self-confidence in the world couldn't shield me from the fact that just like my classmates from my community, I, too, was considered second-class, marked by the place I called home. Those of my friends who lived on the other side of our misfortune – the children with dads, safety and beautiful parks – were rarely allowed to attend sleepovers in my community. Sometimes when I visited their homes, well-meaning parents would gush patronizingly about my neat appearance and my ability to string a few sentences together.

Even my extended family avoided visiting us. My own aunt, a haughty woman with a husband and a house (major accomplishments for women of that time), warned my cousins against 'picking up the habits of the unruly children' in my community the few times they visited. She, like so many adults around us, spoke these words with little regard to their weight, and little appreciation for the ways children intuit such things. Much like the underage sex trade that swallowed up Britney and other girls in my community, I didn't understand the full extent of what was happening, but I knew it was wrong, and that it had something to do with where I lived.

Mapping Chaotic Geographies

In the spring of 2015, I decided to visit the social housing community of my childhood with a photographer. With his help, I wanted to document the specific design features that shaped our experiences in the community – including the sex trade and Britney's murder. As we turned into the complex, the trip became an uneasy crawl toward an unresolved past.

We parked beside an above-ground garbage bin regurgitating chicken bones, baby diapers and empty soda bottles. A few feet away, an elderly man riffled through a pile of colourful baby clothes next to a soiled floral mattress and one red shoe that seemed desperate for its companion. Looking up at my old balcony in the sky, I remembered how small we all were as kids – and how small we sometimes felt.

Having researched place-making and crime-prevention models while completing graduate work in environmental studies, I instinctively began to audit the community from both a child's perspective and a professional eye. The doorways along the outer perimeter sink inward and were still covered with view-obstructing awnings. These dim alcoves provided excellent coverage for Mikey the Pimp's drug deals, and also created an uneasy feeling for children walking past the building's shadowy perimeter. Out back, the wood and sand were entirely obstructed by the building's height and girth. All of these design features contravened the precepts of natural surveillance. A principle of Crime Prevention through Environmental Design, natural surveillance seeks to focus as many eyes on a space or place by using simple and effective design strategies like lighting, landscape and the siting of doors and benches. Jane Jacobs similarly espoused the virtue of the 'eyes upon the street' in the compact working-class neighbourhoods of New York's East Village.[8]

When we walked around to the front of my former building, I noted another set of design deficiencies. As we entered, I found myself standing atop what appeared to be the very same carpet, now worn through to the rubber, that I walked across on my way to school each morning thirty years earlier. Aside from a security guard who turned a blind eye to the happenings in the building, there was no access control – no external fences, low walls, shrubs or even an intercom system to hinder criminals like Mikey the Pimp. In the winters when it was cold, he and his clientele were never inconvenienced. They had full access to interior spaces within my building. Instead of the parking lots, ravine and the park out back, his clients were directed to warm, accessible spaces, like the laundry room and the stairwells, where they could devour their purchase of crack or a young girl in relative comfort.

My building wasn't the only problematic place in the community. The clichéd social housing basketball court – mythologized as a site of hoop dreams and a launching pad for upward mobility – was located close to the row houses where Britney and her family lived. Like many of our public spaces, the court was hidden a couple of flights below street level. Like my building, it too lacked access barriers, natural surveillance and safe-circulation paths. There was a single opening, which doubled as both entrance and exit. The younger boys in the community cut a hole in the fence to create an escape route from the police who sometimes beat them up or the older local guys who 'jokingly' pummelled them as part of their initiation into manhood. Instead of recognizing the dangers of having a single gateway serving as both an entrance and exit, or paying attention to the natural pathways carved out by residents, the housing provider installed prison-like metal bars around the sides and top of the fence, as if to make escape that much more difficult.

During the summers, we weren't whisked off to cottages – heck, we didn't even have a local pool! – so the guys played basketball in this reinforced metal cage while the girls watched. There was an air of pageantry about these games. Many girls would get dressed up, doing their hair and watching the guys play without ever being given any space or time on the court. Though his silky shirts and layers of gold chains hindered him from actually playing ball, Mikey the Pimp lurked around the court, likely recruiting or keeping an eye on 'his' girls. I was an awkward-looking tomboy with zero interest in lip gloss, and the whole ritual struck me as bizarre.

I didn't want to hang around the court anyway; I had other plans. By the time I was twelve, I'd made business cards out of lined essay paper, and secured three babysitting clients for the summer. Sometimes I would treat my friends to french fries at a local hamburger place or purchase Popsicles from storeowners who eyed us suspiciously as we walked through aisles stocked with overpriced white bread and powdered milk. The burger place and variety store were situated in a strip plaza atop a really steep hill that lacked both a pedestrian walkway and speed bumps. Because of the drug and sex trade in the community, an increasing number of cars sped in and out of the complex.

On one of our trips to the variety store, a driver forgot to put on the emergency brakes and his car began to roll down the hill. In an instant, it was rocketing through the air toward my friend Mindy. She tried to outrun it, but the car landed on top of her, crushing her pelvis. Mindy spent the entire school year in the hospital. The design of that complex, coupled with the criminal activities it facilitated, was lethal.

Gender-Based Safety Issues

Most everyone perceives social housing to be unsafe, and at the same time very few people understand the dimensions of the peril – especially gender-based violence. Despite the fact that single mothers and their children make up the vast majority of social housing residents, the violence in these communities is almost exclusively defined by gun and gang activity, centralizing young men. As a result, municipalities, public funders and private donors direct millions of dollars toward safety and prevention interventions meant to address these narrow issues while overlooking others.

To some extent, I get it. Guns and gangs scare people. Public bloodshed and body bags are compelling political instigators that impact everything from tourism to economic development and neighbourhood renewal. By contrast, women's safety issues tend to be both interpersonal and domestic, egregiously veiled from the public realm and public discourse. Women are neither frightening perpetrators nor unusual victims.

A watershed research study, the 'Quality of Neighbourhood Life Survey' conducted in eastern Ontario in 1999, revealed the dimensions and impact of gendered violence across six social housing communities. It was distributed by stakeholders of such communities, including community centre staff, to 1,200 households. The findings revealed that the rate of physical violence in social housing was higher than among most married/cohabitating women surveyed in North America. The victimized women tended to be younger, and reliant on welfare or disability payments for their livelihood. In addition to dealing with the stresses of poverty, the study concluded that women living in social housing faced significant incidents of violence and harassment.[9] While all women across race and class face the risk of sexual harassment and violence, the intersection of poverty and gender creates unique vulnerabilities for women living in social housing.

Mikey the Pimp, and other predators – drug dealers, pedophiles, domestic abusers and even unconscionable staff – regard social housing communities the way the fox views an unattended chicken coop. A community filled with poor women and girls who have few opportunities, limited access to the larger city and uncultivated personal agency creates prime conditions for the kind of exploitation and criminal activity that rarely make the evening news.

I now realize it was no accident that Mikey the Pimp preyed on Kate and her mother. Kate was uncomfortable in her skin while her mother endured the kind of social housing poverty that chisels away at self-worth. She was welfare-poor. Her caseworker would ask her about her lovers, the brand of her laundry detergent, and then shame her for not having a job. To compound these intrusions, she didn't receive enough benefits to pay her rent and also eat during the last week of the month.

My mother, and others in the neighbourhood, chose to work at less-than-secure jobs in an attempt to escape the additional indignities of the welfare system. Kate's mother lacked the fortitude, mental or physical wellness, or capacity to follow their example. I'm infuriated and deeply saddened by the way she failed to protect her daughter, and allowed her home to be used as a base for the underage sex trade in which a number of girls like Britney became entangled. At the same time, I recognize that she was a second-class citizen within a group of second-class citizens. She undoubtedly suffered a sense of lowered self-worth.

Also, I'm pretty certain that Mikey the Pimp, initially, was less than clear with his intentions to exploit Kate and her mother. I recall something that resembled a courtship. From the outside looking in, it was obvious that this thirtysomething man and this very young teenager were not involved in the kind of romance that many girls my age read about in corny preteen chapter books. But for Kate, I'm sure the attention and small gifts – and I do mean very small gifts, as Mikey the Pimp didn't even drive a car – meant the world to her. The romance, however dubious, proved short-lived. Almost immediately after he moved in, domestic fights spilled into the hallway and lobby of the building.

Anthropologist Philippe Bourgois's highly respected study of social marginalization in East Harlem adds further context to the gendered violence in social housing communities. He proposes that this deplorable behaviour is a poor man's expression of a 'crisis in patriarchy' and reduction of 'masculine dignity' hastened by a lack of opportunity and the isolation of public housing towers.[10] Unpacking dignity in relation to gender, place and class adds valuable texture to this multi-faceted narrative.

I've witnessed how the shared suffering and lack of opportunity delineated by Bourgois sometimes creates a form of unhealthy solidarity and silence when issues of violence arise. In some instances, gendered violence is justified by residents, while in others there isn't even language to protest. For instance, in the social housing community where I grew up, domestic violence was referred to as a private quarrel and gang rape was referred to as 'running train' on a girl. Without a firm sense of self-worth and connection to the larger world, many residents did not have the language to properly describe the violations within the community.

Even if Kate or her mother could find the words to protest as the situation worsened, they would have had little recourse. Reporting Mikey the Pimp to the housing provider would likely mean an increase in rent or, worse, an eviction. And reporting Mikey the Pimp to the police would result in a loss of much-needed resources or, worse, safety.

Both mother and daughter were caught between punitive social housing policies and a very real physical threat. Such a quandary is not specific to the sex trade. Countless women in social housing find themselves coupled up with less-than-stellar men for nominal financial assistance. When these partnerships go awry or become violent, the women have few options, and often choose to endure unsafe conditions to protect their housing.

Toward Dignified Design

In tenth grade, after my mother completed her post-secondary education and moved us out of social housing, I was invited to have dinner at the home of a new friend. Her father was an engineer and her mother a nurse. Their home was beautiful, comfortable and filled with spirited debate. Her father, the warmer and more progressive of the two, encouraged his guests to share ideas and tell their stories. Forgetting – or perhaps ignoring – the fact that I had been raised in a social housing community, my friend's mother began to harshly criticize a single mother, much like my own, for raising children in one of 'those' neighbourhoods. Her father noted my discomfort. 'It's easy to judge poor people when you can afford the high cost of dignity,' he said.

There's a powerful but largely unacknowledged correlation between our wide-scale housing-affordability crisis and the cost of human dignity. Scale up to 10,000 feet and consider the entire spectrum of this issue: think about deplorable housing conditions across many Indigenous communities and the need to amend unfair treaty agreements. Think about the sub-prime mortgages that caused tens of thousands of American families to lose their homes. Think about women and children languishing up to three years in shelters intended for short-term stays. Think about elders on fixed incomes unable to feel secure in their twilight years. Think about people living with developmental and physical disabilities who can't access supportive housing. Regardless of circumstance, people across this spectrum will tell you that their own particular housing crisis isn't merely about bricks and mortar. It's about our inherent right to safe, comfortable and dignified shelter.

Addressing housing issues, particularly social housing issues, is a massive challenge for our society, and especially our increasingly polarized and segregated cities. Social housing provision models, policies and funding formulas vary tremendously. As previously mentioned, the dilemmas we're facing have emerged from the toxic combination of poor design and intentional economic inequality. Indeed, these issues, emerging over several decades, extend well beyond the design purview. But at the same time, the character of communities in large part emerges from buildings and their surrounding environments. It's entirely possible for low-income neighbourhoods to be socially stable places, and designers have an integral role to play in co-creating better and more dignified social housing.

Buildings are a concrete articulation of economies, history, culture, values and aspirations. Their height, girth and orientation inform the quality of relations between people and places. It's also true that buildings serve many functions. Some are appreciated for their aesthetic value while others focus on high-energy performance and environmental resilience. As the name suggests, social housing should have an explicit social goal.

While there are no infallible approaches, human rights – with an emphasis on inherent desire and cultural rights, social planning and human-centred design – offer a powerful framework for centralizing dignity. I'm especially interested in the potential of a human-centred design framework that squarely places a focus on investigating and resolving social problems. It's an immersive process wherein the individuals for whom the design is intended play a leading role in the design process. For example, in some instances, designers will engage communities outside the formal and often restrictive consultation processes set out by municipalities.

This approach works best when community members are not simply observed, surveyed or asked to provide superficial feedback. Instead, education and relationship-building should be employed to co-create knowledge and design solutions. Given that each situation is unique, the process should be iterative and guided by deep collaboration with community members and professionals across silos. Designers should consider a handful of important questions:

- *What is the social goal of social housing?*
- *What are my personal or professional biases that may inadvertently hinder my work on social housing projects?*

• How do we (meaning the design team and community members) define dignity?
• How can we apply this shared definition to this particular process and place?
• Have I taken into account the capacity, resilience, community networks and aspirations of the individuals who live here?

Another strategy for realizing the goal of social housing through dignified design is acknowledging that the mixed-income redevelopment model – the development of market-based housing on land owned by municipal agencies and using the proceeds to rebuild social housing stock – is not a magical fix. This seems counterintuitive, given the economic challenges facing social housing agencies, as well as the need to desegregate poverty. However, just as root-grafting fruit trees can result in the transfer of bacteria, so it is that attempts to redevelop mixed-income communities atop years of both design and social dysfunction won't necessarily solve the underlying problems.

Such acknowledgements are also important given the intense degree of internalized stigma experienced by those living in social housing. People on the receiving end of degrading ideas and stereotypes often begin to believe the aspersions and 'live down' to every horrible thing that is projected onto them. Conversations about internalized stigma tend to be centred on race, homophobia and mental illness, but this kind of self-loathing also afflicts people living in social housing.

Long before Mikey the Pimp's arrival in my childhood community, many residents expressed various forms of internalized stigma – urinating in public spaces, senselessly destroying doors and laundry machines, improperly disposing of garbage and lashing out at fellow neighbours for small infractions. This is not to suggest that my community was devoid of proud and supportive individuals; some of the most resilient and kind people I've ever encountered lived in my neighbourhood. That said, it's important to understand that years of class segregation created complex subcultures, misplaced anger and intergenerational trauma, all of which need to heal.

For these reasons, cross-class – or mixed-income – communities can further agitate feelings of inferiority or self-consciousness for social housing residents. Living next to neighbours with greater financial and social capital can accentuate the canyon across classes and daily struggles. These spaces are never without tensions, as social housing residents generally lack the experience, agency and healthy entitlement to occupy equal space and participate in place-making processes.

Certainly designers cannot be expected to single-handedly address internalized stigma and the multitude of other social housing issues. The best mixed-income redevelopment or community garden project can't reimagine social housing if residents don't deem themselves worthy of safe, beautiful and connected communities.

This observation leads to a critically important and delicate proposal – just as design contributes to social conditions, so do the people on the receiving end of design. I can't solely blame 'bad buildings,' systemic design inequity or even Mikey the Pimp for all the problems in my community. Poor and even poorly housed people are accountable, too.

I say this recognizing my many privileges – I've been blessed with a high degree of fortitude, a second-grade teacher who mentored me for decades, a good group of friends within and outside of my community, a father who loved me from a distance and a mother who clawed her way out. I know the ground is uneven and that people in social housing are dealing with despair, resettlement, precarious employment and everyday survival. To compound these issues, relations with police and, sometimes, housing staff are contentious. So it's understandable but entirely unacceptable that everybody keeps their heads down when terrible things are happening. This lack of accountability is a part of what I think about when I'm awakened by Britney's memory in the middle of the night.

As I reread that 2010 article about her murderer, I'm saddened by the many ways that city-builders and community members failed a young girl who was too valuable to be twice disregarded. And so I'll tell you that Britney was not an insignificant girl from an insignificant neighbourhood. Although older, and undeniably 'cooler,' she was kind and always said hello to us younger kids. She was beautiful, with brown hair and freckles that fluttered across the tip of her nose onto her cheeks. She was my friend's older sister, and to this day the grief of her murder remains etched in his face.

And she is not the only one lost to the shortcomings of social housing. My Facebook network tells this larger story. The vast majority of my social and professional network is comprised of people I met after my mother moved us out of the community. However, I remain in touch with a couple dozen childhood friends from my days in social housing. While my friends and colleagues with greater financial resources and options are completing graduate degrees, travelling and preserving the planet, my childhood friends are dying. A thirtysomething mother slipped into a coma and succumbed shortly afterwards. An athlete who had grappled with his homosexuality for decades overdosed. A bystander at a gathering was mistakenly executed.

My anecdotal observations are supported by numerous reports, like a 2010 *Hamilton Spectator* study that linked class disparities to a twenty-one-year gap in life expectancy between that city's most affluent neighbourhoods and its poorest neighbourhoods.[11] But this issue is not just about a body count. Many other surveys highlight another kind of death – a slow spiral into hopelessness, internalized stigma and disconnection from the city. For example, in 'The Built Environment and Mental Health,' published in 2003, Gary W. Evans asserted that high-rise housing was adverse to the mental health of mothers with young children, and that there are indications that poor quality housing overall increases psychological distress.[12]

But we don't need another report to tell us what we all experience on the streets daily. As urban places become more intensified, it's impossible to avoid encountering the multitude of issues spilling over from social housing communities into public consciousness. Crime once associated with the inner city is now visible in the vibrant public square, and many people have become numb to homelessness. Meanwhile, coffee-shop chatter often centres on soaring rental costs and the declining possibility of home ownership. We're being forced to completely rethink our notion of home, housing types and the role of mixed-income communities. Why not add human dignity to the urgent conversation about social housing design?

Walking Through Loss:
A Critical Visit to an Old Neighbourhood
Photography by Taha Muharuma

For me, walking has always been a political and humbling act. Social disparities, unsung local leaders and informal gathering places are revealed when we navigate communities on the ground level. In the spring of 2014, I initiated a walk through the social housing community of my childhood – a reckoning with loss and residual despair. It was an exploration of the tension I've carried, having lived across class lines and vastly different communities. But it wasn't just personal. As I walked through my old neighbourhood, I contemplated the egregious affordability crisis across the country and committed to working towards the co-creation of dignified social housing.

– Jay Pitter

Reconsidering Revitalization:
The Case of Regent Park
Jay Pitter in conversation with Sandra Costain

Well before the redevelopment of Toronto's downtown Regent Park neighbourhood had been completed, the $1 billion project was heralded as a success – a self-financed model for the revitalization of neglected social housing communities here in Canada, and perhaps beyond. In fact, in a February 2016 feature, *New York Times* writer Dan Levin declared that the transformation of the neighbourhood, long dismissed for its poverty and crime, was a 'model of inclusion.'[1]

While the Toronto Community Housing Corporation (TCHC) plan should be recognized for its approach to developing mixed-use and mixed-income neighbourhoods, such declarations may be naive and premature.

Ensuring that there were a variety of affordable rental units, market town homes and condominiums, recreational and cultural facilities, and businesses was a good start. Few would argue with the ideal of a diversity of residents raising families, learning, enjoying green space and working alongside each other. But many outsiders, including planners and community development advocates, might overlook the complexity of the residual issues stemming from the community's legacy of poor design and systemic marginalization, and its ongoing challenges with crime and safety. What's more, they may not understand the sense of loss felt by long-time residents, and the lingering class tensions that surface when affluent condo buyers move into a space that most of the city once avoided. Indeed, while many people may miss – or minimize – these complicated issues, Sandra Costain, a respected and long-time Regent Park community leader, sees them every day.

Sandra lived in Regent Park for the first twenty-three years of her life. Although the neighbourhood was discounted in the media and in the city's imagination, she recalls many beautiful things about Regent Park. The notion that someone would feel nostalgic about an apparently notorious public housing project runs counter to all the dominant narratives, and raises some troubling questions about the motives behind its redevelopment.

Growing up with her mother and father, Sandra was surrounded by a village of 'aunties' – a local network of women who showered her with love and looked out for her. She also remembers a time when all of the spaces in the community were wide open and accessible: permits were not required for barbecues or street parties, and she had a grand time at the local ice rink or playing an evening game of 'kick the can.'

Sandra doesn't deny the shortcomings of Regent Park. There was a lot of fighting and public drinking, and the 1980s ushered in a destructive drug trade. And, of course, there were the kinds of divisions that plague many public housing communities – between Black and white residents, and between the residents who lived north of Dundas Street and those who lived on the south side.

In spite of the community's challenges, Sandra carried with her a pride in her neighbourhood, a feeling that endured even after she moved out to attend Ryerson University to study social work. Sandra decided to stay connected to Regent Park so her son could experience the wonderful 'village feel' she enjoyed as a child. She also wanted to make a difference in the neighbourhood, and has been doing so for over a decade, working in a leadership role for a local service agency. In a conversation in early 2016, Sandra discussed post-revitalization Regent Park from the perspective of a former resident who has spent her career working in and for the community. She shared a critical yet hopeful analysis of the community's ongoing transformation:

Where do long-time Regent Park residents and the owners of the market condos interact?

The way you phrased that question is interesting. It's important to be clear that there isn't one unified and homogenous group of long-time Regent Park residents and another group of condo owners. The residents who've lived here before the revitalization are comprised of many communities – people from many African countries, people from South Asian countries, people from Caribbean islands, people from Eastern European countries. All of these and other groups of long-time residents were still trying to figure out how to live with each other when the new residents arrived. It's important to keep this in mind.

What an important distinction – thank you. Yes, the same is true of the public housing community where I grew up ... so many people thrust together by class rather than choice, and trying to figure things out. So let me rephrase the question: where do people in the community across experiences interact most?

Whether Regent Park residents have been here for generations, several years or they are brand-new, the place where people connect most is at the big park, the one right off the boardwalk. That is where the blending is happening.

What does this blending look like?

People are parenting. Well, mostly the original or long-time residents are parenting. Lots of people in this community who've recently moved here are young adults who are not necessarily parenting. They don't have children, but they have nieces and nephews or friends with children. Plus, there is a small group of young families among the new residents who are also coming out to the park.

So people across the various 'class' and cultural groups are parenting their little people together?

Well, they're using the space at the same time, but not together, I wouldn't say that. Children are children, so they're playing together. But there's been some tension between the adults.

What kind of tension?

It's really disheartening, some of the things that are happening. Like everybody and their sister wants to get in on the action because the community is so high-profile. In the summer, complete strangers come to the park and start handing out free things to residents they assume are living in public housing.

So we're outside on a Friday – we do this Show Love event every Friday in the park. There's music and food; people really enjoy themselves. Then these people from outside of the community show up and start handing out bread.

What!

Yes. Sometimes it's shorts and soccer balls, but sometimes it's bread. And then the great divide between residents really shows. Because if you earn a good living, you're probably not going to accept the free shirt or ball, but if your income is $12,000 per year you might get in line for that free bread. And these people coming in here think that because residents are poor or because they read about the community – that they can come into our park and give away stuff and make people line up for bread without even considering how that may make them feel, especially now in front of their new, financially better-off neighbours. We're trying to do something new in this park and people are not being thoughtful about the people here, about exposing their need.

There must be a way of giving that involves consent and dignity ... especially in a public place like the park.

Exactly. There are also other situations in the park. This one time, a toddler from the condos, maybe two and a half, had one of those wooden bikes with no pedals. Like one that cost a couple hundred dollars, and he puts the bike down. And this other little guy, living in a public housing unit, jumps on the bike and starts riding it. Well, the mother of the toddler totally freaks out and starts talking about her child owning the bike. But it hasn't been like that here. Before, if you came to the park to play, it was understood that everything would be shared. When people don't have a lot, there is little talk about ownership and that stuff. You share.

It didn't end up being horrible, but it did go on for a long time, and the incident shows the way different residents value things or different social rules. People are not on the same page with that stuff yet.

I did hear about a serious incident in the Daniels Spectrum building between a little Asian boy, I think, and an older white gentleman. Do you know about that?

I do. This little boy, around eight or nine years old, was running in this beautiful brand-new building with pure excitement and accidentally stepped on the shoe of the older man. And the man called him a 'dirty c-word.' People were *really* upset. This was reported to people operating the space. There's a monthly tenant meeting and it was discussed there. It took months to resolve, but the man who spewed out this ugly racist slur to the little boy was made to apologize.

I've heard that story a few times now and it's always upsetting. I'm glad the community and Daniels Spectrum came together to address the issue. While we're on the topic of the Daniels Spectrum building, though, I'd love to get your thoughts on that.

It's an interesting building. Daniels Spectrum doesn't have that home-away-from-home feel that the girls' program I ran out of the demolished Blevins building had.

Funny, right? That building, a modernist high-rise designed by architect Peter Dickinson, was shrouded in so much language around violence and disrepair, and so many young women I meet talk about the amazing work you did out of that building. Like you've literally mentored two generations of young women out of that building, women who've gone on to post-secondary education.

Yeah, I still remember when that program started. The unit we were assigned was filthy-dirty, and I asked the girls to meet me there on the weekend to clean up. I promised them homemade spaghetti, but secretly thought there was no way these girls are going to spend the day trying to clean up that awful mess. I almost didn't purchase the ingredients for the spaghetti because I was sure they would be so put off by having to rip up old dusty carpets and scrub down every single surface in that place. I showed up with groceries and a ton of cleaning supplies, fully expecting to be scrubbing away by myself. I was so surprised to see these girls, many of them so negatively labelled, show up with old clothing and head scarves, ready to work. That building was a disaster in many ways, but we created a beautiful space in that apartment unit, right from day one.

When the city shows up with their plan and narrow questions, they don't hear these kinds of stories. They aren't really looking for them, and so the ways we've done a good job of creating community here, even with all of its problems, get missed.

This example really shows how redevelopment is about design, better buildings, and it's also about people who care – people who show up and create space for others.

Thanks. I mean, I carry so many great memories from that apartment unit and – Well, back to the Daniels Spectrum: that space is very important, too, in a different way. It's obviously gorgeous. On the lower level they now have space on Fridays. Many groups use it, so it's flexible, which is good, but you can't put roots down there. You have to pack up after programming ends. That's not entirely bad, because the space is always changing and responding to the community's needs, but it is different.

Community work, real neighbourhood-building, doesn't always happen like that. It extends beyond regular working hours, and young people need permanence. But one thing I really like about the Daniels Spectrum is that it is a space for exceptional youth. The programs aren't all about a need or service. Young people in this community now have a place to be excellent – to be exceptional – and that's important here and in every other public housing community.

Great point. I remember in my old public housing community there weren't any spaces to be exceptional, unless you include the basketball court. Clearly someone or a group of people didn't anticipate that we might also be interested in literature, science or astronomy.

Exactly. I like that about the Daniels Spectrum. Our youth *deserve* more spaces to be exceptional. To do things that other people in the city do – take classes, experience art and hear speakers. It's so good for them not to feel ashamed to invite their friends into the community. They deserve that.

But we also have to be clear that the Daniels Spectrum isn't for youth facing lots of social barriers and personal challenges. People need to remember that young people in this neighbourhood are still involved in the sex trade, still carrying loaded weapons, still unemployed, still struggling with mental health issues. We can't leave these youth out in the cold.

Do you have any other concerns about redeveloped spaces?

Well, access is a concern. There are obviously the concerns about fees for many of these new spaces. Although there are subsidies, many of the fees are still too much for low-income residents and sometimes even for service agencies doing a lot of work with very small budgets. In cases where there aren't any fees and buildings have been greatly enhanced, there's another, emerging issue of access. People from outside of the community, who don't actually need to use some of these spaces, are taking up space here.

What is a specific example of this?

Well, at the aquatic centre. It's a beautiful pool. We have a group of long-time child-development workers doing really important and hard work for relatively little pay. I know that some of them want to use the pool during their lunch break, but you have to sign up each day, on-site, to gain access. Well, all of these middle-class and wealthy women from other communities with perfectly fine amenities, I'm sure, drive in here and fill up the spots before the workers get their break. So these women doing great work in the community aren't able to get access.

The lack of fees, newfound neighbourhood popularity and sign-up structures sometimes create access issues for residents and workers who have been here long before the redevelopment process. Also, we have to stop pretending that these amenities are actually for these people. I believe the developer, the City and Toronto Community Housing have redesigned these amenities to capture the interests of the new, higher-income residents.

Another example of an accessibility issue is the new Athletic Grounds. It is now completed, and there is not yet any word about fees or processes for accessing the space, but people are playing on it daily. Charging a kid a fee just to pick up a ball and kick it around isn't going to go over well in this community. Plus, requiring them to organize formal teams rather than spontaneously play pickup games like they are used to will create another accessibility issue. Or requiring local groups to apply for funding – that's going to create a barrier.

These kinds of constraints will create resentments, and the young people will find a way to circumvent all of that formality and financial inaccessibility. It will create undue conflict and class tensions. The social development planning and operation plans are very important in ensuring that these new spaces are accessible to all members of this community.

When I led a walk here a couple of years ago with local residents, one of the big themes that came up was the importance of informal gathering places. With all of these new programmed and formal spaces, are people still able to gather informally?

One thing poor people know how to do is make a lot out of next to nothing. Because the old Regent Park was so poorly designed, we didn't have certain spaces like party rooms and rooftop spaces, so the community created their own spaces. When people see residents outside gathering with music playing, eating, even braiding each other's hair or maybe drinking a little bit, it isn't the picture-perfect Regent Park they want. But we've lived so long without formal or properly designed spaces, it's natural to gather outside. Also, the units are so small sometimes that being outside is a way of breathing and escaping isolation and cramped living quarters.

It's important to know that people will still want to gather informally, outside of beautiful buildings. People will want that sense of freedom and street-level connection. And it will take time for some residents to even learn how to be comfortable or how to behave in some of the new spaces. I think both kinds of spaces are needed. In my experience, having people gather, formally and informally, keeps eyes on the streets, helps us to stay abreast of needs and potential serious conflicts, and builds a sense of belonging.

Do you notice any other differences or tensions across residents groups?

The most visible one everyone can see are the dirty windows. It's that simple. You have townhouses that look exactly the same, but the one way you know who the long-time public housing tenant is and who is a new tenant paying market rent are the dirty windows. Condo owners pay fees to upkeep their lawns and windows, but TCHC barely has any money to upkeep its housing units.

This is a huge problem, because we must remember that at one time the same buildings being bulldozed and criticized now were once gleaming and considered the answer to the community's problems. We can't place too much hope in these buildings. We need to think about things like ongoing maintenance, accessibility and creating more community cohesion. Also, you have some women walking around in high heels that cost hundreds of dollars in a neighbourhood where people are struggling to find grocery money at the end of the month. There have been some robberies.

Do you think this will work … this whole redevelopment scheme?

I need this to work for people who lived here before all of this – the people who lost their neighbours through the relocation process, people who have seen cherished spaces brought down to the ground, people who are trying to find a new place for themselves in their own neighbourhood. I need it to work for them.

Model Citizens
Andrea Gunraj

Kehinde Bah was only twenty-one when he was invited to join the board of an organization serving youth. In 2000, the early days of his civic leadership work, he was just starting to become known beyond his Blake-Jones neighbourhood, an almost perfect square of streets nestled south of Danforth Ave. Blake-Jones is designated as one of Toronto's 'Neighbourhood Improvement Areas,' with its high rates of unemployment, school dropout and marginalization.[1]

Although Bah recognized the invitation as an opportunity because he'd be one of the few young Black men at the decision-making table, he also experienced an intense sense of pressure, too. 'I would put it in my mind that I had this responsibility to be here,' he says, 'because we don't get to be here because we can't afford to have our voices heard in these spaces.'

The day of the organization's annual general meeting arrived, and it was taking place far outside the streets familiar to Bah. 'The lady just told me, "Just come to this address for this time," and it was like, she didn't think nothing,' he says. 'I had to scrounge up bus money and it was the last of my change.' While he identified the correct subway station, he boarded the northbound bus instead of the south-bound one he needed to take. 'Keep in mind, I'm from Blake,' he recalls. 'I didn't know the world. I didn't know the city. I hadn't been around places, especially on my own.'

When he finally realized he was going the wrong way, he got off the bus and headed south on foot. 'I ended up having to walk all the way down because I didn't have any more money,' he says. 'By the time I got there, the meeting was almost over. I had no idea where I was. I could've been on the moon.'

Bah's experience wasn't unlike the confusing journey many people face when they try to navigate urban decision-making systems that have rarely included their voices. Toronto's hyper-diversity doesn't necessarily translate into representative engagement and leadership. All sorts of social and economic factors affect an individual's ability to participate in civic life, and those factors even determine which citizens are more likely to emerge as civic leaders.

We can describe those individuals most enabled to participate and get recognized for their involvement as 'model citizens.' They don't achieve that status by mere effort. Decision-making structures, either intentionally or by default, are set up to privilege their voices. By virtue of class, language, education, social identity and profession, model citizens stand apart from those city-dwellers who aren't listened to and haven't mastered the language and mannerisms of public engagement. This imbalance, which seems built into a system ostensibly designed to canvass public opinion, represents a major obstacle in a hyper-diverse, multilingual city like Toronto. It prevents local government from understanding how its actions impact all its citizens, whether model or not, and ultimately undermines the effectiveness of local democracy.

But it's not a one-dimensional reality either. Bah's story suggests that non-models do succeed in breaking through, even as they face their own barriers, risks and pressures. They can become what I term 'outlier change-makers,' who, by exercising and sharing their own knowledge and skill, influence urban decision-making. While their involvement can be powerful in representing the needs and assets of non–model citizen communities, outliers face a heavy burden in their role as voices for those who aren't typically engaged by municipal decision-makers. Moreover, we shouldn't conclude that the consultation status quo works just because individuals like Bah find space to express their views. Municipal officials must try harder to broaden the doorways to civic leadership and engagement, and to build voices and opportunities beyond the familiar faces of model citizens and the few others who make it in.

Fragmented Engagement

Author and activist Jane Jacobs was an outspoken advocate for neighbourhood-level leadership in urban planning from the 1960s through the 2000s. From New York City to Toronto, she championed bottom-up planning so citizens would drive city development and infrastructure decisions. Her influence still reverberates through the consultation mechanisms involving municipal decision-makers and everyday people.[2]

But this engagement model hasn't played out in balanced ways. Some citizens simply participate more than others, and their involvement tends to be better recognized and rewarded. Their skills, language, race, ability and other identity factors allow them to work effectively in a system well-suited to the expression of their needs and ideals. Jacobs's model of public engagement has worked out in a rather lopsided way.

A few years ago, I witnessed this lopsidedness in the northwest Toronto suburb of Rexdale, another Neighbourhood Improvement Area. City staff and councillors were hosting a town-hall meeting at a local community centre to discuss the impact of a recent shooting and what could be done to prevent similar tragedies. I entered a packed room of mostly racialized residents, many of whom identified as newcomers, women and subsidized-housing tenants. The contrast between guests and hosts was immediately clear: the only white people who showed up were either city staff or councillors.

But a deeper disconnection also emerged. Staff and councillors wielded the lexicon of municipal government jargon and referred to the city's bureaucracy in a way that took their own specialized know-how for granted. Residents were certainly open about their confusions and frustrations in the process. The participants in this exercise communicated over and past one another, using two different languages: that of the insider and that of the outsider. As the atmosphere grew increasingly tense, I lost track of what concrete outcomes had emerged.

The absence of a common civic language is a problem. In a 2001 essay, University of Maryland urban geographer John Rennie Short described the growth of 'balkanized cities' in the U.S. where urbanization is accompanied by resident disparities, particularly between downtown and suburban dwellers, especially those 'middle-income whites and upper-income Blacks and whites moving out from the central cores.' While it takes place against a political background of metropolitan fragmentation, this social balkanization is more signifi-cant than municipal borders. It disadvantages urban dwellers with less access to power and keeps community groups at odds with one another, unable to act on mutual interests. As Short says, 'there is civic engagement and civic engagement. Not all of it is necessarily good.'[3]

It's easy to assume this kind of fragmented engagement happens only in famously segregated U.S. cities like Detroit and Birmingham. But such social divisions are apparent in decision-making and engage-ment in Greater Toronto as well. The Diversity Leads report, published by Ryerson University's Diversity Institute in 2014, addresses repre-sentation of women and 'visible minorities' in leadership across the GTA, both among elected officials and in other areas such as appoint-ments to government agencies and boards. In 2014, women occupied 32.5 percent of all senior leadership positions even though they make up 51.5 percent of the population. Visible-minorities, meanwhile, occupied only 12.8 percent of leadership positions but accounted for 53.7 percent of the population.[4]

According to research published in *Canadian Ethnic Studies* in 2008, new immigrants and some non-European communities are less likely to vote and participate in volunteer activities, clubs and organ-izations. This is especially the case for immigrants who came to Canada between 1991 and 2001, many of whom have lower incomes and less English or French than Canadian-born citizens and pre-1991 immigrants. Those immigration trends have continued since 2001.[5]

The connection between language and engagement cannot be underestimated. The inability to communicate in the language of migration is like being left without a voice. But many newcomers are unable to access language classes because of unmet child-care needs, resource and time constraints, high levels of unemployment and little knowledge of opportunities for participation. '[A]t a time when social networks might be most needed,' according to an essay by immigrant health researchers Yvonne Lai and Michaela Hynie, 'participating in social network may actually increase immigrants' stress and distress, rather than contributing to their well-being.'

Interestingly, urban complexity itself can represent a barrier to newcomer participation. For new immigrants, large metropolitan areas with a highly diverse mix of residents can create a sense of isolation and disconnectedness. Smaller cities may actually better foster social integration. Other barriers also play a role in newcomer disconnection. Interviewing twenty-one newcomers, Lai and Hynie concluded that 'community organizations were unaware of the unique experiences and needs of new immigrants and this discouraged [newcomers] from participating.'[6]

Older citizens, especially those limited by health, social resources or income, also face obstacles when it comes to civic engagement, according to a study by two University of Berkeley public health experts.[7] And active citizenship for lesbian, gay, bisexual and transgender communities, observed Ann-Marie Field, a Université du Québec à Montréal researcher in a 2007 analysis, may be thwarted by gendered notions of citizenship, which are 'closely associated with the institutionalization of heterosexual and male privileges.'[8]

Model Citizens

The reality of fragmented engagement has been recognized and tackled by reformers like Toronto-based Dave Meslin, who advocates for more open and accessible participation in municipal decision-making.[9] There are also examples of city-led initiatives to broaden engagement, such as the 'Feeling Congested?' campaign – geared toward improving transit and mobility – and the Toronto Youth Equity Strategy.[10, 11] But these efforts can't do enough to balance the heavily tipped scales in urban engagement and leadership.

Toronto city councillor Kristyn Wong-Tam is often involved in city-led public consultations like working groups and design charrettes. A variety of methods are used to publicize these events – mail-outs, flyer drops, newsletter announcements and social media. 'Even with all those tools deployed to try to extract community input,' she says, 'what I find happens is that you have, oftentimes, very similar voices speaking about their particular concerns and those certain types of voices tend to be repeated over and over again.'

As Wong-Tam puts it, these voices tend to be those citizens who can attend an evening meeting featuring two hours of English dialogue. They are usually living in the downtown core, white, middle to upper income and older than forty. 'When you have a city as diverse as Toronto,' she says, 'and when you have government policy that's being informed by public input that only extracts a certain type of feedback, then what ends up happening is that you have people speaking in an echo chamber.' She describes it as 'a monoculture that largely gets represented, and it's the voices of that monoculture that influence policy.'

The people who engage, the model citizens, usually belong to well-established urban networks. As American sociologist Robert Putnam explained in his seminal book, *Bowling Alone: The Collapse and Revival of American Community*, 'social networks, and the norms of reciprocity and trustworthiness that arise from them' is key.[12] In fact, social capital is directly linked to high socio-economic status, which is the basis of political participation, as University of Calgary political scientist Brenda O'Neill points out in her analysis of human capital and civic engagement.

O'Neill identifies education as one of the most important variables under the umbrella of socio-economic status, and high educational attainment is a particularly strong indicator of civic participation. It not only provides knowledge, language and skills that enable engagement, but it also heightens an individual's acceptance of democratic structures and can foster an inner desire to be politically informed. In other words, O'Neill concludes, the educated model citizen 'buys into' the premises of democracy, even if they aren't always fulfilled as promised.

Higher education also tends to lead to better-paying employment. Wealth provides model citizens with enabling factors like free time, child care and disposable income for donations to causes and parties. These individuals are also more likely to be in professions that allow them access to political information and skills conducive to civic engagement and leadership. They start off with an educational advantage and get to practice and sharpen that advantage on paid time.[13]

The point, as Parissa Ballard, Laura Caccavale and Christy Buchanan note in their 2015 research on civic engagement, is that model citizens are 'civically oriented.' They hold attitudes that create responsibility, trust, tolerance and intentions to engage, and they enact behaviours useful to community service.[14] But an inner civic orientation cannot be pulled apart from environmental and social factors. Those who are accustomed to being attended to and are given voice in civic processes will likely be more civically oriented.

There are gender differences in civic engagement, too. O'Neill shows that women's participation in voting has risen to the level of men's, and their informal engagement, in areas such as community volunteerism, is even greater than that of men. But in formal positions such as city council and government boards, they are not well-represented. This lower access to formal leadership could result from cultural factors, like gender norms, and practical barriers, like women's lower earning power. The model citizen with the highest levels of influence, then, is more likely to be a man.

Lastly, there is the age factor. O'Neill shows that the model citizen is less likely to be a younger person. The reasons are complicated – perhaps a combination of generational shifts in beliefs and attitudes about formal state structures, as well as what people tend to value at different life stages. Whatever the reasons, O'Neill notes that younger people vote less often, join fewer interest groups and political parties, and are less aware about politics.[15] But as Ballard, Caccavale and Buchanan point out, younger people with high socio-economic backgrounds are more likely grow up to gain social and political power. Model citizens, in other words, are more likely to pass on advantages, clout and 'civic savviness' to their children.[16]

The other side of the analysis about the political success of model citizens is that they engage with a system of municipal governance that creates space for them to articulate their views. 'There are some built-in inherent biases that we all have in terms of what an expert looks like,' Wong-Tam says. 'And I find that we don't often capture people's lived experiences.' When she does see participation of 'non-model citizens,' it is more often in areas like poverty-reduction strategies than in technical fields like city-building and planning. It's worth noting that the technically complex decision-making often evolves from the advice of professionals such as geographers, planners, designers, architects and transportation engineers, whose opinions are highly esteemed and carry weight with policy-makers.

The reliance on experts and technical analysis in itself presents an imbalance in whose voices are most listened to when decisions are made. And whether or not they are experts in these fields, model citizens benefit from the 'professionalization' of municipal advice. 'When you have model citizens who have a certain aesthetic and have a certain vocal presentation that we see repeatedly, whether it's through mainstream media or just who we imagine a leader should be or what an expert should look like, then their voices will carry more weight,' Wong-Tam says. It is bias added to bias – decision-makers, she says, are not trained to hear beyond a contributor's accent, skin colour, clothes and vocabulary.

Outlier Change-makers

Rose Streete, a leader in her Mississauga neighbourhood, explains how her civic activism is grounded in perilous life experiences that would have prevented most others in her circumstances from having anything to do with public engagement.

'Nine years ago, I lost it all,' she says. 'I was homeless, penniless; I went to a shelter with the running shoes on my feet. And I was pregnant with my fourth child.' Despite all that, Streete had a tremendous drive to do something to affect change during Toronto's so-called Summer of the Gun. During those months in 2005, thirty-three young people, many of them Black, lost their lives to gun violence. 'At that point, I had two Black youths growing up. I could see the differences and say, "Not my child," which often parents do. Or I could look at the similarities and say, "It could be my child."'

Streete became an active change-maker in her shelter and community using strategies she developed when navigating her own housing barriers. 'I realized, okay, I just need to keep understanding more of how these guidelines work,' she recalls. 'What are these policies and how do they work for and against people? And what are the loopholes? Where do they bind themselves? Where do they not make sense?'

She carried the strategies forward to her housing residence in the Ridgeway neighbourhood, an area then marked by high crime, over-policing, marginalization and low engagement. 'I believe in making intentional communities. So I moved in intentionally because I saw scores and scores of Black youth always standing on the roadside. Now I had the opportunity to go in and do something about it.'

Streete decided to become a community champion – an outlier change-maker. 'I know on one hand, the system thought I was going to fail,' she says. 'They thought I was going to go in there and go through a baptism by fire. But I went in there and I did what they were afraid to do.' She became a leader and integrated creative methods, like arts and documentary, into her engagement practices. Streete successfully advocated for improvements to local park infrastructure, new community events and enhanced police-community relationships. But she was only invited to a formal neighbourhood strategy table after doing a significant amount of the work on her own. 'It was a bonus for them to have found this worker bee that was willing to do the work for them, because there's no liability for them,' she says.

Similarly, Kehinde Bah worked in community and found himself at policy and decision-making tables. From 1999 to 2002, he was a member of the Toronto Youth Cabinet, serving as chair and vice-chair. Bah worked with young people and bureaucrats to address issues of concern to marginalized youth. Yet when he joined the Cabinet, going to city hall was like entering a different world. 'I always felt like they didn't take someone like me seriously where I came from,' he says. But he was driven by the desire to reduce injustice and create an identity for himself outside of his neighbourhood. 'We were coming from very vulnerable positions, so oftentimes the issues that they're talking about impacted me and impacted the people around me, and that voice wasn't really being heard in this kind of space. I felt that maybe I could do something about that.'

Bah explains that there were people in key positions at the Youth Cabinet who helped him develop his outlier change-maker identity. They looked like him, encouraged him to take up space and showed him new skills. 'I didn't really mean to be a leader or to know how to talk to white people,' he says. 'Young people from a place like Blake, they might have white people in the centre that they're at or whatever, but it's not the same as talking to some stranger and being like, "I know you have power and I need you to use your power to provide this so that we can do that." That's very, very hard to do.'

Rose Streete views her transformation into an outlier change-maker as a strategic one. She speaks of the social change process as a 'tactical mission' marked by rocky terrain, dead ends and exposed wires. 'There are always going to be opposing forces,' she says. 'You learn about the forces that are with you and the forces that are against you.' Still, she notes that community champions walk a lonely road. Streete cites an example of work she did to address police-youth tensions in her Ridgeway community in 2005 and beyond: 'I did have a vested interest because I had Black youth of my own. I did have a vested interest because I understood poverty – I was living it all of the sudden. I did have a vested interest because I'm also a contributing part of society and I believe we can live better lives.'

But in the end, her lobbying for needed neighbourhood infra-structure and her efforts to help reduce the police-youth tensions were successful because 'neither side trusted me.' She proved to all participants in the debate – parents, police and neighbours – that she was looking out not only for their interests and ease, but also for the safety and well-being of young people in the community.

Municipal officials, perhaps not surprisingly, may bristle at the suggestion that local government excludes low-income people or racialized minorities. Some bureaucrats, in fact, have mandates to boost those voices. Laura Metcalfe, a community development officer with the City of Toronto, is helping to build the Toronto Youth Equity Strategy, which aims to improve services for youth most vulnerable to involvement in serious violence and who have minimal access to supports. 'A lot of the civic engagement that's happening in marginal-ized communities is under-acknowledged,' Metcalfe says, noting that most of the civic leaders she has worked with in areas like Jane-Finch are women, racialized and have lower incomes. 'That's also part of how privilege plays out,' she adds. 'The voices that might get covered in the newspapers or on the radio or on TV are not necessarily all those voices. But those voices are there. I know who they are. I see them. I work with them.'

Both Streete and Metcalfe point to the complicated, real-world dynamics of civic participation. Those who are marginalized may have less access to civic engagement and leadership experience. As Streete knows from her own experiences, the work they do may not be acknowledged in official circles. Only certain types of citizen involvement are likely to be profiled, measured and counted. The model citizens with the most power and voice are best positioned to be recognized for their civic involvement, but they are by no means the only ones who are engaged.

Metcalfe sees herself as an enabler, someone whose job it is to open up more space for engagement and leadership. 'That's one benefit of working with the city,' she says. 'We're the closest level of government to residents. There's a more immediate link, I think, at the municipal level, which is an advantage here.' Kristyn Wong-Tam also considers herself an enabler, and advocates for enhanced inclusion through mechanisms such as distributing information in multiple languages and accommodations like child care and sign-language interpretation for meetings residents are expected to attend. Many of these practices and services are not the norm, and they happen piecemeal across city initiatives. 'If we're to provide service for our residents,' Wong-Tam says, 'I expect us to provide services to those residents in a universally acceptable way.'

Expanding engagement also reduces the pressure on those few who do manage to get a seat at the table. Streete speaks of being targeted as a 'snitch' because of her high visibility in a neighbourhood with so few grassroots leaders. Others are forced to make equally difficult trade-offs. 'There were so few of us in the room,' Bah says of his time in the Youth Cabinet. He was unemployed and, with the hours he dedicated to this leadership role, he wouldn't have been able to hold down a job. 'It was an exploitation I was aware of, but I just couldn't turn down. I wrapped up my identity in this role of leader, in this role of hero to my block.'

Broadening Engagement and Leadership

Despite the advocacy of individuals like Wong-Tam and Metcalfe, systemic efforts to amplify the voices of non-model citizens continue to fall short. The costs are great. It means urban governments don't have the ability to understand how their policies and actions impact all citizens. More fundamentally, the project of local democracy is foiled because so many citizens are functionally disenfranchised on the level of decision-making closest to their lives. If disenfranchisement happens at the lowest level of government, how much more pronounced might it be at higher levels? The lack of broad engagement, in fact, calls into question the very legitimacy of policy-making.

The lack of diverse engagement and leadership impacts individuals and communities in other ways, too. Various urban sociologists and geographers point to the negative outcomes associated with exclusion for large swaths of the city – higher unemployment, limited access to resources, increases in morbidity and mortality, even in some cases social unrest.

What can be done to broaden civic engagement and perhaps avoid these negative outcomes? Trust-building is an essential first step, and looking for opportunities for non-models to take a lead will help. 'Marginalized and disenfranchised communities are tired of being co-opted,' says Wong-Tam. 'They have to survive their day-to-day existence, and the systems of oppression are real. We can't come into the discussion with only our value statements on the table, without asking them what we can do for them and only asking what they can do for us.' She suggests that meaningful empowerment involves not only having citizens at decision-making tables but also sharing power. 'Let them run the meetings the way they need to run the meetings in the format they want with their cultural customs, and when they're ready, they'll let us know what they think.'

Civic-engagement theorists propose a range of solutions, everything from improving access for marginalized groups to membership on panels, boards and advisory committees, to creating stipends and reimbursements to help offset the costs of doing the time-consuming work of civic engagement. Others highlight the value of building accessible virtual spaces, more child and attendant care, and expanded translation services. Given the multiplicity of languages spoken in Greater Toronto and the number of newcomers who come every year with first languages other than English or French, the translation of documents, meeting announcements and other tools related to public engagement is crucial.

Municipal officials must also work harder to identify non-model leaders, like Rose Streete, who are already engaged in civic work in their communities, but often outside official structures. Local leaders must also encourage connectedness among neighbours from an array of socio-economic and ethnocultural backgrounds.

And just as lobbying organizations are a part of the political process, non-profit organizations can act as intermediaries to build the contributions of non-model citizens. Kelly LeRoux, a Wayne State University political scientist, notes that social-service non-profits and/or those organized around group identities such as ethnicity are particularly useful in providing space and support for marginalized people to amplify their own voices.[17] Faith-based organizations are an important part of the non-profit landscape, particularly for newcomer populations. Livianna Tossutti, Ding Ming Wang and Sanne Kaas-Mason's 2008 study found that religious behaviour was the most consistent predictor of engagement in public affairs. They note that 'declines in institutional worship, without an accompanying increase in personal worship, can be expected to have adverse consequences for democracy and civil society.'[18] While engaging with faith-based organizations as intermediaries can present challenges in secular contexts, the potential these organizations have to grow civic participation among newcomers cannot be ignored.

But beyond these ideas, municipal governments must enforce the breadth of engagement with targets and requirements. If non-models are not meaningfully engaged in the process of developing policies or practices, then political leaders should withhold making decisions until their views have been properly solicited. And in the end, these solutions won't be successful without challenging the way those who make policy tend to think. This could include anti-bias education and better accountability structures for decision-makers.

In the hyper-diverse urban communities of the twenty-first century, we need new mechanisms to recognize the engagement and leadership of those whose input has been traditionally ignored, and we must then imbed their views directly into the way we build our cities.

Many thanks to Kehinde Bah, Laura Metcalfe, Rose Streete and Kristyn Wong-Tam for sharing their expertise and experiences, as well as to Gord Perks for supportive background information.

A Tale of Two – or Three – Cities:
Gentrification and Community Consultations
Mariana Valverde

Just east of Toronto's downtown, two busy streetcar lines meet at the corner of Broadview and Queen East. At that well-travelled intersection, the New Broadview Hotel's imposing neo-Romanesque bulk is the dominant landmark on a late Victorian main street almost untouched by the postwar building boom. Although the arrival of film studios on nearby Eastern Avenue in the late 1990s gave rise to Queen's trendy cafés and shops, few rich people wanted to actually live in the area – until a few years ago, when Streetcar Development quietly began to build tasteful high-end condos. These mid-rise buildings were raised on warehouse-type sites that did not require the developer to tear down Victorian houses, which meant that few locals noticed – until, in the summer of 2014, Streetcar took over the New Broadview and revealed plans for a tasteful, 'heritage' boutique hotel.

My neighbours had generally disliked the hotel because it housed a notorious strip club called Jilly's. Thousands of people going by on streetcars and on foot had long been a captive audience for the outsized, stereotypical pictures of semi-dressed women that marked the building's exterior, so many locals saw the change in ownership and use as a positive development. As a feminist, I had never been thrilled to see photos of young women in provocative poses dominating a key street corner. But, as I often used to say to my complaining neighbours, 'Hey, Jilly's is the one thing that stands between us and total gentrification!'

The Jilly's/New Broadview makeover was widely publicized in the *Toronto Star* and other media. But the larger social and economic context of extreme and highly localized gentrification in the Queen-Broadview area had only recently become apparent to the city-planning apparatus. Yet many of us in the neighbourhood had taken note. Well before the Jilly's sale, some concerned local citizens decided to take active measures to influence city policy so as to minimize the exclusionary effects of the upscaling of Queen East.

Public meetings on gentrification organized by the Ralph Thornton Community Centre in 2012 and 2013 initially stirred people to action. And after the Real Jerk, a venerable Jamaican restaurant across the street from Jilly's, was forced to close in 2013 (to later reopen at the un-gentrified corner of Gerrard and Carlaw), area residents formed Planning South Riverdale (PSR), with the aim of ensuring that the neighbourhood remained inclusive and affordable. Also in 2013, city planners decided to hold several community consultations in the area. The members of PSR, including myself, saw these as opportunities to raise awareness and ensure that city policies and planning rules supported social inclusion.

Like many other cities, Toronto has developed sophisticated protocols for community consultations about planning issues. But just who is actually consulted? And how exactly are those people consulted? Many people (including some authors in this collection) have wondered whether planners and the consultants hired to help them ought to revise their consultation methods so they do not unwittingly ignore the very people who are most at risk of being displaced in rapidly changing neighbourhoods like Leslieville, where Jilly's was situated.

But few models of genuinely inclusive urban planning consultation exist. The PSR group, concerned about the growing spatial and economic inequality of the neighbourhood, designed and carried out a series of alternative consultations in Leslieville in 2013 and 2014. Our unofficial consultations ran in tandem with two official city consultations: one concerning the establishment of a Heritage Conservation District in the small area just east of the Don River that is known as Riverside, and another geared to producing the architectural and height guidelines for Leslieville's commercial heart (Queen Street from Degrassi to Jones).

The Official Story

In Toronto, main streets, officially known as 'avenues,' are governed by a policy promoting limited intensification. Along many wide avenues in the inner suburbs, the problem is low density and too many parking lots. On older downtown commercial strips, such as Queen East in the Leslieville and Riverside neighbourhoods, the problem is instead that skyrocketing real estate prices and rents are threatening to turn the lively high streets of the Jane Jacobs type into canyons of high-end condos and boutique restaurants.

The Heritage Conservation District designation study aimed to preserve at least the architecture of the neighbourhood – though heritage designations can hinder local efforts to ensure that the area remains inclusive and affordable, as the replacement of Jilly's by a proposed boutique hotel underlines. Initially, the city's Leslieville 'avenue' study seemed to hold more promise, since 'affordability' and 'inclusivity' were part of the mandate.

The planning department had hired an outside consultant to run the community consultations, which took place over several months and demanded a great deal of energy from participants: four public events, solicitation of feedback through emails and phone calls, plus four further meetings of a select 'stakeholder' group.

The city held an initial 'open house' in a school gym, offering information about the avenue study, as well as three other planning reviews going on at the same time. For most residents, it was too much technical information. Few aside from professional planners and architects could keep the different studies straight. What's more, the open-house format has problematic political implications – city staff (and architects or planners hired by the city) come up with plans for a neighbourhood, and public participation is limited to reacting after the fact.

Between October 2013 and April 2014, the city held three more public sessions, each featuring short and tightly managed presentations of official plans followed by round-table discussions with participants (known in planning-speak as 'charrettes'). One evening, the people attending this session were all asked to think about the neighbourhood and its resources, identifying 'assets' and going on to suggest 'improvements.' The city's consultants dutifully gathered the input and summarized it at the next meeting. At another session, participants had to think of words that described the area: predictably, watchwords like *creative, energetic, diversity, inclusive* and *cosmopolitan* predominated.

Besides those four public meetings, the city convened four sessions with a select 'stakeholder advisory group.' A member of PSR asked to participate and was included, but it wasn't clear how others were chosen. The group included two established community agencies, but their representatives did not attend regularly; the rest of the participants were either homeowners or local business people. The low-income tenants living in the hundreds of units of subsidized housing nearby and the apartments above the Queen Street stores were not represented. The terms of reference for the stakeholder group noted that 'a few spots were reserved for local professionals with skills/experience in urban planning, urban design or architecture.' Low-income tenants, by contrast, were not specifically sought out.

At stakeholder advisory committee meetings, some participants attempted to raise broader social issues, asking how the urban design guidelines for the Leslieville stretch of Queen Street would help low-income residents. They repeatedly raised the question of affordable housing and the disappearance of shops and restaurants that had served lower-income residents for years. City staff fielded these queries politely, even agreeing with the sentiments – but by their very politeness, staff furthered the mistaken impression that social inclusion issues would be represented in the avenue study report. It was only after repeated probing by critical residents that city planners reluctantly admitted, late in the process, that neither affordable housing nor affordable retail were within their purview. The purpose of the exercise turned out to be limited: to set height limits and design guidelines for future development by builders like Streetcar.

While the city's staff and consultants expressed vague support at those meetings for socio-economic diversity, the official record included only the following comment: 'We [the city] do not intend to eliminate any affordable or social housing.' The planners knew all along that the purpose of the exercise, in legal terms, was to produce architectural guidelines. Their polite and 'inclusive' attitude had the effect of misleading participants about the nature of the exercise.

While attendance at the stakeholder group meetings fell (there were initially twenty participants, but that figure dropped to eight), the continued participation of progressive activists meant that official city reports did note the exclusionary effects of the gentrification of Queen Street East, but only in the context of heritage preservation:

> In recent years there has been an increase in specialty shops in the study area. The increase in specialty shops may push out the businesses that residents may currently depend on. This can be an opportunity as new types of businesses transform the area into a destination, but can also become a threat as businesses that meet the needs of local residents get pushed out.[1]

This bland statement was as far as the official record went in acknowledging the exclusionary effects of commercial as well as residential gentrification. But fortunately, while waiting for the city's reports, PSR's members did not put much faith in the official process, and instead undertook their own data-gathering and consultation exercises.

Focus Groups with Marginalized Residents

Though theoretically open to anyone, official public consultations on planning questions tend to draw homeowners, business owners, better-educated residents and those undaunted by such discussions. Urban neighbourhoods, of course, include many other people – shift workers who can't get to meetings, newcomers who don't yet have the language skills to follow the conversation, single parents who can't find or afford child care and, of course, people who exist on society's fringes – those who are homeless or just barely hanging on, and for whom the prospect of spending time in meetings discussing new land-use planning rules is eclipsed by the daily challenges of survival.

PSR's members recognized that those residents who had the most to lose from gentrification were unlikely to respond to the usual city mechanisms for soliciting public input. We decided that the group should go to where the most marginalized members of the community spent their time, instead of expecting them to attend public meetings. PSR organized four focus groups, in a supportive housing complex, a shelter, a health centre and a facility for older street-involved men. Overall, forty-one people turned out, including several new-immigrant seniors.

Besides changing the consultation venues, the group also broadened the conversation. PSR took two questions from the official process – 'What do you like best about the neighbourhood?' and 'What would you like to see improved in the neighbourhood?' – but also added questions about the area's existing services and stores.

Changing the frame of reference elicited important insights into the ways in which gentrification increases the pressure in the lives of those who live in such areas. Many people told us they no longer bank and do grocery shopping in the Riverside/Leslieville area, but go across the Don River to the Regent Park area, where there are retailers geared to lower-income consumers. Others said affordable clothing and shoes were no longer available in the area. Many poorer residents said during the sessions that they felt more at home on Parliament Street, despite the long walk, than among the cappuccino bars of a neighbourhood many had lived in for years.

The most revealing finding was that the loss of one particular store or service might have a snowball effect. If a shop that is essential to poor people's lives (a pharmacy, a bank, a hardware store) closes down, either due to the different shopping habits of new gentrifiers or because upscale restaurants and bars can afford much higher rents, its long-standing customers may well move many of their other activities to a more distant area as well. In one group, for example, several people mentioned going as far as Queen and Parliament to access shops and services. Another group appeared to have the same experiences.

The most consistent finding, emerging spontaneously in three of the four focus groups, was the desire for a coffee shop that would be open in the evening and welcoming (whether due to prices or to atmosphere was unclear) to low-income neighbours. 'It's all high-end now,' observed one older man living in transitional housing. 'There is nobody around after 9 p.m.' Given that within five minutes' walk of where the focus group was being conducted there are several higher-end bars and pubs that are busy late into the evening, it seemed this man meant that there was nobody around like him, or nobody with whom he felt an affinity. Participants in the other focus groups complained that the last remaining low-end doughnut shop (a Coffee

Time at Dundas and Broadview) had been transformed into a high-end bridal-wear store. Leslieville's many espresso bars sell caffeine, obviously, but these long-time residents don't even see such establishments as coffee shops.

These are highly practical concerns: what happens when there are no more affordable supermarkets at which to buy groceries, or a declining number of local health professionals serving clients on provincial disability or welfare? But prices are not the only issue. There are also cultural processes of exclusion – at one session, an older, dishevelled man complained bitterly about how most of the parkette behind the New Broadview Hotel had been turned into an off-leash dog park. Others echoed his point. The reason? That park had previously been heavily used by the low-income tenants living above the Jilly's bar and in a nearby supportive-housing building as a good place to go for a smoke. Now it had been colonized by condo-owners with dogs.

Overall, the low-income residents who participated in PSR's focus groups felt they'd been marginalized in their own neighbourhood by the proliferation of high-end restaurants and specialty stores – cupcake shops were mentioned with particular scorn. Despite that, city-planning officials had never sought to document how these doubly marginalized low-income residents actually used their own neighbourhood.

The Store Survey

The PSR also decided to document the impact of commercial gentrification by conducting an in-person store survey, something else the city's planning staff did not do. Going from store to store during the winter of 2013–2014, the PSR team ambitiously surveyed all the properties on Queen Street from the Don River to Jones Avenue – about two hundred establishments. The volunteers then systematically rated each establishment on a scale of one to six – with one being most economically and socially accessible, and six being least accessible.

We found that an astonishing 37 percent of storefronts fell into the 'six' category – not just high-end restaurants and bakeries, but also a range of other shops, from organic butchers to a specialty bicycle store to high-end home-décor shops. The second-largest category was stores that rated a 'five,' with 26 percent of the total. Thus, almost two-thirds of all the businesses on that stretch of Queen Street East appeared to cater not only to gentrifiers generally (a category that can include lower-income artists) but specifically to well-off gentrifiers. When the survey was updated eight months later, the proportion of high-end shops had increased to over 70 percent.

Just as interesting, however, was the finding that businesses of a distinctly low-end character still existed in considerable numbers: 11 percent of the stores were rated as either 'one' or 'two,' including a pair of very cheap Chinese restaurants, two pharmacies catering to those on provincial benefits, an auto-body shop, rundown variety stores and two low-end restaurants in which patrons seemed to mainly drink bottled beer.

So while Queen East has a surprisingly resilient low-end retail sector and a flourishing super-high-end retail scene, it is lacking in mid-range shops and services, such as a Tim Horton's. The store survey exposes a microcosm of Toronto's 'three cities' – University of Toronto sociologist David Hulchanski's mapping analysis that reveals increasing income polarization between neighbourhoods from 1970 to the present. Queen East is a place where Toronto's three cities coexist within a single neighbourhood, where the rich (who here predominate, unlike in the city as a whole) and the remaining poor (who are getting poorer) are squeezing out the middle class.

While writing this article, I took a break to buy food at Rowe Farms (a good example of a category 'six' business), which is next to one of the few remaining working-class diners – Jim's, at Logan and Queen. When I first moved to the area, in late 1991, I used to bitterly complain to my east-end partner that we had to walk all the way to the Danforth for an espresso. The only local restaurant I patronized was Jim's – and only to get rotisserie chicken to take home. Today Jim's continues to be popular with tow-truck drivers and cops, as well as some locals. But one of the city's 'Development Proposal' signs has ominously gone up. Three adjacent lots (Jim's, the mechanic next door and a postwar church) have been bought and assembled by a higher-end condo developer. The builder has offered to rehouse the occupants of the Red Door Shelter, which rents space in the church, by way of a 'community benefit' given in order to gain extra density. But Red Door's success, which makes the liberally minded locals feel good about ourselves and our neighbourhood, contrasts sharply with the area's seeming indifference to the fate of Jim's working-class patrons.

Planning students are today encouraged to care about social inequality. But a progressive conscience is one thing, and planners' legal tools are another. In South Riverdale, residents who attended evening meetings at some trouble and expense were not clearly informed that maintaining the area's affordability was not on the planning agenda. When the narrow architectural focus of these official consultations became clear, many of us felt betrayed by city staff.

But the silver lining was that a tiny community group like Planning South Riverdale could obtain information from marginalized people who do not attend public meetings. The group's volunteers managed to organize and successfully run focus groups that generated valuable perspectives that had eluded city planners and paid consultants, who weren't, it must be said, looking for those kinds of insights. We concluded that if they wanted, planners could devise ways to 'outsource' some consultations to individuals who are already trusted community members, instead of always using professional consulting firms. Clearly, when we went to the places where marginal people live and gather and feel empowered to speak, we were far more successful at soliciting meaningful input than when city staff issue notices and hope people will interrupt their routines to attend a scheduled meeting in an official location.

Neighbourhoods in Toronto and elsewhere have become increasingly polarized spatially and socially. Tasked with planning socially, economically and culturally complex urban communities, city staff and ultimately politicians, who have the authority to change the rules, are going to have to find new approaches to ensure that those at risk of being displaced or ignored have some say in the changes washing over their city and their neighbourhoods.

Mobility in the Divided City
Eric Mann

It's a chilly Monday morning in February and Maria is heading to work. She's waiting for the No. 60 bus at Steeles and Bathurst, on Toronto's northern edge. She faces a long commute to the downtown salon where she works as a hairdresser, a job she's held since emigrating from Bulgaria with her two children in 2007. The bus will take her to Finch subway station, a terminus that serves 90,000 commuters each day. From there, Maria travels from the postwar inner-suburban city to its pre-war urban core. Door to door, it's a ninety-minute trip, on a good day. Commuting takes a large chunk out of Maria's day – time she'd rather be spending with her kids.

Maria's experience is typical for those who commute from the city's suburbs – and the inner suburbs in particular, where rapid transit is in short supply. While Toronto's booming, transit-connected core attracts new jobs, wealthier residents and plentiful amenities, the auto-dependent suburbs remain stuck in traffic. The Toronto Region Board of Trade notes the average daily commute has reached eighty minutes, which puts Toronto dead last when compared to nineteen cities in North America and Europe. As congestion worsens, those who live in the suburbs feel left behind, with limited access to the enhanced quality of life downtown. And that's a shame, because the inner suburbs are also home to many of the city's recent immigrants – highly motivated city-builders, like generations before them, who are ready to leave their mark on Toronto.

When we talk about transit, we must talk about more than just commute times. We also have to talk about connecting residents to the opportunity to build a more cohesive, prosperous city. We need a debate about transit equity.

Since Ontario established Metrolinx in 2006, the agency has been tasked with planning, integrating and expanding the region's transit systems. Its major tool is a thirty-year vision for the Greater Toronto and Hamilton Area (GTHA) called the Big Move. The plan calls for investing $50 billion to build 1,200 kilometres of rapid transit by

2031. The first wave of construction includes big projects, like the expansion of Union Station, the new airport express train, a subway to neighbouring Vaughan and bus rapid transit corridors in York and Peel regions.

The Big Move aims to provide rapid transit service within two kilometres of 80 percent of residents. The plan also points out that delivering transit equitably to all people in the region is important: 'Access to frequent, fast and affordable transit is ... crucial for equity and social cohesion.'[1]

How and where we deliver transit plays a significant role in where city-dwellers choose to live and, by implication, the health of their neighbourhoods. According to a 2015 survey by the Royal Bank of Canada and the Pembina Institute,[2] GTA residents with the means to do so are reducing their commute by living closer to transit, work and amenities, even if it means giving up a big house and backyard. Yet the unintended result is increased polarization, with wealthier households clustered in residential enclaves close to transit and office nodes.

This pattern began in the 1970s, when congestion was on the rise, and transit-connected neighbourhoods began to increase in value at the expense of the auto-centric suburbs.[3] Today, the most desirable neighbourhoods exhibit an urban structure and density that supports walkable connections to services, jobs and public spaces. In contrast, the city's low-income neighbourhoods tend to be located within the auto-dependent inner suburbs – postwar areas developed at low densities, and generally lacking pedestrian-friendly connections to daily needs.

The results of this city-scale migration are shocking. While growth and development have dramatically improved the quality of life downtown, investment and incomes within the inner suburbs have declined. In 1970, low-income neighbourhoods made up 19 percent of the city's geography; by 2005, such neighbourhoods comprised over half of the city – 53 percent. Almost all of these neighbourhoods – in Etobicoke, western North York and Scarborough – have poor access to rapid transit.

Toronto is not unique in this regard: the central areas of global cities with abundant transit – places like London, New York and Hong Kong – are experiencing similar concentrations of wealth, accompanied by high-skill, high-paying industries and desirable neighbourhoods. As cities sprawl and commuting times lengthen, the wealthy are paying more to live in core areas. American economist Paul Krugman argues that the resulting pattern of gentrification feeds on itself: as more high earners move into urban centres, these centres begin offering more jobs and amenities – restaurants, shopping, entertainment – that make them even more attractive, and more financially inaccessible.[4]

This polarization is concerning for many reasons. Among the most serious is that where we grow up may directly impact our future. A recent study of five million lower-income families across the U.S. showed that every year of exposure to a middle-class neighbourhood environment improved a child's chances of success.[5] The authors, Harvard economists Raj Chetty and Nathaniel Hendren, suggest five characteristics of place linked to strong upward social mobility: less segregation by income and race, lower levels of income inequality, better schools, lower rates of violent crime and a larger share of two-parent households.

Transportation investments, if directed appropriately, can invigorate and revitalize disadvantaged urban areas. York University cities researchers Douglas Young and Roger Keil have dubbed Toronto's 'in-between city' as a zone that demands prioritized transit investment, as well as measures to increase the supply of affordable transit-oriented development.[6] Such policies, they argue, would not only alleviate the lack of jobs, housing and amenities in lower-income areas, but also recognize public transit as an essential mechanism for allowing low-income families to move from poverty to economic self-sufficiency.

There are many opportunities to improve the reach and accessibility of transit, from the downtown to the city's outer fringes. To understand which steps to take, we need to know more about where we are now. We need to consider how the built form of the postwar inner suburbs compares to both the downtown core and the outer 905 suburbs developed since the 1980s. But to truly understand the goal of transit equity, we must also consider the daily commuting experiences of ordinary people as they move around the city.

The Downtown

On a Tuesday afternoon, my friend Mike, who works for a major Canadian bank, finishes his day's tasks and walks down the block to pick up some groceries. He lives with his partner in a downtown condo beside a subway station – a perfect location. Mike estimates that almost all of his daily needs are within a fifteen-minute walk or short subway ride. Life couldn't be more convenient. Since moving to Toronto fifteen years ago, Mike has always made transit a priority in deciding where to live. But that's not a lifestyle choice: Mike is legally blind, so access to the subway is non-negotiable. 'The issues around mobility that normally come with this disability actually go away when transit is at your fingertips,' he says, adding that the time he saves travelling allows him to spend his evenings helping with a vision research organization and a cycling network he co-founded. 'If I had to commute, I would not be able to pursue my community and volunteer work.'

But Mike doesn't actually work in one of the downtown bank towers; he once did, but three years ago his employer announced his position would be shifted to a suburban office park accessible only by private vehicle or a tortuous transit ride. If he continued to live downtown, his commute would take two hours each way, a trip involving a subway and two buses. Instead, Mike searched for other options, and found another banking job that allowed him to work from home.

While Mike's disability has driven his location choices, many other people have gravitated to core areas out of a desire to spend less time commuting. Since the mid-2000s, downtown Toronto has experienced tremendous growth and investment – condo towers rise at a record pace, and the area has also seen a huge influx of knowledge jobs. This residential growth has fuelled a corresponding resurgence in new retail and restaurants, cultural destinations and other amenities. Not coincidentally, much of the new growth is focused around subway stops, Union Station and streetcar routes.

Each year, about 15,000 new condo units are brought to market across the City of Toronto. The number of new rental apartments under construction reached a twenty-five-year peak in 2015, driven in part by the demand for downtown living without the high cost of ownership. Market research firm Urbanation estimates that 6,523 purpose-built rental apartments – numbers not seen since before the virtual collapse of rental construction in the 1990s – were under construction during the third quarter of 2015.[7] About 70 percent are located in the old City of Toronto, and three-quarters of those units are within a fifteen-minute walk of a subway station. Only a quarter of the downtown work force commutes by automobile. Thanks largely to the vibrancy of the core, the *Economist* ranked Toronto the world's most livable city in 2015.

But growth has brought challenges. As in other prosperous cities, prices for ground-level housing in the central core are rising faster than construction costs and incomes. The Bank of Canada has warned that many homebuyers in this market are carrying unsustainable levels of mortgage debt, making their monthly payments vulnerable to an inevitable rise in interest rates.

Some policy analysts, like U.S. economist Jason Furman, have called for measures to ensure that the inward migration of wealth doesn't price everyone else out of the market. Land-use restrictions, according to Furman, chair of the Council of Economic Advisors during the Obama Administration, are the most likely culprit. The solution is to find ways to increase the housing supply.[8]

Toronto's Official Plan limits the scale and density of development within so-called 'stable' residential neighbourhoods while directing growth to mixed-use areas and arterial corridors served by transit. However, a recent study suggests there is much work to be done to achieve this goal. Despite the downtown condo boom, fully 86 percent of new GTA residents settled in low-density subdivisions on the suburban edge of the region between 2001 and 2011. (During the same period, some inner suburbs actually declined in population, likely due to an aging population, and out-migration to more desirable areas.)

So what does accessible and equitable transit look like for those who live in the downtown core? Affordable transit fares certainly, but it's also critical to address affordable housing. First, through incremental change, to achieve a greater mix of affordable housing within a short walk of rapid transit stations, along existing and planned corridors, like Eglinton Avenue. Affordable housing that appeals to families, like townhouses and stacked towns, as well as two- and three-bedroom apartments, constructed using lower-cost wood frame, which is now permitted up to six storeys. Second, opportunistic change to revitalize or unlock the value of surplus, or underutilized public lands, to (re)shape new transit-oriented, mixed-income communities, in partnership with the private, co-operative and non-profit sectors, such as those projects being developed by Toronto Community Housing, Options for Homes, Waterfront Toronto, the Toronto District School Board. Third, through policy measures to spur or require greater investment in community services, like daycare and park space.

The Inner Suburbs

When Maria and her children first arrived in Toronto, they lived in a modest townhouse in Richmond Hill, on the GTA's northern fringes. When Maria found work downtown, the commute proved too long and stressful, so they explored affordable options closer to the core, and settled on an apartment near Bathurst and Steeles, one of Toronto's postwar inner suburbs. Despite that move, Maria still had to take a bus and a subway to reach her new job.

Like many such inner suburbs, the Bathurst and Steeles neighbourhood grew dramatically in the 1960s from a small village to an auto-centred suburb, thanks to the construction of highways, subdivision development and the construction of large-scale infrastructure by the Municipality of Metropolitan Toronto, then the regional government.

Urban highways like the 401 and the Queen Elizabeth Way reinforced a car-centric structure of low-density postwar neighbourhoods. As former Toronto mayor John Sewell points out in *The Shape of the Suburbs: Understanding Toronto's Sprawl*, a typical suburban residential neighbourhood holds just 3,300 residential units per square mile, while the same area downtown has 7,000 units.[9] This means amenities and services in the suburbs are far more dispersed, and not within walking distance. A resident in the city's core can expect to travel 6.4 kilometres a day by car and a further 3.2 kilometres by transit, while a resident in the suburbs travels an average 22.5 kilometres per day and 3.2 kilometres by transit.

For Maria, the toll is significant, and she is not alone. From the 1950s to the 1970s, Toronto's postwar suburbs saw the development of hundreds of high-rise apartments on arterial roads, many marketed to middle-income earners. These buildings proved to be affordable options for many new immigrant families.

Toronto, in fact, contains the largest concentration of high-rise residential buildings in Canada and the U.S., with some 280,000 apartments. Yet those in the inner suburbs have poor connections to services or rapid transit. At the same time, studies indicate that residents of these buildings are less likely to own a vehicle, and would benefit greatly from new rapid transit.

When planned successfully, rapid transit corridors can unlock new development within walking distance of transit stops, providing a greater mix of new housing, jobs and other services. If combined with policy measures to support new affordable housing – such as inclusionary zoning, a policy that mandates developers to set aside a certain proportion of units as affordable – then the benefits of the investment are likely to reach more residents, including lower-income families.

Metrolinx and the City of Toronto claim to understand this potential and are planning to extend service to lower-income areas of Scarborough, Etobicoke and North York. The challenge is how to do it. Take Scarborough, where much of the developed area is designated as 'stable residential neighbourhoods.' These low-density communities can't generate enough ridership to support rapid transit, and redevelopment is tightly regulated in these zones. Similarly, most of Scarborough's employment lands are fiercely protected for their important role in accommodating warehouses and distribution centres. But these sorts of commercial uses don't generate nearly the density of employees needed to justify rapid transit.

As a result, the areas where higher-density redevelopment is most likely to occur include arterial roadways. These corridors have plenty of underutilized land suitable for new development, including strip plazas, parking lots, car dealers, undeveloped lots and mixed-use land parcels with retail on the ground floor.

Since the early 2000s, Toronto council has considered successive proposals to extend rapid transit to areas like Scarborough – a frustrating and controversial process exploited by politicians like the late former mayor Rob Ford, who pushed for costly subways while lobbying against the construction of relatively less expensive light rail transit running in their own rights-of-way on major routes.

As of 2016, a political consensus had coalesced around a plan that would see three rapid transit modes in Scarborough – regional express rail, a subway extension and a network of LRT routes. Together, the proposed lines put about 64,000 Scarborough residents within walking distance of twenty-six new rapid transit stops – far more than any previous scheme. The compromise also replaced the political debate between subway and LRT advocates, with a more tailored approach that better aligns the level of service to Scarborough's diverse mix of quiet suburbs, medium-density corridors and high-density urban development nodes.

The plan aims to keep a one-stop subway extension. In this regard, it's about accepting half loaves as better than none; funds for the scaled-back subway will finance the LRT lines instead.

How does this latest plan improve transit equity in a postwar suburb like Scarborough? City staff note the proposed lines pass through eight of Toronto's thirty-one Neighbourhood Improvement Areas, so designated because residents often experience unnecessary and unjust differences that lead to inequitable life outcomes. By funding LRT transit investment through these communities, the plan improves mobility for lower-income families who now rely on crowded buses or spend much of their incomes operating vehicles. A wider network of rapid transit will allow more residents to live without a car, freeing income for other daily needs.

The 905 Region

Lareina is an optometrist and part owner of an eye clinic along Hurontario Street in Mississauga, a sprawling suburban municipality immediately west of Toronto. Five years ago, after enduring long commutes from her home in Markham, a northeastern GTA suburb, she purchased a condo at the south end of Hurontario, in Port Credit, a quiet residential community adjacent to Lake Ontario. The move was strategic: her commute was cut to just ten minutes by car. In a few years, she looks forward to riding the proposed Hurontario LRT to work. 'Being so close to work, it's faster to take transit than to drive my car and park,' she says. 'It's also nice to get some fresh air. It will be so easy just to hop on and off the LRT.'

The Hurontario LRT, which will provide frequent service on a dedicated right-of-way, is planned to run from Port Credit to the northern boundary of Mississauga, with connections to the Port Credit and Cooksville GO rail stations, as well as to Mississauga City Centre, a primary area for compact, higher-density development and an employment hub for the region. The LRT is one of several 'next wave' Metrolinx projects, which together account for about 70 percent of proposed spending. They represent a game change for regional mobility by extending rapid transit between the 416 and 905 regions – and between and within growing 905 municipalities as well.

Mississauga has evolved from a sleepy suburban bedroom community into a diverse city with a more dynamic economy and growing density. But underlying this transformation is a sobering truth: Mississauga has run out of farmland to develop new residential subdivisions, the revenue from which has helped keep the city out of debt for two generations. To replace the shortfall, Mississauga is luring developers to build new towers on underutilized lands surrounding its city centre and along busy arterial roads. And the LRT is a key part of the pitch.

An LRT is perfectly suited to suburbs where there's not enough density to support subways, but where demand exceeds what local buses or streetcars can accommodate. Typically, densities of over one hundred people per hectare are required to justify subways, which can move up to a thousand people every two to three minutes. In comparison, LRTs can accommodate about four hundred people every four to six minutes, which fits well with the planned densities along Hurontario. While not as frequent as subways, LRTs deliver a more predictable service than local buses, because they run in a separated right-of-way instead of mixed traffic. These are key benefits, intended to sway 'choice riders' who might otherwise drive to work.

Lareina and her husband, Rohit, plan to have kids soon. Living close to transit was a deciding factor in their recent search for a larger home along the same corridor. They liked Port Credit, but worried about competition for properties in this popular area. So they looked strategically at their expenses. By selling one of their cars, they were able to buy an older townhouse in Mineola, over a kilometre north on Hurontario Street. For Rohit, their new home is a five-minute walk to the nearby Port Credit GO rail station, which means he can get to his downtown engineering firm in just forty minutes. A recent study by the Pembina Institute estimates that for each car removed from a household budget, about $200,000 more can be carried on a twenty-five-year mortgage.[10]

Of course, not everyone has a car to trade in for a larger down payment to live near transit. That's why Mississauga councillor Carolyn Parrish sought to link affordable housing policy to the development of new transit infrastructure.

Peel Region, which encompasses Mississauga, has the province's longest waiting list for affordable housing. To ensure that new development along the corridor provides a range of housing choices, Parrish persuaded council to consider mandating minimum inclusionary zoning provisions, requiring developers to include at least 10 percent affordable housing units. 'The people who need the transit most, especially in a place like Mississauga, are displaced,' she said.

During one 2015 council meeting, Parrish's motion to study inclusionary zoning measures was supported by local resident Paula Torres, who lives in a deteriorating apartment building in Cooksville, a mixed-use urban centre along the LRT corridor targeted for higher-density growth. The area is also home to a large proportion of lower-income households, earning an average of just $26,000 per year. In Torres's building, a one-bedroom rented for $1,100 a month in 2015, or roughly half of the earnings of these households. Torres fears that once construction of the LRT begins, the apartment will be sold to a developer, who will tear it down to build condos priced out of her reach.

Inclusionary zoning is in use in over two hundred communities across North America. New York City mayor Bill de Blasio aims to use inclusionary zoning and other policies to build 80,000 new affordable units across his city by 2024. His plan targets areas that would otherwise continue to gentrify, worsening the pattern of income polarization across the city. While inclusionary zoning will generate only a portion of the planned units, it goes beyond most other cities by requiring that developers add lower-rent apartments if they want to build in east New York and other rezoned areas. Crucially, the policy combines with public investment in street beautification, new schools, enhanced parks and small businesses, with the aim of creating more complete communities that cluster jobs, amenities and services within a short walk or transit trip from home.

Mississauga is not the only municipality seeking new powers to address an affordable-housing shortfall. Since 1999, the City of Toronto has made fourteen separate requests to the Ontario government to allow for inclusionary zoning for developments that include more than twenty units. The requirement would be offset by fast-tracked approvals and other incentives. In 2016, following three separate reviews of planning policies, the provincial government announced its intention to bring forward new legislation to grant municipalities this authority. To illustrate the potential, consider that between 2005 and 2015, Toronto approved almost six hundred multi-unit residential projects, representing 109,433 new housing units. If the city had an inclusionary zoning policy that set aside 10 percent of new units as affordably priced, Toronto would now have created 10,000 lower-cost apartments, housing approximately 20,600 people. Without inclusionary zoning, the city developed just 2,800 affordable units from 2010 to 2015 – a figure that hardly dents Toronto's affordable-housing waiting list, which exceeds 95,000 households.

Mississauga hopes the LRT will also attract new employers along the corridor and to the city centre, where no new office buildings have been constructed since 1992. The LRT will have connections to the GO Transit regional rail service, and other GTA rapid transit services, like SmartTrack and the Mississauga Transitway, linking the city centre to a much wider labour force from neighbouring 905 munici-palities such as Brampton, as well as the 416 area. Over time, the aim is for the LRT to provide the convenience that allows more people – like Lareina and Rohit – to live, work and play along the corridor.

It's been eight years since Maria and her kids first arrived in Toronto from Bulgaria. During that time, various transit schemes have come and gone while she waits for a shorter commute, more time with her kids and a better life in a more walkable, vibrant community. This year, Maria's son Martin started classes at the University of Toronto, a big step toward his dream of becoming an architect. 'I love it here,' Martin tells me, over a plate of dumplings at one of his favourite restaurants near the university's downtown campus. He still lives with his mother in the suburbs and, like her, commutes to the core each day. On nights when he's working late, he crashes on a friend's couch, or sleeps in the studio space provided for students, to avoid the long and expensive cab ride home. Maria hopes he'll have better housing options in the future.

For people like Maria, who want a better future for the next gener-ation, we owe it to ourselves to build a more connected, vibrant city. Beyond the numbers, this is about overcoming a sense of inevitability in the face of auto-oriented sprawl and replacing a decades-old pattern that continues to separate home from work, but also rich from poor. As we plan transit, we should strive for a more community-driven process of city-building. It's a paradigm shift, and a reminder that we once invested huge sums for the public good. The transit network we use today was built generations ago to serve a much more compact city. Then, as now, we had to connect diverse immigrant communities to a walkable urban structure and mix of uses. Those investments set the stage for the vibrant city centre we enjoy today.

Our job now is to invest in a future that reconnects the core with the suburbs, realigns plans for affordable housing, jobs and transit, and brings the region's residents closer to the opportunities they seek in the world-class city to which we aspire.

Toward More Complete Communities:
Business Out of the Box
Alina Chatterjee

The Big Picture

Toronto as we know it today is a city of neighbourhoods, but not all neighbourhoods are the same. Much has been written over the last decade about the shifts and changes that have accompanied increased density and poor planning – racialized poverty, precariousness of employment and lack of access for many Torontonians to affordable housing, transit and healthy food. Low-income areas of the city that are most disproportionately impacted are the 'inner suburbs' – those postwar communities that were not planned for the type and diversity of population growth the city now experiences.

For newcomers who face formidable and systemic obstacles to entry into the labour force, small businesses and micro-enterprises have become a more attractive alternative. Unfortunately, there are many barriers for entrepreneurs, most importantly access to affordable retail or commercial space. In the downtown core, zoning regulations allow for mixed-use and mixed-income communities, but space is scarce and prohibitively priced. On the other side, there is plenty of retail and office space available in the inner suburbs, but current zoning rules do not allow for commercial and residential uses to exist side-by-side.

The increasingly concentrated poverty in inner suburban neighbourhoods is especially visible in postwar 'tower communities' – the hundreds of high-rise slab apartments that are socially, economically and geographically isolated. Residents contend with poor transit, disrepair and little reasonable access to services and amenities. There is an urgent need for drastic and non-traditional interventions, including ways to allow these buildings to become launching pads for new small businesses.

In fact, the entrepreneurial spirit of successive newcomer groups has long shaped our cities, and in particular inner-city communities.

To make room for this kind of entrepreneurial energy, the City of Toronto is introducing a new land-use designation, the Residential Apartment Commercial (RAC) zone, to create the conditions that will allow small businesses to take root and thrive in Toronto's tower communities.

These new regulatory levers and tools can transform low-income tower neighbourhoods through the use of interventions designed to provide platforms for newcomer entrepreneurship. Such changes will change the urban fabric of the high-rise, racialized apartment communities that characterize Toronto's postwar neighbourhoods.

About Business out of a Box

'Business out of a Box' is a social-franchise model that evolved out of a 2010 economic development program at Scadding Court Community Centre known as 'Live Local Market.' SCCC staff recognized the importance of finding new ways to support low-income newcomers and create effective pathways for these residents to become economically independent. The community centre, located between the Atkinson Co-operative housing complex at the intersection of Dundas West and Bathurst streets, decided to retrofit shipping containers and offer them as affordable retail space, initially targeting low-income immigrants and youth. Rents begin at $11 per day, including electricity.

The uptake was tremendous, and SCCC could not keep up with demand for space in these containers. The project expanded and, in 2011, was renamed Market 707. There are currently eighteen small businesses operating in the market, including several eateries, a barber, a bike repair shop, a clothing boutique and a cellphone repair stall. According to the *Toronto Star*, 126 entrepreneurs were on the waiting list for spaces as of mid-2015. Revenues increased by 188 percent between 2011 and 2015.[1]

Winner of the Special Jury Award at the 2013 Toronto Urban Design Awards, Market 707 uses community economic development to animate streetscapes and limit reliance on grants and the charitable sector. This concept has successfully provided affordable retail space to low-income, newcomer and youth entrepreneurs. It has also increased access to locally made products and revitalized the area in a fresh and organic manner. The Market 707 model – using shipping containers to provide low-cost space for upstart businesses – has attracted city-wide interest as a way to fill gaps and open doors for a wide range of entrepreneurs and communities.

Responding to surging demand for modular markets, the Business out of a Box (BoB) social-franchise model provides tools and resources to help people in other communities create similar initiatives where they live. Since its inception, moreover, BoB has received significant coverage from local and international media outlets.

The BoB value proposition is unique because shipping-container markets create low-rent economic development opportunities for local entrepreneurs, convenient access to new retail venues for the residents of tower communities, animated public spaces around the bases of those apartment complexes and, perhaps most important, the fostering of social connections within these dense residential spaces.

The Value Proposition

In many cities around the world, the creative use of shipping containers to address commercial infrastructure shortages is not a new idea. Revitalized shipping containers create spaces for living and working, and also reshape urban spaces. Known as 'cargo-tecture,' such utilitarian structures have been used as schools, disaster relief shelters, housing units, health clinics, laboratories and markets in the developing world. Cities like Cape Town, Soweto, Mumbai and Dhaka rely on cargo-tecture because it is cost-effective, environmentally friendly, mobile and durable, as well as easy and fast to construct.

More recently, we have seen retrofitted containers used in Western countries as studios, office spaces, bars, restaurants, swimming pools, nurseries, garages, student housing and sports centres. Many of these innovative uses can be seen in Montreal, Sydney, Copenhagen, London, Zurich, Seattle, Utrecht, Amsterdam, Gwangju and others.

Shipping-container retail spaces create low-cost, pedestrian-friendly opportunities for both consumers and entrepreneurs. Entrepreneurs can test ideas in a low-risk environment, while enhancing community life by providing access to products, services, programs, food, events and more. Ultimately, the reanimation of these spaces helps local economies and creates vibrant streetscapes for residents from all walks of life.

These modular markets also offer compelling solutions for suburban environments where there is a lack of street-level, affordable retail space. They can be purpose-designed, retrofitted and connected to one another to create tailored spaces.

Case Studies

According to SCCC executive director Kevin Lee, the entrepreneurs who have established businesses in Market 707 come from a wide range of backgrounds – young entrepreneurs with post-secondary degrees, pensioners, new Canadians and youth from low-income backgrounds. 'It's a variety of different people that we have here,' Lee told the *Toronto Star*. 'They're not all just poor. You have to have a mix, both culturally and socio-economically.'[2]

The businesses in Market 707 include:

• Spin Can Cycles, a successful bicycle repair shop originally run by two recent high school graduates. Co-founder Chase Brokenshire, who was nineteen when he launched Spin Can, says Market 707 was the only way he could have started the business without start-up capital. Absent affordable space, he could not have realized his vision of a niche service for quick, on-the-spot repairs at reasonable rates.

• Kanto by Tita Flips, a Filipino eatery run by Diona Joyce. A former pharmaceutical sales representative in the Philippines, Joyce became an inadvertent restaurant proprietor in Toronto. She came to Canada in 2001 'kind of by accident' after helping a friend apply for landed immigrant status. She initially worked as a cleaner in a McDonald's and later took on telemarketing jobs before starting a small catering operation in 2007. As that business grew, Joyce opened Kanto in 2012 in Market 707. Her cuisine has drawn widespread media attention, and won a 2015 People's Choice Award at the Kultura Filipino Arts Festival. Her goal, she told the *Toronto Star*, is to bring Filipino food into the mainstream of Toronto's ethnic culinary offerings.[3]

• Gushi Chicken, founded and operated by Shinji Yamaguchi, an aspiring chef who also assists the well-known Japanese restaurateur Sang Kim. Yamaguchi trained as a high-precision machinist in Japan, but couldn't establish a career and decided to move to Toronto to pursue entrepreneurial opportunities in the food business. After doing an apprenticeship, he tried a pop-up kushikatsu eatery at Harbourfront in 2013, but the business didn't attract customers. Undaunted, he invested in a container at Market 707, and began building a profile for kushikatsu in a city more accustomed to hot dogs. Gushi's growth since then has been so robust that Yamaguchi is looking for space to secure more permanent locations. 'Gushi aspires to becoming a king of street food,' Yamaguchi told *Nikkei Voice*, a Japanese-Canadian magazine. 'I want people to say that they can't talk about street food without knowing Gushi.'[4]

• Bombay Street Food, founded by Amreen and Seema Omar. Originally from India, the sisters-in-law drew on recipes from their travels to launch the stall at Market 707. They leveraged the profits from that operation to introduce their Indian street-food concept at pop-up markets in other parts of the city. In early 2016, they opened a permanent restaurant on Bay Street. 'This restaurant will help us put a real focus on authentic Mumbai street food,' Seema told *Post City Toronto*. 'We've got a menu already, and we're tweaking it.'[5]

The Business Model

The basic operating premise for the Business out of a Box model is that up to four small businesses share low-rent space in a forty-foot container, potentially recouping their capital investment (equipment, interiors, etc.) within three to five years. sccc functions as the operator of the overall market.

Once it identifies a location and entrepreneur tenants, sccc purchases and transports the containers to approved sites and develops a long-term repayment plan tailored to each operator. They target low-income and newcomer entrepreneurs, who pay rental rates that range from $11 to $14 per day, and also finance any retrofits they require for their container. Food-based businesses must adhere to public health regulations, which means specific retrofits for water and sink access. sccc pays for electricity, and provides access to a water source at the community centre. Thanks to low overhead costs, business owners can save and accumulate profits, as well as pass on cost savings to their customers. Through rental revenues, sccc provides vendors with services such as promotion, marketing and business development.

Initially, Market 707 relied on outreach and promotion led by sccc to find tenants for the first stalls. The centre focused on recruiting vendors from nearby Alexandra Park, a low-income co-op whose residents access 80 percent of sccc's social programs and services. As interest grew, more containers were purchased with support from foundations, municipal economic development funds and profits from rental income.

Today, there is a long waiting list of entrepreneurs eager to make Market 707 their new business destination, and the BoB franchise model is in demand all over Toronto. Revenues are such that sccc no longer subsidizes Market 707's project coordinator, the administrator overseeing daily operations. As a result, the centre has been able to develop the BoB franchise concept around the city.

To be eligible to participate, vendors must meet at least one of the following criteria: they must be a newcomer to Canada; a youth under thirty; a first-time business owner. They may also employ other newcomers or youth. As the market evolves, and the BoB model takes root in other locations, sccc has diversified the range of non-food products and services available.

How can BoB change neighbourhoods?

Many low-income newcomers have turned to starting small businesses as a means of achieving decent livelihoods and financial stability. Recognizing that poverty has moved to Toronto's postwar inner suburbs, and especially the tower communities in those areas, zoning permissions – and specifically the introduction of the new RAC land-use designation for high-rise apartment towers – have the potential to play a critical role in creating conditions for renewed local economic development and social prosperity. These communities can leverage the Business out of the Box franchise model to create inexpensive retail spaces at the bases of these towers for aspiring local entrepreneurs.

The versatility of shipping containers can also address a host of community needs in tower communities and elsewhere, such as the Welcome Hut visitor orientation centre at Evergreen Brickworks in Toronto. The concept is increasingly being explored for housing in Vancouver.[6] Given the diversity within tower communities, and the service gaps their residents face, such low-overhead modular markets are well-positioned to provide local economic development opportunities at a grassroots level.

The tower communities are not the only potential venues for the BoB approach. The concept has also been used to animate parks, create greenhouses and commercial kitchens, and activate temporarily vacant development lands, including:

> *BoB in McCormick Park – Friends of McCormick Park*, located in north Parkdale, had been trying for years to find a way to serve food in the park. Unfortunately, the kitchen in the Mary McCormick Recreation Centre was not suitable for preparing commercial meals and the snack bar at McCormick arena wasn't interested.
>
> After working with the community and local councillor Ana Bailão, sccc launched McCormick Park Café in the summer of 2014. Operated by Aangen Community Centre, the café boasts fresh farm produce as well as healthy meals and snacks from shipping containers.

BoB and Toronto's First Shipping Container Greenhouse – The greenhouse at SCCC had been in a state of disrepair for several years. While the City was not prepared to invest in a new one, the centre needed the facility for much of its programming, which is geared toward a community garden, community kitchen and food security issues.

As an alternative to public funding, SCCC partnered with Giant Container Services to create what is now Toronto's first container greenhouse, fully operational since 2014. The produce is used for the centre's community kitchen programs and is also donated to Toronto food banks.

BoB and the Development Opportunity – Since 2013, SCCC has partnered with real estate developers in other parts of Toronto to promote and market the BoB concept. Concrete towers and vacant lands awaiting development present opportunities for advancing the shipping-container retail concept as a way to create new markets for existing vendors and provide opportunities for emerging entrepreneurs.

Developers have recognized the value of being able to promote local commercial activity on planning building sites as a way of attracting condo buyers. The connections created allow SCCC to explore more permanent BoB markets when these projects are complete and filled with new residents. For BoB, the real value for such pop-up markets lies in the social and economic benefits for the small businesses coming through SCCC's program.

BoB and Toronto Community Housing – In 2015, SCCC partnered with Toronto Community Housing to launch a request-for-proposal process that allows neighbourhood groups to nominate locations that could benefit from a BoB market. The goal is to develop two self-sufficient venues in underserved inner suburban neighbourhoods. The centre will help successful franchisees finance and set up their businesses for an annual fee.

It will be important to test how the BoB model functions in economically challenged neighbourhoods whose residents represent a very different market than the downtown consumers who use Market 707. Factors expected to impact success include affordability, local need, accessibility, security and the involvement of community-based organizations to host and incubate the businesses. The learnings from the two pilot projects will inform how BoB will evolve and adapt to different local microeconomies over the long term.

The Future of BoB

The use of shipping containers to create local economic activity among racialized, low-income and youth entrepreneurs has created a ripple effect across the city that speaks to the potential of BoB as a powerful city-building and place-making tool. The versatility of containers allows for neighbourhood beautification and reanimation of vacant or neglected space, but the value proposition also brings economic life and jobs, which are key to building vibrant and healthy communities.

These social dividends can be seen clearly through the partnerships that have emerged among diverse neighbourhood stakeholders – community centres, elected officials, foundations, developers, architects, government departments, design professionals, educational institutions, law firms, aspiring entrepreneurs and, most importantly, local residents. Such public-private partnership projects build social capital, skills and connections; strengthen the capacity of those traditionally excluded from entrepreneurial markets; break down barriers in highly diverse communities; and foster more complete and inclusive communities.

Going Beyond Representation:
The Diversity Deficit in Local Government
John Lorinc

One afternoon in February 2016, a tense mood hung over the politicians gathered in Toronto's council chamber. They had convened to debate the latest development in the city's struggle to balance the consumer demand for the Uber ride-sharing service with the fierce objections of the taxi industry and its thousands of drivers, many of whom had blockaded the downtown two months earlier.

With a proposed legal strategy on the agenda, the spectator seats filled with dozens of irate cabbies. Following a few speeches by pro-taxi councillors, David Shiner, who has represented an affluent suburban ward for over twenty years, took the taxi industry to task for failing to use Uber-style apps.

Suddenly, the chamber erupted in shouting, and the police hastily cleared the angry cabbies from the room. As Sam Moini, a taxi industry spokesperson, later told the *National Post*, 'If the food was taken from your children's mouths … and you have a city councillor stand up in council (and) say, "you guys don't have the same technology that Uber does," which is a complete lie, of course you're going to get enraged.'[1]

When the session resumed, Kristyn Wong-Tam, a downtown councillor, stood up and acknowledged the proverbial elephant in the room: 'The issue here is also around race,' she began, obviously distressed by the conflict and the verbal assaults on a few of her council colleagues. 'There are times when we don't pay attention to race and our places of privilege.'

As in many big cities, Toronto's taxi drivers are overwhelmingly non-white, and mostly newcomers, many from South Asia or the Middle East. According to a 2012 federal study, over 80 percent of cabbies in Toronto are immigrants. What's more, the report noted, immigrant drivers tend to be 'much' better educated than their Canadian-born counterparts, with almost half having completed multiple post-secondary degrees, including 225 who were either PhDs or MDs.[2]

Subsisting on meagre cabbie salaries or juggling multiple part-time jobs, many drivers have watched their incomes drain away as Uber has soaked up an ever-greater market share. What's more, while Toronto actively courts tech companies and the young urban professionals they employ, municipal officials seem much less inclined to defend the workers who operate at the fringes of the labour force, despite the city's oft-stated slogans about the strength of its diversity.

'We are conditioned to respect white-collar work and perfectly spoken English,' Wong-Tam said later. 'We have folks in the council chamber who are not in a place of comfort. We're not responding to their realities.' The question, indeed, is why the city's governing body failed to understand that the Uber issue is just as much about the economic stresses facing newcomers as it is about cheap rides.

While dozens of major cities are struggling to regulate Uber, the controversy here has underscored the gap between Toronto's much-touted ethnocultural diversity and the socio-economic indicators that show the steadily widening divisions between the city's rich and poor, many of whom live in concentrated enclaves far from jobs, transit and services. In fact, municipal politicians and top bureaucrats tasked with implementing their policy decisions generally don't reflect the city's demographics, says Wong-Tam. 'When I ride the transit, I see the face of Toronto. When I go to meetings at city hall, I don't see the face of Toronto.'

It is more than a little ironic that in a region with a larger portion of foreign-born residents than almost any other global city, Greater Toronto's municipal politicians are mostly white, mostly male and mostly middle or upper middle class. According to a 2011 study published in the journal *American Behavioral Scientist*, Ryerson University political scientist Myer Siemiatycki points out that the proportion of visible minorities on Toronto council actually dropped between 1997 and 2006 – from 12 percent to 8.8 percent (the 2016 figure is 11 percent).[3] Greater Toronto's suburban municipal councils have a comparable lack of diversity, even though those regions have even larger immigrant and racialized communities that have grown dramatically in the past generation.

'Why,' Siemiatycki asks, 'are immigrants and minorities so statistically under-represented in the City of Toronto?' He also poses a related question: does that lack of representation have an impact on the way these municipalities plan, deliver services and enforce regulations, such as those governing cabs? The answer turns out to be complex and paradoxical – a story about 'both the political inclusion and exclusion' of newcomers, low-income and non-white residents, but also the systemic failings of a municipal electoral system that seems programmed to hoard political power while simultaneously promoting the virtues of diversity. 'We have to go beyond just representation,' says Wong-Tam. 'We have to talk about integration and social inclusion. We're not even close.'

In 2008, four Canadian political scientists published the first comprehensive, quantitative study of the representation of immigrants, women and minorities in Canadian cities. The results, 'Electing a Diverse Canada,' are not especially surprising.[4] According to a 'proportionality index' developed by the researchers, the elected politicians in Canada's eleven largest cities (at the time) were disproportionately male, while the three other categories were all under-represented, in some cases significantly. For the period covered by the survey, several cities – Halifax, Regina, Saskatoon – had no visible-minority politicians, and a few others – Montreal, Ottawa – did only marginally better. Edmonton, interestingly, had the largest proportion of racialized and foreign-born politicians, faring considerably better than Toronto, a city where almost half the residents were born outside Canada.

These metrics are at best blunt measures: in any representative democracy, the collective makeup of the government never holds up a precise mirror to the body of people who elect it. What's more, the head count – by race, gender and country of origin or, for that matter, sexual orientation, ability and economic status – reveals little about the underlying electoral dynamics, the quality of individual politicians and the degree to which those elected officials can represent the interests of their constituents. Tokenism, obviously, is not the solution.

In fact, one of the study's lead authors, University of Ottawa political scientist Caroline Andrew, points out that some analysts now argue in favour of moving beyond identity politics to 'substantive representation,' focusing 'on the results or the impact of elected officials on policies or programs.' Still, as she writes,

> there is a common-sense reality check that reminds us that legislative bodies made up entirely of middle-aged White men make us uncomfortable, no matter how politically attuned they are to voters' ideas. This discomfort indicates that we feel some degree of numerical representation to be a necessary element in political representation ... It is not necessarily the exact replication of the general population that is needed[,] but certainly a mix of individuals from the groups that comprise the general population.[5]

Yet if it's true that we accept the importance of a greater 'mix' and inclusiveness in the local governments serving hyper-diverse urban regions, why do our municipal politicians come mainly from a comparatively narrow demographic?

While large-scale immigration – from Ireland, Italy, Eastern Europe and China – began to significantly reshape Toronto's predominantly white and Anglo-Saxon population in the late nineteenth century, the levers of municipal government remained firmly in the hands of an Anglo-Irish Protestant elite whose members belonged to Orange Order and Freemason lodges. Despite that political reality, a baker named William P. Hubbard, an Afro-Canadian whose parents had fled slavery in the 1840s, became the first Black citizen in Toronto (and Canada, in fact) to be elected to public office, in 1894. Within a few years, the popular east-end alderman was named deputy mayor, and later worked with Sir Adam Beck to ensure that Ontario's hydro-electric generators remained in public hands.

It took almost half a century for city council to open up further, first with Nathan Phillips, Toronto's first Jewish mayor (elected in 1955 after serving for years as an alderman), and then with the wave of Italian-Canadian municipal politicians who took office in the late 1960s and 1970s, representing dense working-class wards in the west end. Toronto council gradually admitted other politicians with diverse backgrounds – Eastern European, Asian, South Asian, LGBT and Latin American, as well as a growing number of women.

Yet municipal councils in Toronto and the surrounding suburban regions remain, for the most part, far more homogenous, in every category, than the constituencies they represent. Large and internally diverse ethnocultural communities – Asian, South Asian and African or Afro-Caribbean – have barely been represented on council. 'It is really striking,' says McMaster University political scientist Karen Bird, who has studied diversity in both Canadian municipal governments as well as their counterparts in countries like Germany and Denmark. 'Canada's municipal sector compares poorly with municipal governments in other countries, including those you'd be surprised by,' she says.

The causes are nothing if not tangled – a reflection of the social complexity of these urban regions.

In some parts of Toronto, immigration settlement patterns have changed since the postwar period, when newcomer groups tended to cluster and could build the critical mass needed to elect politicians. Today, with much larger wards that have become home to newcomers representing many different nationalities, there's no longer a critical mass. 'White candidates tend to win in those wards,' says University of Toronto Mississauga political scientist Erin Tolley, who studies media representation of diversity. In some cases, she adds, white candidates become the default choice because of rivalry or mistrust among different ethnocultural communities. (There's no lack of diversity among those *seeking* public office, however. A scan of the candidate lists suggests that in most wards, the people running for public office do reflect the ethnocultural mix of the city.)

Based on her research, Tolley points out that minority candidates are often treated differently by reporters – not necessarily maliciously, but in 'unconscious' ways that reinforce stereotypes about the archetypal office-holder. The coverage of non-white or immigrant politicians tends to place more emphasis on their backgrounds and demographics. She also cites the attention given to accents (e.g., Olivia Chow during the 2014 Toronto mayoral race), as well as attention to the *lack* of an accent. Ontario NDP deputy leader Jagmeet Singh, who represents a Brampton riding, is often described as 'articulate,' notes Tolley, who reads such characterizations as a coded way of saying that the thirty-seven-year-old politician doesn't have a South Asian accent. 'Nobody would make comments like that about a white candidate.'

Andray Domise, a marketing professional who ran for council against late former mayor Rob Ford in a north Etobicoke ward in Toronto's 2014 election, adds that both journalists and other candidates may cast non-white or immigrant candidates as somehow representative of their own tribes. Domise, who is of Caribbean descent, sought to avoid being pigeonholed as a 'Black candidate' who is subtly expected to represent Black residents from a broad range of backgrounds. Rather, his goal was to expose Ford's neglect of low-income immigrant and culturally diverse communities in the ward. On the campaign trail, he hammered away at how Ford's cuts to social services, transit and recreation compounded the economic challenges and divisions facing residents in areas like Rexdale. 'The disdain and lack of respect for people of colour is staggering,' he says.

Race and language played a disquieting role in that election. The *Toronto Sun* ran an editorial cartoon that used racial stereotypes in its depiction of Chow. Other candidates reported hearing a lot of anti-Muslim sentiment at the door; indeed, Munira Abukar, a young woman running in northern Etobicoke, had to fend off racist taunts after someone scrawled 'GO BACK HOME' on her campaign signs and brochures. For his part, Domise found himself countering a high-profile candidate well-versed in the art of 'code-switching.' Ford, he says, could adopt a Jamaican patois to appeal to Black voters. 'We don't normally get a lot of that from politicians,' he muses. 'We're often quick to adapt to white culture.'

Quite apart from these troubling undercurrents, Domise points to a structural problem preventing low-income candidates from inner-suburban enclaves like Rexdale from gaining public office. In the sprawling wards of post-amalgamation Toronto (some with as many as 60,000 residents), fundraising is critical. But candidates from less affluent areas, even those with extensive social and community networks, have little chance of raising the necessary sums. Nor can most of those residents – especially women – take time away from their jobs to mount a competitive campaign. Domise, who had to quit his job to run, adds that restrictions on contributions from corporations, non-profits and unions, created in the mid-2000s in the wake of a corruption scandal, have created further barriers. 'A lot of minorities don't see a path to leadership,' he says. 'The system favours the richest and best-connected people because they can raise money.'

Yet San Grewal, a long-time *Toronto Star* reporter who covers municipal politics in the suburban 905 region, says the lack of municipal representation is also connected to cultural attitudes about local government that trace back to some groups' home countries. In both South Asia and Mainland China, he observes, local politicians lack prestige and clout. 'Municipal politics are not highly regarded,' he says, adding that in the large Indo-Canadian communities in Mississauga and Brampton, community leaders seeking political influence are more focused on federal and provincial parties and seats. The flip side of this story, adds Grewal, is that while dozens of visible-minority candidates have run in local elections in Mississauga and Brampton, the majority are fringe figures who end up cancelling out one another's votes.

Entrenched cultural attitudes in some predominantly ethnic neighbourhoods add further twists and turns to this story. Alejandra Bravo, a progressive education activist who came to Canada from Chile as a child, has run three times for council in a dense, ethnically mixed west-end Toronto ward where working-class neighbourhoods abut rapidly gentrifying ones. While Bravo, now a director at the Broadbent Institute, had the backing of the local NDP machine, she encountered resistance from older Italian, Portuguese and Latin American voters who told her a young mother shouldn't be running for elected office. Some older immigrants, she observes, experienced social exclusion themselves, but they also rejected attempts by a younger generation of activists to address those divisions politically.

If there's one point of broad consensus about the chronic diversity deficit in Greater Toronto's municipal councils, it is the problem of incumbency. Municipal councillors, once elected, are exceedingly difficult to unseat because elections take place in a 'low-information environment,' as Tolley says. Without a party system, platforms or any straightforward methods for evaluating their voting records, councillors trade on name recognition and run on anodyne promises – building community, safe streets, nice parks. Says Siemiatycki, 'It's very hard to cast an intelligent ballot at the municipal level.'

Because there are no term limits on municipal office holders, councillors tend to enjoy lengthy stints in local government, and few lose during elections. On the 2014–2018 Toronto council, for example, twenty-six of forty-four councillors have either held their seats for long stretches (twenty years or more), worked previously as staffers for their predecessors or had a family connection to a well-known office holder. In the 2014 City of Toronto elections, thirty-six of thirty-seven incumbents who sought re-election won, and did so with comfortable majorities, according to the Toronto Election Study, a multi-university research project.[6]

The problem is even more entrenched on some suburban councils, says Grewal. 'The seats on council tend to be treated like property. They're handed to friends, families and staffers.'

'The power of incumbency is so great that it needs to be examined,' adds Bravo. '"Diversity is our strength" is an aspiration. It's great if you're comfortable. But if not, it breeds resentment that can be exploited … '

In the 2014 municipal race in Hamilton, voters in a downtown ward with lots of newcomers and low-income residents sent entrepreneur Matthew Green to city hall – a first for a blue-collar city that had never elected a Black member of council (Hamilton has a long history of electing councillors with roots in working-class Italian and Eastern Europe neighbourhoods).

Since taking office, Green has energized residents with a series of well-attended meetings to hash out issues affecting their neighbourhoods, including carding by Hamilton police. His presence, says Karen

Bird, 'has absolutely made a difference,' and has forced city council to confront previously ignored issues, such as racial profiling. 'You get different kinds of discussions that hadn't taken place before,' Bird observes. 'It certainly made councillors pay much more attention and want to hear more of those diverse voices across the city.'

The point of broadening representation on local councils is not to check off boxes or shift municipal politics to the left. Rather, as Siemiatycki says, the goal is to bring a wider range of experiences to bear on debates about how socially intricate urban communities are governed, planned and regulated. 'You never know how identity issues and the experiences that flow from identity will manifest themselves politically,' he observes. 'But the benefit of the doubt should always go to inclusion rather than exclusion.'

He cites a 2012 showdown at Toronto council during Rob Ford's term, when the former mayor, a fierce critic of public sector unions, moved to outsource city hall's cleaning staff to save a relatively small amount of money. While left-leaning councillors predictably opposed the move, they found an ally in a centrist councillor who'd mostly supported Ford's agenda – Ana Bailão, a rookie councillor for a west-end riding with large numbers of Portuguese and Latin American immigrants.

During the debate, Bailão recounted how both she and her mother had worked for non-unionized contract cleaning companies after they'd arrived to Canada. 'My mom had to have two jobs,' she said in an emotional speech to council. 'At age fifteen, I was cleaning offices downtown for two years. I know this industry, and these are new immigrants coming to this country … These are the most vulnerable people in this city.'[7] Those grim formative experiences, Siemiatycki recounts, allowed Bailão to ask council, 'How much is that savings worth to you?'

For each of those stories, however, there are others that underscore how city councils comprised primarily of middle-class homeowners have, at key moments, made choices with grave implications for less affluent residents – for example, sharp cuts to already-overcapacity suburban bus routes that serve as the exclusive or primary means of transportation for tens of thousands of Torontonians, many of them newcomers, tenants and low-income workers.

(Interestingly, Olivia Chow, early in her 2014 mayoral campaign, pledged to reverse those cuts, which were a key part of Ford's aggressive cost-cutting agenda. While she lost the race, John Tory, the winner, moved swiftly upon taking office to reverse the cuts in an attempt to demonstrate that he was attuned to the social impact of fiscally driven policy choices primarily of interest to property taxpayers. Tory, however, demonstrated that he has a tin ear for contentious issues such as overly aggressive or racially biased policing.)

Wong-Tam, who notes that the senior-most ranks of Toronto's civil service bear scant resemblance to the city's ethnocultural and socio-economic makeup, argues that the problems go beyond council politics. The city's bureaucratic machinery, she observes, isn't set up to gauge the impact of municipal programs and services on specific populations. Wong-Tam says the city should be disaggregating data on who actually uses services to determine whether council's policies, many of them approved with an eye to extending services to under-served communities, are actually hitting the mark. She points to cities like Boston, Los Angeles and Montreal, where bureaucrats must now use a 'gender equity lens' to assess the impact of programs. 'If you address the needs of diverse women,' says Wong-Tam, 'you will catch all sort of other diversities.'

Other observers point to the way insufficiently diverse councils can fail to respond to important planning issues that arise, sometimes rapidly, as community demographics shift. San Grewal points to a bitter 2012 debate in Brampton about bylaws governing basement or second suites, which had been illegal until the provincial government required municipalities to update their policies to allow for such uses.

With many such suites rented by recent immigrants, predominantly white homeowner groups in Brampton mounted a strenuous campaign to oppose them, arguing that the legalization of these apartments would lead to overcrowding in local schools and parking problems. While basement suites represent as an important source of affordable accommodations in a rapidly growing city with long waiting lists for social housing, few councillors were prepared to oppose outspoken ratepayer organizations. 'That voice was drowned out overwhelmingly by councillors who were against basement suites,' says Grewal. 'You need that diversity of views to ensure that constituents are properly represented.'

But there are stories where councils tacked in the opposite direction. Erin Shapero, a former Markham councillor and one of the first women to win elected office in that municipality, recalls how council began to accommodate the community's growing ethnocultural diversity. In the early 2000s, soon after she was elected, Shapero, who is Jewish, noticed that council meetings were scheduled to coincide with the High Holidays in the fall, a practice that posed problems for Markham's growing Jewish community. When she raised the point, council moved to adopt a calendar that recognized a range of cultural festivals and holidays.

She also pushed to find better ways to incorporate the input of diverse communities into how the city planned public spaces, such as local parks. After learning that the predominantly Asian residents living near a proposed park didn't care for the minimally landscaped space, she set up a broadly representative working group to collaborate with an artist, a facilitator and municipal parks officials to co-create a space that better reflected the neighbourhood's goals. The result: a park that includes a space for tai chi practice, seating that allows visitors to face one another and a therapeutic pebble path, but also a basketball court.

'In the end, consensus was really how we designed the park,' says Shapero. 'We need to shake up city planning because it doesn't reflect the diversity of Greater Toronto communities. We talk about inclusive communities, but it won't happen unless we do things differently.'

Over the years that I have covered local politics, I've frequently heard local politicians and Toronto urbanists inveigh against the prospect of injecting party politics into the day-to-day work of municipal government, which, they insisted, shouldn't be subjected to partisanship, whipped votes and ideological posturing.

But is our current system of municipal government, with its strong bias toward homeowners and incumbents, capable of addressing the extraordinary social complexity of a region like Greater Toronto? Are our municipal institutions geared to respond to urban hyper-diversity? The question is rhetorical: certainly, the incumbency narrative on its own proves our local governments are wired to stubbornly resist the introduction of new ideas, new faces and new voices.

It's worth noting that in the private sector, best practice among corporate boards now emphasizes the systematic replacement of directors at regular intervals. The reason: fresh perspectives are vital to large and complex institutions. It's important to replenish and reinvigorate. If the principle holds for a multinational, it must surely apply to municipal councils tasked with governing intensely complex urban communities.

Term limits, of course, would help counter the incumbency advantage, although there's no guarantee that councils would become more inclusive as a result. Other ideas for opening up municipal politics in Toronto began to surface in the mid-2000s, and coalesced into a push for electoral reforms designed to mitigate the impact of the so-called first-past-the-post system, which accords victory to candidates with the most votes, even if their tallies are well below 50 percent.

Municipal election reform advocates like Dave Meslin have argued for an automated runoff system known as 'ranked ballots' that will produce winners who reach elected office with a clear numerical majority. While the provincial Liberals adopted a policy allowing municipalities to run ranked-ballot elections, Toronto council rejected the prospect in 2015, despite years of lobbying and advocacy work by Meslin and other reform activists.

Yet when I asked various municipal government experts about how they'd confront the homogeneity of local councils, none felt that ranked ballots would lead to better and broader representation. 'I don't see any evidence that ranked ballots will help increase diversity,' Karen Bird says. 'Parties will increase diversity.' Myer Siemiatycki agrees: 'The parties are now the vehicle of inclusion.'

Indeed, political parties of all stripes at the federal and provincial levels seem to be doing a much better job at nominating a diverse range of candidates to stand for election. As Bird notes, 'I see how effective the party system has been at reaching out to new voters and immigrant communities.' (The party system also fosters a cleaner form of accountability because individual candidates are always measured against their party's platforms and voting records.)

Bird points to examples in European cities like Copenhagen and Arhus, where the percentage of racialized councillors actually exceeds the proportion of newcomers or minorities in those cities, and this despite the fact that Denmark's state and national governments in recent years have been dominated by right-of-centre parties with anti-immigrant political agendas. The reason: a party-based municipal elections system with so-called 'open lists,' which means voters choose both the party and specific candidates. The structure, Bird explains, encourages the parties to recruit candidates from immigrant or lower-income communities.

Those candidates, she adds, 'are not only coming from the left-wing parties. The centre-right is also running those candidates. They are in parties pretty much across the political spectrum.'

In a hyper-diverse region like Greater Toronto, the stakes couldn't be higher. Clubby politics, voter disengagement and a chronic disconnect between municipal government and the complex communities it serves have fostered a form of political marginalization that amplifies the social, economic and spatial sorting that has become the dominant dynamic in the evolution of the city's neighbourhoods.

We are, therefore, confronted by a critical choice – between a more inclusive and responsive local government capable of bringing in new voices, or a dominant and entrenched political class that directs municipal resources at an ever-narrower slice of the urban population.

As Siemiatycki warns, 'We underestimate the extent to which this recurring exclusion carries with it a ripple effect.'

Brampton, a.k.a. Browntown
Noreen Ahmed-Ullah

I live in a suburban Ontario town where the visible minorities are now the majority. Brampton – a.k.a. 'Browntown,' 'Bramladesh,' 'Singhdale' – is just like the nicknames imply: mostly brown.

On our street of new semi-detached homes, I see brown and Black families, mostly immigrants. Strip malls consist almost entirely of Indian-only grocers, sweet shops and stores selling fancy South Asian clothes. My drive home off Highway 427 is lined with places of worship: palatial Sikh gurdwaras, a monumental Hindu mandir and a soon-to-be-built mosque. The only church in the area is a tiny historic landmark.

At the walk-in clinic, brown and Black families. At Service Ontario on a weekend, of the thirty people in line, only two are white and they are related. At the nearby library, an entire section carved out for Punjabi and Hindi books. And on Diwali, 'the festival of lights,' the night sky above Gore Road is lit up on both sides, crackling with competing fireworks displays.

I am no longer surprised when staff at a local Canadian Tire speak to me in Punjabi, or grocery stores advertise Diwali and Eid sales. Sobeys recently opened a supermarket in the heart of Brampton called Chalo Freshco, or 'Let's Go, Freshco,' marketing it as the first Canadian grocery store designed for 'desis,' or those of South Asian descent, offering everything from spices and basmati rice found at an Indian grocery store to Indo-centric vegetables and ready-to-eat tandoori chicken and snacks.

On any given day, groups of women in colourful shalwar kameez (tunic and baggy pants) stroll vigorously along the sidewalk, getting in their daily exercise. Men in brightly hued turbans and flowing white beards bike to the neighbourhood park to hang out with friends.

Sometimes I wonder if I live in India or Canada.

But I am not complaining. For someone who has lived her entire life as a minority – and a very visible one, thanks to the hijab covering my hair – this environment is a welcome change. I am with my own kind.

According to Statistics Canada's 2011 National Household Survey, visible minorities made up two-thirds of Brampton's population – five years later that number is likely higher (and it renders the bureaucratic label 'visible minority' obsolete). Nearly 40 percent of Brampton is South Asian, with Sikhs representing almost 20 percent of the population. What are the top three languages spoken in Brampton after English? Punjabi speakers comprise nearly 22 percent of the town, Hindi 9 percent and Urdu 3.8 percent. Not surprisingly, they're all languages originating on the South Asian subcontinent.

I love that I can walk to the Asian Foods grocery store down the block when I've run out of coriander or turmeric, or when I'm craving some samosas. Who needs a neighbourhood 7-Eleven when all my favourite comfort foods are a stroll away? Need to get your legs waxed or your eyebrows threaded? Every few blocks there's a salon operating out of someone's basement.

I also love that I don't stick out like a sore thumb. As a South Asian Muslim, Indian on my dad's side, Pakistani on my mom's, I feel like I finally fit in. I am part of the non-white majority. I don't need to worry about someone judging me by my hijab or hurling racist comments. I don't have to deal with the patronizing tone of a white person in a mall parking lot, talking down at me about some asinine rule like I don't speak English.

The brown people who live here love Brampton. It's like being in India, but with free health care, good schools and clean streets. Yet even as we revel in this urban enclave, we know in our hearts that the Brampton that is emerging is not a good thing. Google 'Brampton' and 'ghetto,' and you'll find plenty to read. Brampton gets labelled as a ghetto largely because of the city's high concentration of visible minorities, especially South Asians.

As a writer who has documented and experienced true urban decay south of the border, I know that 'ghetto' is a racially charged word that conjures up images of heavily populated slums, often segregated neighbourhoods occupied by minorities. It's a disparaging term – one that historically was used for enclaves occupied by Jewish Europeans and now used more often to describe – especially in America – urban Black poverty.

Regardless of whether Brampton is or isn't a ghetto, that label alone is an ominous marker. It raises tough questions about the future of a city that's been profoundly reshaped by the immigrants who've made their homes here.

Until August 2014, I was a reporter in Chicago, covering the inequities of the city's public school system and writing about disenfranchised African-American youth. Neighbourhoods on Chicago's south and west sides – now, those are true urban ghettos. Here in Brampton, you don't have abandoned homes boarded up, acting as magnets for prostitution and drug dealing. The city isn't shutting down schools. Gang members are not opening fire at children playing on sidewalks.

So if Brampton is not a ghetto, what is it?

The sprawling suburb of subdivisions, with its high South Asian (specifically Sikh) population is what's called an 'ethnoburb' – a middle-class suburb occupied by an ethnic group. Besides the Vancouver suburb of Surrey, as well as London, England, the Brampton area is home to one of the largest Sikh communities outside of India. How it got to be that way is a lot like the story of other ethnic enclaves going back generations – people followed friends and relatives.

'It's an interesting case because you have this clustering and clumping of particular people through market processes and social relationships,' says York University professor Roger Keil, who researches global suburbanization. 'Immigrants from a particular ilk living together – that's the common history of immigration from the Lower East Side of New York City to nineteenth-century Vienna.'

In Brampton's case, the clustering was triggered by developers who kept buying farmland and converting it into endless subdivisions. Jobs at the airport also fuelled the expansion, attracting South Asian immigrants first to Malton and then nearby Brampton. Within a generation, Brampton transformed from Canada's flower-growing capital to its ninth largest city. The population boomed from 234,445 in 1991 to 523,911 in 2011, with that number now reaching nearly 600,000.

But the rapid demographic turnover has not been lost on long-standing residents.

Racial tensions ignite over everything from permit battles for a new temple to fireworks regulations for Diwali. In 2014, anti-Sikh flyers distributed by the immigration reform group Immigration Watch Canada – entitled 'The Changing Face of Brampton' and asking residents 'Is This Really What You Want?' – sparked outrage among Sikh community groups. Another flyer distributed in March 2015 warned of the city's dwindling 'European' population, implying the decline was a result of 'white genocide.'

Whether it is 'white genocide' or 'white flight,' few would dispute that the town has lost a sizable chunk of its white population. And while academics shy away from using the term 'white flight' to describe what happened to Brampton's white families, residents speak freely about what they observed in their own neighbourhoods.

Back in 2005, when Dr. Gurjit Bajwa moved into his Castlemore subdivision of 3,500-square-foot homes, there were about fifteen white families, out of 105. Many of those white families are now gone, with South Asians making up half the subdivision. Another 20 percent of the families are Black. This transition occurred in one of the wealthiest parts of the city, where homes are valued at almost $1 million.

The forty-five-year-old ER doctor at Etobicoke General Hospital doesn't know what drove the white families away, but he knows he too has faced the stigma of living in Brampton. Bajwa, who is Sikh, says in the beginning he wouldn't even tell co-workers he lived in Brampton, instead naming the neighbourhood.

'I would say I lived in Castlemore,' he says. 'There was a negative connotation to Brampton. People wouldn't say it, but it would just be a non-verbal cue like a rolling of the eyes, or "Oh, I see." They were thinking: "You live in a ghetto. You're a doctor – you could be living anywhere you want. You could be living in Rosedale if you wanted to. Why do you choose Brampton? Why do you choose to live in a ghetto?"'

So why *did* he move to Brampton?

'Two reasons,' Bajwa says. 'One was housing prices. In the more established areas of Mississauga, Vaughan and Markham, the housing prices were higher. Here, they were 10 to 15 percent lower. The other reason is that flocks tend to migrate together. If you have one community moving, they tell their relatives.'

Mrs. R., who immigrated to Canada from the West Indies forty years ago, watched her neighbourhood change during the fifteen years she lived in Brampton.

'My street was very diverse. We had West Indian, South Asians, Italian, Portuguese, Vietnamese, Filipino and Caucasian,' she recalls. 'By the time we left in 2015, the neighbour on the left, who was Italian, was now South Asian. And the one on the right, who was Korean, was now South Asian. You'd walk into a bank that was mixed and now you see South Asian managers and South Asian bank tellers. You'd have to be living under a rock to not see that things were changing.'

And the non–South Asians didn't always welcome the changes. Some were upset that older Punjabi and Hindi immigrants seemed to be getting by without having to learn English. Because South Asians didn't call out a friendly hello, or because all South Asian homes had basement apartments, or because of their 'smelly' cooking, some people just didn't like having them as neighbours. They watched the welcome mat being laid out by businesses like banks, and were filled with resentment. When they had immigrated here from different parts of the world, no one made services like opening a bank account easy for them.

'I've been here longer, and I feel like an outsider,' a Black resident tells me.

Pardeep Singh Nagra, a well-known Sikh activist who rose to fame in Canada after a court victory against the Canadian Amateur Boxing Association over his beard, is the executive director of the Malton-based Sikh Heritage Museum of Canada.

His path to Brampton is a lot like the trek of so many Sikh immigrants in the Toronto region. The first stop for his dad and uncle, who immigrated in 1971, was the Little India neighbourhood along Gerrard Street and the gurdwara on Pape Avenue. Then, once their wives and children immigrated from India, the families bought their first joint home – ten people under one roof in a semi-detached in Malton. They moved a few times in the area, eventually following relatives and friends to Brampton in the early nineties.

Nagra has carefully collected artifacts documenting Canadian Sikh history. He's helped curate exhibits at the museum, detailing Sikh achievements like the first gurdwara in North America, built in Vancouver in 1908, and the first RCMP officer allowed to wear a turban, in 1990. Modern-day Canadian Sikh heroes include local boy Jagmeet Singh, the deputy leader of Ontario's NDP; YouTube sensation Jus Reign; Navdeep Bains, the new Canadian Minister of Innovation, Science and Economic Development; and Harjit Sajjan, the decorated Canadian soldier turned Liberal defence minister.

Yet, despite the long history in this country, Sikhs are still not accepted as Canadians, says Nagra. That's why a city with a large South Asian population gets labelled as a ghetto, he says.

'There are enclaves in Toronto for the Jewish community, the Italian community and even the Asian community,' Nagra says. 'The negative is only associated with brown skin, whether it be Blacks or South Asians. There are only two places outside of Toronto that are labelled as ghettos – Brampton and Scarborough. It is racism. It's naive not to think race doesn't play a role in what gets labelled as a ghetto.'

Racism is also a factor in why an influx of Sikh immigrants watched white families leave and other white families opting not to move to Brampton, Nagra continues. He points to the language in the anti-Sikh flyers and racist comments that surface during city council meetings on temple permits.

'At what point do I get freed and get to be seen as Canadian?' Nagra says. 'Is it being born here? Is it having citizenship? Is it cheering for the Leafs? Is it playing hockey? Is it having some maple syrup? Doing the Terry Fox Run? As long as I am not seen as a Canadian, my existence here offends people because of what I choose to wear. They can't exist in my space. They're offended that I exist in their space.'

The process of immigration, settlement and social harmony isn't inevitable. In fact, it needs to be worked on. Forward-looking municipalities actually try to create links between their various ethnic communities to counter resentment and flight.

Kristin Good is an associate professor of political science at Dalhousie University. In her 2009 book, *Municipalities and Multiculturalism: The Politics of Immigration in Toronto and Vancouver*, she argues that local governments – not just their federal and provincial counterparts – have a role to play in helping communities deal with multiculturalism and the racial tensions that may arise as a community becomes more biracial than multiracial.

'As Brampton transitioned from a more diverse multicultural immigration base to a more concentrated South Asian population, that concentration creates a perception of cultural takeover in a municipality among long-standing residents and can lead to particular kinds of multiculturalism challenges,' Good says. 'My theory predicts that you'll see more of a backlash when there is concentration. Part of it is the perception that the immigrant group doesn't want to integrate. Part of it is the sense of cultural takeover and the loss of being the majority in the place. And part of it is that certain types of developments are perceived to cater to particular ethnic groups, and sometimes that makes long-standing residents feel excluded.'

In such cases, municipalities need to step in and foster intercultural understanding between the groups. But Brampton's municipal leaders never took that critical step. In fact, Good found that politicians in neither Brampton nor Mississauga had planned or reacted well to their minority population in the early 2000s. 'They were unresponsive,' she says. 'What they didn't do were all of the things that more responsive municipalities did that follow a multicultural model of citizenship, rather than one based on a hands-off, laissez-faire assimilation approach to immigrant integration.'

In her research, Good found that more responsive communities actually created separate divisions within municipal government whose officials engaged their diverse communities and oversaw access and equity in the city's employment practices and services. These municipalities also provided grants to community organizations helping new immigrants integrate and promote positive ethnic relations, and finally they took steps to incorporate immigrants and ethno-racial minorities into the political process and municipal decision-making.

In Brampton, visible minority representation on city council and in city hall was a problem back when Good's book was published, and it's still a problem today.

Gurpreet Singh Dhillon was elected to Brampton council in November 2014. In a town where the visible minority is now the majority, Dhillon is the sole non-white councillor. 'It's 2015, but our council, for whatever reason, does not reflect the city,' he says. 'I would like our council, and our city, to be more aware of who is living in this city and what their cultural needs are.'

Case in point: disputes over the use of city parks. During the summer of 2015, Dhillon organized an opportunity for residents to vent concerns to city staff about their requests for more park gazebos, shelters, tables, benches and porta-potties not getting approved. City staff couldn't understand the need for the requests, but meeting face-to-face with one-hundred-plus residents has now led to findings that Dhillon hopes will influence Brampton's next master plan for its parks.

'Our parks are designed for passive use – you come in, you go out. In India, though, people socialize and congregate at parks,' Dhillon says. 'City staff have been handling some of their concerns for years, but they've never actually been to these parks. The staff doesn't live in Brampton. They have no clue about people's needs, their cultural practices.'

The city also needs to hire municipal officials, police and firefighters who reflect the community, says Bajwa, who actively campaigned to defeat Brampton's long-standing mayor, Susan Fennell, in 2014.

'One of the ways you promote cross-cultural barrier breakdown is by having government appear to reflect the nature of the community,' Bajwa said. 'The staff at city hall should be – if not 35 percent – at least 15 to 20 percent South Asian, but it's not. The police officers you hire should be approaching that number, so that when police officers go to houses where those complaints arise, they know who they're talking to. They can deal with people in their own language, they can understand the complainant's background and can easily solve problems that way.'

Brampton residents have a point. If you look at Ferguson, Missouri, where the fatal shooting of an unarmed Black teenager in 2014 by a white police officer sparked the Black Lives Matter movement, minorities make up at least two-thirds of the population but the police department is predominantly white. The disconnect between the community and racial representation on the police force is a problem afflicting many American cities struggling with police brutality in African-American and Latino communities.

Prof. Jeffrey Reitz, director of University of Toronto's Ethnic, Immigration and Pluralism Studies, doesn't believe that municipal governments, which are challenged by limited access to tax revenue, alone bear the blame for failing to integrate the different ethnic communities in Brampton. He says the national multiculturalism program, which has a mandate 'to build an integrated and socially cohesive society,' was cut by about a third to $7 million a year under the Conservatives. The program not only provides funding to organizations to take on projects and events promoting multiculturalism, but also undertakes public education initiatives – like Asian Heritage Month and Black History Month – that promote diversity and help break down barriers.

'Back in the seventies and eighties, it was much more funded than it is now, even without adjusting for inflation,' Reitz says. 'I don't think the whole burden should fall to municipal governments, because multiculturalism is a national program with national implications.'

Canadian cities may boast that they never fell victim to racism and avoided the kind of white flight that led to the destructive segregation in many large cities south of the border. But the Brampton story reveals that we have our own version of white flight, and before we figure out how to manage hyper-diverse and increasingly polarized cities like Greater Toronto, we need to reflect on our own attitudes about race and ethnic diversity.

White flight played a crucial role in making Chicago one of the most segregated cities in America. When Blacks began moving to the city from the Deep South during the first half of the twentieth century, political leaders used racially restrictive covenants to dictate where Black families could live. Even after the Supreme Court struck down these covenants, homeowners' associations maintained the status quo by discouraging members from selling to Black families. It wasn't until white families began moving out in droves that Black families began moving in, eventually creating the city's predominantly Black South Side.

In what many consider Chicago's most dangerous neighbourhood – Englewood – the white population dropped from 89 percent to 31 percent between 1950 and 1960. Today, Englewood is 98.5 percent Black, 0.6 percent white and 0.4 percent Latino. With business and industry following the white population, neighbourhoods like Englewood succumbed to violence. Public schools there today are among the worst in the city. At one local high school, which was the subject of a *This American Life* documentary, twenty-nine teens were shot in one school year alone. Even as I was reporting on life in this neighbourhood, high schoolers would lift up their T-shirts and their pants to show me gunshot wounds like seasoned war veterans.

When the mayor closed nearly fifty schools in 2013, another disenfranchised community on the West Side, North Lawndale, was hit particularly hard. The community, which is 92 percent Black, saw two elementary schools and a high school shut down. In communities where the achievement gap kept widening, closing schools – essentially divestment, since residents would end up with fewer school options – was the city's solution.

The disparity between Blacks and whites is so wide in Chicago that the *Atlantic*'s Ta-Nehisi Coates declared in the summer of 2015 that it's almost like Blacks and whites don't live in the same city. In fact, many Black youths in Chicago have never visited downtown. They remain isolated in their crumbling, violent neighbourhoods.

I fear that same disparity for the Toronto area's brown and Black populations. As the GTA becomes further divided along racial and socio-economic lines, will ethnic enclaves become the vehicle through which we create haves and have-nots in this city?

Already, insurance rates in Brampton are the highest in the GTA. I discovered this when I moved to the city and had to insure my car. An insurance agent told me this was because of the high rates of crashes and fraudulent claims in Brampton.

Similarly, Brampton's public schools are increasingly serving only brown kids. Families that can afford it send their children to private Catholic schools, while public school teachers complain about a lack of ESL supports for the large number of students who are still learning English. Some believe race also played a part in Brampton residents losing out on an LRT expansion that would have connected them to the GTA, helping them get to Mississauga and other transit connections faster. The city's long-time older, white residents, who didn't want anything to disrupt their downtown neighbourhood, convinced city council to vote down the proposal and give up $1.6 billion promised to the project by the Province of Ontario. Newcomers had fought hard for better commuter options.

Does this accelerating dynamic create other forms of social dysfunction, such as concentrated poverty, elevated crime rates and chronic unemployment? Urban expert Keil says the risk of that exists only if business and industry fail in Brampton.

'Ghettoization is often linked to racialization and is often driven by the collapse of a certain industry, like Detroit, which lost one million people,' Keil says. 'The ghettoization and segregation of African-Americans in Detroit has more to do with the downfall of the auto industry and the loss of tens of thousands of jobs.'

In Brampton, Keil adds, we need to look out for those places where immigrants have found employment in the low-paid service sector, like warehouses and factories: 'If there's continued job loss in those places, a loss of income and wealth, then I'd fear those places might become the job deserts and service deserts that we have seen in the inner suburbs of Toronto over the last generation.'

Finally, the evolution of Brampton raises questions about the nature of multiculturalism in the GTA. Does the presence of ethnic enclaves mean we remain with our own people, and have little interaction with others?

Ethnic enclaves have their pluses – in the Sikh community's case, political success. Sikh activism and the area's high concentration of Sikh votes not only brought Justin Trudeau to Brampton three times during his campaign, including a packed rally attended by thousands a few days before the election, but Trudeau also mentioned the city in his victory speech after it proved to be a pivotal battleground for candidates – all five ridings in Brampton went red this year. In 2011, they had all voted blue.

Ethnic enclaves also give immigrant groups power because the electoral system rewards them for large numbers and high concentration.

But at what cost? That high concentration also drives away people who could help make the community more multiracial, and better connected to the city-region at large.

'Political success is one of the benefits, but I don't think that benefit is good enough,' says Bajwa, the physician. 'Ideally what you should have is a mixed community. Ghettoism is very bad. It's bad for everybody. It's incumbent upon all of us to reach out to our neighbours, whoever they are.'

We will have to wait and see how Brampton continues to evolve. Keil says no community remains stagnant. Second- and third-generation South Asians may choose to move out of the city. Or white families could choose to move in.

As it is, Bajwa says a few white families have begun trickling into his subdivision. On a recent day, I saw a white couple buying fruit and vegetables at an Indian grocer in my neighbourhood. And a few months ago, a white family moved into a home two doors down. Their dazzling Christmas decorations – the only ones I can see on our street – defiantly stake their claim to a spot here.

I'm itching to ask them: 'Why Brampton?'

Life in the City In-Between
Shawn Micallef

It's easy to miss the people for the landscape, especially if the landscape isn't conventionally handsome, like Toronto's inner and outer suburbs. A little too modern, perhaps, or a little too car-centric: a jumble of shapes and spaces that don't fit together. These are the everyday spaces of Toronto, where a few million people live and work among a mishmash of concrete towers, hydro corridors, wood and brick storefronts, and civic projects of varying scale and grandeur. The layers have built up and roots have grown deep, though. It's a landscape best seen not in widescreen but in a close-up, where the people are revealed and impossible to ignore.

Conclusion
J. David Hulchanski

All cities are subdivided. The divides are social, economic, ethno-cultural, physical and more. What matters is the type and strength of the divisions. Are they good or bad? Which ones are increasing and which are decreasing? Recognizing and then openly discussing unde-sirable trends among a wide circle of stakeholders is the first step in turning them around – finding ways to build cities that are less divided and more inclusive.

We now have a much better understanding of the nature of these urban divides, thanks to a growing body of research, as well as the accounts contained in these pages. They reflect the broader divisions within society. In a highly urbanized nation, we can easily locate where certain trends reside and measure degrees of change and concentration. Yet, too often our civic leaders fail to acknowledge – much less talk about – some of our most undesirable but most signifi-cant social and economic divisions. For many affluent city-dwellers, it is easier to celebrate diversity, give occasionally to charities and speak of Toronto's inclusive intention to build 'one city.' Those who live comfortably and can benefit from what the city has to offer, it seems, would rather not dwell on inequality and the injustices of racism, sexism and prejudice arising from class, gender, race, religion and other divides.

Why should we worry about the significant social and spatial divides that rising economic inequality is exacerbating? Why bother attempting the difficult task of being serious about inclusive city-building? The British social epidemiologist Richard Wilkinson, who studies the relationship between the distribution of income within a nation and key indicators of health and social problems, offers up a compelling answer: 'Inequality promotes strategies that are more self-interested, less affiliative, often highly antisocial, more stressful, and likely to give rise to higher levels of violence, poorer community rela-tions, and worse health.'[1] Swirling macroeconomic forces, in turn, intensify those inequalities. 'While the [2007–08] recession took a toll on all of us,' observed Sen. Ratna Omidvar, executive director of the Global Diversity Exchange, 'it had a particular deep impact on recent immigrants, with their unemployment rates being twice that of others. The narrative of doctors driving cabs and engineers delivering pizzas is not just local mythology, it is quite real.'[2] More equal societies, by contrast, are more cohesive, inclusive and healthier for all – and not just for those at the lower end of the income gap. They demonstrate greater resilience and have fewer significant divides.

When I came to Toronto to study urban planning in the early 1970s, I was surprised by how orderly and well-maintained the city looked, especially in comparison to what was happening in U.S. cities. I now know that the Toronto of the 1970s was mainly a middle-income city: two-thirds of the city's neighbourhoods were middle-income compared to less than one-third today. There were some low-income neighbourhoods (about 25 percent of the city; now 50 percent) and some high-income neighbourhoods (about 16 percent; now 21 percent). I was able to get around the city easily because the Yonge subway line and the just-completed Bloor-Danforth line connected the developed parts of the city. The TTC cost twenty-five cents (inflation-adjusted, that's $1.40 today), and you almost always got a seat. My graduate school tuition was $600 per year (about $3,400, inflation-adjusted), and finding a place to rent was easy.

During my first week in Toronto, to get to know the city better, I asked a friend: where are Toronto's 'slums'? Though he noted that no area had the sort of concentrated poverty that existed in some U.S. inner cities, he circled on a map a couple of the more rundown parts of Toronto. One Sunday afternoon, I walked around one of those areas, Cabbagetown. I saw Victorian-era houses with poorly maintained porches and lawns. Some were rooming houses, and it seemed many were divided into rental apartments on the main and upper floors. There were children everywhere. Houses in Toronto sold for about $30,000 ($180,000, inflation-adjusted). In 'rundown' Cabbagetown, houses were even cheaper fixer-uppers, affordable for people with lower incomes.

That entire area of the city to the west and south of Cabbagetown housed average and low-income working people who were mainly white. The newly developing suburbs in Scarborough, North York and Etobicoke were home to the vast and growing postwar group of middle-income families. A single income could buy a house, a car and support a large family in the cheaper central city or in the nice, new, middle-class suburbs. This began to change in the late 1970s. Some of the baby boomers who had been renting in the central area while they were students wanted to stay in that area when they were able to buy.

Neighbourhoods in the core were being 'renewed,' mainly by demolishing houses to make way for clusters of private-sector rental high-rises, such as St. James Town next to Cabbagetown. Further south, I visited Canada's first public housing community, Regent Park, and a newer modernist high-rise public housing community nearby, Moss Park. The adjacent area closer to downtown was known, at the time, as skid row. A 1977 Toronto Planning Board report, aptly titled 'Report on Skid Row,' noted with some alarm the steady loss of both flophouses (how many today know what a flophouse was?) and rooming houses. That report did not yet use the term 'homelessness' because 'homeless men' referred to individuals who were not affiliated with a family home and the support that provides. They were transient and lived in cheap apartments, rooming houses and flophouses. They were homeless, but not unhoused.

The Toronto of the 1970s was indeed a divided city. Still, it was far less divided and, as we've seen in the preceding chapters, much less socially complicated than the Toronto of today. Neighbourhoods were indeed changing, but in a way that at least acknowledged – and then attempted to be inclusive to – the needs of all social groups. A great deal of private and public rental housing was being built in the central area as well as in the suburbs. The City of Toronto built the St. Lawrence neighbourhood – with about 3,500 housing units, half of them social housing – with an innovative site plan that maximized the number of at-grade family units. The city expanded the transit system and made improvements to all forms of physical infrastructure. There were many social agencies and community services where they were needed, in the lower-income central neighbourhoods.

Neighbourhood change continued, of course, but with a difference. The change no longer consisted of building private or public rental housing. What we now call gentrification had begun. It was initially referred to in Toronto as 'white painting,' a reference to the practice of sandblasting paint off the brick exteriors and adding white trim. One social class began displacing another social class.

What happened to the Cabbagetown area has since happened throughout Toronto – and other cities in many Western nations – producing a sharper and deeper social and spatial polarization of residents, on the basis of class, socio-economic status and ethnocultural origin. Governments began seriously deregulating and cutting taxes and social spending in the 1990s. Politicians promised that deregulation, individual and corporate tax cuts, austerity in social spending, and a turn to market fundamentalism would leave everyone better off. Benefits would trickle down. A rising tide would lift all boats.

By the 1990s, with public spending severely curtailed, there was no longer a focus on the supply and maintenance of private or public rental housing. Land zoned for higher-density residential was originally intended to be rental. With the introduction of condominium legislation and the increasing acceptance of condo living, most new high-density residential buildings have mainly been for the ownership market. Renters, on average, have about half the income of owners. The gap was about 20 percent in the 1960s, when a great deal of rental housing was built and when new immigrants could still afford to buy the single-family homes that would, in later decades, gain enormously in value.

The private sector can't build for such a low-income group, and investor-owned condo units are filling the demand at the higher end of the rental market. The federal and provincial governments have refused to play any significant role, as they once did. Toronto now has relatively low property taxes for those with the means to own property – a reward to a group that disproportionately votes in municipal elections. The Toronto of the 1970s and 1980s – a clean, efficient and relatively inclusive city that actor and writer Peter Ustinov famously described in 1987 as 'New York run by the Swiss' – is no more.

Is there any good news? A glimmer: those of us who study these trends know what happened. We have also analyzed what explains the divided city trend. The data indicates that four major factors trump anything a municipality can do by itself: changes in the labour market (fewer 'good jobs'); changes in the housing market (higher rents and house prices); changes in government taxes, transfers and fees (mainly helping the highest income group and imposing risk and costs on everyone else); and society's failure to adequately address discrimination in not just the labour market, but also in housing, education and even within social networks.

We need to move beyond the old rhetoric of diversity and recognize that global cities like Toronto have become exceptionally complicated social spaces that defy the easy categories of identity, even as their internal fissures widen. For about two decades, year-by-year changes affecting wages, housing costs and social spending, and our failure to be serious about direct and systemic discrimination, have produced the divided city. But it's also true that year-by-year changes designed to improve the situation in each of those categories should produce a more inclusive Canada, as will some of the solutions proposed in these pages.

Only then will we begin to see cities like Toronto become less subdivided and more inclusive in this, the age of hyper-diversity.

NOTES

Introduction, Jay Pitter

1. Not his real name.

2. J. David Hulchanski, 'The Three Cities within Toronto: Income Polarization among Toronto's Neighbourhoods, 1970–2005' (Cities Centre, University of Toronto and St. Christopher's House, 2010), www.urbancentre.utoronto.ca/pdfs/curp/tnrn/Three-Cities-Within-Toronto-2010-Final.pdf.

3. Walter Benn Michaels, *The Trouble with Diversity: How We Learned to Love Identity and Ignore Equality* (Henry Holt, 2006).

4. Tuna Tasan-Kok, Ronald van Kempen, Mike Raco and Gideon Bolt, *Towards Hyper-Diversified European Cities: A Critical Literature Review* (Utrecht University, Faculty of Geosciences, 2013).

5. Kimberlé Crenshaw, 'Mapping the Margins: Intersectionality, Identity Politics, and Violence against Women of Color,' *Stanford Law Review*, vol. 43 (1993), p. 1241.

Identity and the City, Beyhan Farhadi

1. Eve Kosofsky Sedgwick, *Epistemology of the Closet* (University of California Press, 1990).

2. Evelyn Peters, 'Aboriginal People in Urban Areas,' in *Urban Affairs: Back on the Policy Agenda*, eds. Caroline Andrew, Katherine Graham and Susan Phillips (McGill-Queen's University Press, 2002), pp. 45–70.

3. Indigenous and Northern Affairs Canada, 'Fact Sheet – Urban Aboriginal Population in Canada,' www.aadnc-aandc.gc.ca/eng/1100100014298/1100100014302 (see also www41.statcan.gc.ca/2007/10000/ceb10000_003-eng.htm).

4. See Sunera Thobani, *Exalted Subjects: Studies in the Making of Race and Nation in Canada* (University of Toronto Press, 2007).

5. See Wayne Roberts, 'Whose Land?,' *NOW*, July 11, 2013, nowtoronto.com/news/whose-land.

6. According to the Public Relations Society of America, 'Pigeonholing occurs when qualified individuals are assigned to projects that relate to their race – regardless of whether they are experts in that group's expectations and needs or if they even identify with that group.' www.prsa.org/Intelligence/Tactics/Articles/view/6C-030440/101/Diversity_Dimensions_Pigeonholing_A_trap_for_pract.

7. Laura Cockburn, 'Children and Young People Living in Changing Worlds,' *School Psychology International*, vol. 23, no. 4 (2002), pp. 475–485.

8. The data supports her experiences of systemic discrimination, as students of Somali descent not only face marginalization in their Toronto communities, but, as a result, drop out and face expulsion at significantly higher rates than their peers. See Katie Daubs, 'TDSB's Somali Task Force Recommends Better Student Support,' *Toronto Star*, August 30, 2013.

9. See also Stephen Michalowicz, 'The City Known as Dixon,' *Torontoist*, December 11, 2008, torontoist.com/2008/12/a_place_called_dixon/.

10. Susan Fainstein, 'Cities and Diversity,' *Urban Affairs Review*, vol. 41, no. 1 (2005), pp. 3–19.

11. Katherine Graham and Susan Phillips, 'Another Fine Balance: Managing Diversity in Canadian Cities,' in *Belonging? Diversity, Recognition and Shared Citizenship in Canada*, eds. Keith G. Banting, Thomas J. Courchene and F. Leslie Seidle (McGill-Queen's University Press, 2007), pp. 155–194. See this source for an excellent overview of the literature on diversity in Canadian cities, as well as a discussion about the various ways cities approach and respond to diversity. For the

purposes of this essay, I am referring to diversity as pluralism – the coexistence of peoples with different beliefs, traditions, values and interests. This may or may not be limited by identity categories, though; as Graham and Phillips point out, 'evidence suggests that most urban municipalities neither collect much information on diverse communities – beyond the basic census data that comes across their desks – nor make effective use of what is available.' (See also Beth Moore Milroy and Marcia Wallace, 'Ethnoracial Diversity and Planning Practices in the Greater Toronto Area: Final Report' [CERIS Working Paper 18; Joint Centre of Excellence for Research on Immigration and Settlement, 2002].)

Doing Immigrant Resettlement Right, Doug Saunders

1. Kare Vernby, 'Inclusion and Public Policy: Evidence from Sweden's Introduction of Noncitizen Suffrage,' *American Journal of Political Science*, vol. 57, no. 1 (2013).

Wasauksing–Vancouver–Toronto, Rebekah Tabobondung

1. As was the case throughout Latin America, North American Indigenous peoples also survived a history of colonization that included an onslaught of racist, genocidal policies. Unlike in Guatemala, during the last century the Canadian state has been reluctant to outright mass-murder Native people. Instead, other gross human rights violations, such as the legislated residential schools and the banning of ceremonies such as the Sundance and Potlatch have been inflicted (Royal Commissions on Aboriginal Peoples, 1996).

2. Heather Howard-Bobiwash, 'Toronto's Native Roots,' *First Nations House Magazine*, issue 1, p. 6.

3. 'The Doctorine of Discovery Is Less of a Problem than Terra Nullius,' A Reconciliation Project, July 16, 2012, reconciliationproject.ca/2012/07/16/.

4. Statistics Canada, 2006 Census. However, it is commonly estimated that there are over 60,000 Aboriginal people living in the GTA, which accounts for those who choose not to self-identify to Statistics Canada.

5. Well Living House Governance, Well Living House Counsel of Grandparents, St. Michael's Hospital.

How We Welcome, Sarah Beamish and Sofia Ijaz

1. We acknowledge the original peoples and traditional caretakers of this land, including the Haudenosaunee, Anishnaabe and Wendat peoples. Refugee resettlement in Canada takes place on lands from which Indigenous peoples themselves have been forcibly displaced by the settler population, of which we are a part. We do not mistake the absence of war here for peace.

2. The 1951 Refugee Convention defines a refugee as someone who, 'owing to a well-founded fear of being persecuted for reasons of race, religion, nationality, membership of a particular social group or political opinion, is outside the country of his nationality, and is unable to, or owing to such fear, is unwilling to avail himself of the protection of that country.' In Canada some people may be classified as 'protected persons' for the purposes of resettlement, even if they do not strictly meet the Refugee Convention definition.

3. Tom Clark, *The Global Refugee Regime: Charity, Management and Human Rights* (Trafford Publishing, 2004), p. 3.

4. Carlos Teixeira and Wei Li, 'Introduction: Immigrant and Refugee Experiences in North American Cities, *Journal of Immigrant & Refugee Studies*, vol. 7, no. 3 (2009), p. 222.

5. For example, see CERIS, 'Final Report: Refugee Research Synthesis 2009–2013,' pp. 18–19, ceris.ca/wp-content/uploads/2015/05/CERIS-Research-Synthesis-on-Refugees-19-May-2015.pdf, and Carlos Teixeira, 'Barriers and Outcomes in the Housing Searches of New Immigrants and Refugees: A Case Study of "Black" Africans in Toronto's Rental Market,' *Journal of Housing and the Built Environment*, vol. 23, no. 4 (2008), pp. 253–276.

6. An example of this in the GTA is Peace Village, a planned community of about three hundred homes built around the Baitul Islam mosque in Vaughan, established by and for Ahmadi Muslims, many of whom came to Canada as refugees.

7. For example, see Teixeira, 'Barriers and Outcomes'; Robert A. Murdie, 'Pathways to Housing: The Experiences of Sponsored Refugees and Refugee Claimants in Accessing Permanent Housing in Toronto,' *Journal of International Migration and Integration*, vol. 9, no. 1 (2008), pp. 81–101; Jeffrey G. Reitz, *Warmth of the Welcome: The Social Causes of Economic Success for Immigrants in Different Nations and Cities* (Westover Press, 1998); Abdolmohammad Kazemipur and Shivalingappa S. Halli, *The New Poverty in Canada: Ethnic Groups and Ghetto Neighbourhoods* (Thompson Educational Publishing, 2000); Ravi Pendakur, *Immigration and the Labour Force: Policy Regulation, and Impact* (McGill-Queen's University Press, 2000).

8. For example, see Miriam Stewart, Joan Anderson, Morton Beiser, Edward Mwakarimba, Anne Neufeld, Laura Simich and Denise Spitzer, 'Multicultural Meanings of Social Support among Immigrants and Refugees,' *International Migration*, vol. 46, no. 3 (2008), pp. 125–126; and Leah S. Steele, Louise Lemieux-Charles, Jocalyn P. Clark and Richard H. Glazier, 'The Impact of Policy Changes on the Health of Recent Immigrants and Refugees in the Inner City,' *Canadian Journal of Public Health*, vol. 93, no. 2 (March/April 2002), p. 118.

9. Robyn Sampson and Sandra M. Gifford, 'Place-making, Settlement and Well-being: The Therapeutic Landscapes of Recently Arrived Youth with Refugee Backgrounds,' *Health & Place*, vol. 16, no. 1 (2010), p. 116.

10. Laura Simich, 'Negotiating Boundaries of Refugee Resettlement: A Study of Settlement Patterns and Social Support,' *The Canadian Review of Sociology & Anthropology*, vol. 40, no. 5 (2003), pp. 579–580.

11. These numbers vary, but from 2005 to 2009 about one-fifth of government-assisted refugees moved cities during their sponsorship period (see Citizenship and Immigration Canada, *Evaluation of Government Assisted Refugees (GAR) and Resettlement Assistance Program (RAP)* (March 2011), p. 24, www.cic.gc.ca/english/pdf/pub/gar-rap.pdf.

12. Beiser, 'Resettling Refugees and Safeguarding Their Mental Health: Lessons Learned from the Canadian Refugee Resettlement Project,' *Transcultural Psychiatry*, vol. 46, no. 4 (2009), p. 565.

13. For example, Nilüfer Demir's photo of three-year-old Alan Kurdi's lifeless body on a beach triggered an outpouring of compassion among Canadians that resulted in policy changes meant to facilitate resettlement of Syrian refugees (e.g., waiving the requirement that Syrians be registered as refugees with the United Nations).

14. Victoria M. Esses, Scott Veenvliet, Gordon Hodson and Ljiljana Mihic, 'Justice, Morality, and the Dehumanization of Refugees,' *Social Justice Research*, vol. 21, no. 4 (2008), p. 25.

15. Ibid., p. 23.

16. Morton Beiser, 'Resettling Refugees,' p. 565.

17. For example, see CERIS, 'Final Report'; Beiser, 'Resettling Refugees'; and Murdie, 'Pathways to Housing.'

18. For example, see Teixeira, 'Barriers and Outcomes'; CERIS, 'Final Report, pp. 18–19; and Beiser, 'Resettling Refugees,' pp. 558–559.

19. Simich, 'Negotiating Boundaries,' p. 583.

20. Dependant children of dependant children are also included. Ministry of Citizenship and Immigration, Guide 6000 – Convention Refugees Abroad and Humanitarian-Protected Persons Abroad, www.cic.gc.ca/english/information/applications/guides/E16000TOC.asp.

21. In some cases, family can also be the cause of the refugee's displacement – for instance, if someone is fleeing abuse.

22. Poverty Free Ontario, 'Status of Poverty in Ontario,' www.povertyfreeontario.ca/poverty-in-ontario/status-of-poverty-in-ontario/#ftn1; Canadian Centre for Policy Alternatives, 'Making Ends Meet,' www.policyalternatives.ca/publications/reports/making-ends-meet; Statistics Canada, 'Market Basket Measure,' www.statcan.gc.ca/pub/75f0002m/2013002/mbm-mpc-eng.htm.

23. Government of Canada, 'Evaluation of the Government Loan Program, Section 4.6.1, www.cic.gc.ca/english/resources/evaluation/ilp/2015/performance.asp#diff_repay.

24. Stewart et al., 'Multicultural Meanings,' p. 133.

25. In some limited circumstances, this could be increased for up to three years.

26. It generally takes seven to ten years for refugees to attain economic stability (see Beiser, p. 545).

27. Beiser,'Resettling Refugees,' p. 545.

28. David A. B. Murray, 'The Challenge of Home for Sexual Orientation and Gendered Identity Refugees in Toronto,' *Journal of Canadian Studies/Revue d'études canadiennes*, vol. 48, no. 1 (Winter 2014), p. 136, referencing Ala Sirriyeh, 'Home Journeys: Im/mobilities in Young Refugee and Asylum-seeking Women's Negotiations of Home,' *Childhood*, vol. 17, no. 2 (2010), p. 215.

29. While privately sponsored refugees may have their guaranteed incomes 'topped up' in this way, government-assisted refugees (who make up the majority of sponsored refugees) do not. This is one reason government-assisted refugees generally have even lower financial security than do privately sponsored refugees.

30. The UN Resettlement Agency, 'A New Beginning in a Third Country,' www.unhcr.org/pages/4a16b1676.html.

Finding Space for Spirituality, Fatima Syed

1. Royson James, 'Crombie and Council Spurn Prejudice in Fight Over Mississauga Mosque: James,' *Toronto Star*, October 14, 2015.

2. 'Migration, Immigration and Social Sustainability: The Recent Toronto Experience in Comparative Context' (Joint Centre of Excellence for Research on Immigration and Settlement – Toronto, 1999), Working Paper.

Navigating the City with an Invisible Illness, Denise DaCosta

1. Ontario Ministry of Health and Long-Term Care, 'Health Services in Your Community,' 2012, www.health.gov.on.ca/en/common/system/services/psych/designated.aspx.

Culture and Mental Illness, Karen Pitter

1. *Informing the Future: Mental Health Indicators for Canada* (Mental Health Commission of Canada, 2015).

2. Juha Mikkonen and Dennis Raphael, *Social Determinants of Health: The Canadian Facts* (York University School of Health Policy and Management, 2010).

3. Fact Sheet # 1, 'Understanding the Racialization of Poverty in Ontario: An Introduction in 2007' (The Colour of Poverty Campaign), www.learningandviolence.net/lrnteach/material/PovertyFactSheets-aug07.pdf.

4. Priya-Alika Elias, 'The Silence about Mental Health in South Asian Culture Is Dangerous,' *New Republic*, September 23, 2015, newrepublic.com/article/122892/silence-about-mental-health-south-asian-culture-dangerous.

5. Mary Amuyynzu-Nyamongo, 'The Social and Cultural Aspects of Mental Health in African Societies,' Commonwealth Health Partnerships, 2013 .www.commonwealthhealth.org/wp-content/uploads/2013/07/The-social-and-cultural-aspects-of-mental-health-in-African-societies_CHP13.pdf.

6. 'Chinese American Mental Health Facts,' National Alliance on Mental Illness, 2011, www.namisa.org/uploads/5/0/7/8/5078292/chinese_american_mh_facts2011.pdf.

7. J. Rathborne, L. Zhang, M. Zhang, J. Xia, X. Liu, Y. Yang and C. E. Adams, 'Chinese Herbal Medicine for Schizophrenia: Cochrane Systematic Review of Randomised Trials,' *The British Journal of Psychiatry*, vol. 190, no. 5 (2007), pp. 379–384.

8. 'The Culture of Well-being: Guide to Mental Health Resources for First Nations, Métis & Inuit People in Winnipeg,' Winnipeg Regional Health Authority, 2011, hwww.uwinnipeg.ca/hr/benefits/docs-and-seminar-pages/health-wellness/culture-well-being.pdf.

9. Marie McKeary and Bruce Newbold, 'Barriers to Care: The Challenges for Canadian Refugees and Their Health Care Providers,' *Journal of Refugee Studies*, vol. 23, no 4. (2010), pp. 523–545.

10. Kelly K. Anderson, Joyce Cheng, Ezra Susser, Kwame J. McKenzie and Paul Kurdyak, 'Incidence of Psychotic Disorders among First-generation Immigrants and Refugees in Ontario,' *Canadian Medical Association Journal*, vol. 187, no. 9 (2015), pp. E279–E286, doi.org/10.1503/cmaj.141420.

11. Shari Narine, 'Racism Lives and Breathes; A Virus in Healthcare,' *Windspeaker*, vol. 3, no. 12 (2013), www.ammsa.com/publications/windspeaker/racism-lives-and-breathes-virus-healthcare.

12. *Mental Health: Culture, Race, and Ethnicity: A Supplement to Mental Health: A Report of the Surgeon General*, Department of Health and Human Services, U.S. Public Health Services, 2001.

Neighbourhood Watch, Asmaa Malik

1. Tanya Farber et al., 'Growing Discomfort with Neighbourhood Watches "Racial Profiles,"' *Times Live*, November 30, 2014.

2. Sam Levin, 'Racial Profiling Via Nextdoor.com,' *East Bay Express*, October 7, 2015.

3. Terrence McCoy, 'The Secret Surveillance of "Suspicious" Blacks in One of the Nation's Poshest Neighborhoods,' *Washington Post*, October 13, 2015.

4. Asmaa Malik, 'Do I Really Belong in "Inclusive" Toronto?,' *Toronto Star*, May 14, 2015.

Accessing Education, Nicholas Davis

1. Dereck W. Cooper, 'Migration from Jamaica in the 1970s: Political Protest or Economic Pull?,' *International Migration Review*, vol. 19, no. 4 (Winter 1985), pp. 728–745.

2. Alex Glennie and Laura Chappell, 'Jamaica: From Diverse Beginning to Diaspora in the Developed World,' *Migration Policy Institute*, June 16, 2010, www.migrationpolicy.org/article/jamaica-diverse-beginning-diaspora-developed-world (Table 1).

3. Caroline Alphonso and Tavia Grant, 'A Tale of Two Schools: The Correlation between Income and Education in Toronto,' *Globe and Mail*, November 16, 2013.

4. J. David Hulchanski, 'The Three Cities Within Toronto: Income Polarization among Toronto's Neighbourhoods, 1970–2005' (Cities Centre & Faculty of Social Work, University of Toronto, 2010), p. 11, www.urbancentre.utoronto.ca/pdfs/curp/tnrn/Three-Cities-Within-Toronto-2010-Final.pdf.

5. Sam Dillon, 'Large Urban-Suburban Gap Seen in Graduation Rates,' *New York Times*, April 22, 2009.

6. Sachin Maharaj, 'Toronto Has a Two-tiered Education System,' *Toronto Star*, April 18, 2015.

7. Hulchanski, 'The Three Cities,' p. 11.

8. Maharaj, 'Two-tiered Education System.'

9. 'Economic Impact of Immigration to Canada,' Wikipedia, en.wikipedia.org/wiki/Economic_impact_of_immigration_to_Canada.

10. Romana King, 'Toronto's Most Affordable Top School Zones,' *MoneySense*, May 19, 2015, www.moneysense.ca/spend/real-estate/buying/torontos-most-affordable-top-school-zones/.

11. Ibid.

12. Ibid.

13. Patty Winsa and Kristin Rushowy, 'Rich Schools Get Richer Thanks to Private Cash,' *Toronto Star*, February 28, 2011.

14. 'Study: Parents Can Still Make the Grade With Well-Priced Homes Near Great Schools,' TheRedPin.com press release, May 15, 2015, www.firmenpresse.de/pressrelease394303/study-parents-can-still-make-the-grade-with-well-priced-homes-near-great-schools.html.

15. Joseph Berger and Andrew Parkin, *The Value of a Degree: Education, Employment and Earnings in Canada* (The Price of Knowledge, 2009), p. 23.

16. Toronto – Rexdale, Pathways to Education, www.pathwaystoeducation.ca/en/toronto-rexdale.

17. Stanley C. Lartey, My Visit with Leonard A. Braithwaite, C.M., O.Ont., Q.C., (Ontario Black History Society, 2009), www.blackhistorysociety.ca/UserFiles/File/Braithwaite-Life-Story.pdf.

18. Ibid.

19. Ibid.

20. Camille Wilson and Lauri Johnson, 'Black Educational Activism for Community Empowerment: International Leadership Perspectives,' *International Journal of Multicultural Education*, vol. 17, no. 1 (2015), p. 109, ijme-journal.org/index.php/ijme/article/viewFile/963/1035.

21. Ibid.

22. 'Portuguese Lead Drop Out Rate for Immigrant Children,' Canadian Immigration Reform Blog, April 2, 2008, canadianimmigrationreform.blogspot.ca/2008/04/portuguese-lead-drop-out-rate-for.htm.

23. Brian Jacob and Jens Ludwig, 'Improving Educational Outcomes for Poor Children,' National Bureau of Economic Research, Working Paper (2008), www.irp.wisc.edu/publications/focus/pdfs/foc262j.pdf.

Policing and Trust in the Hyper-Diverse City, Nana Yanful

1. Mariana Valverde, 'Enforcing Protestant Sunday,' in *The Ward: The Life and Loss of Toronto's First Immigrant Neighbourhood*, eds. John Lorinc, Michael McClelland, Ellen Scheinberg and Tatum Taylor (Coach House Books, 2015). Police used the provincial Lord's Day Act to force Jewish merchants to close on Sundays.

2. Police Services Act, 1990.

3. Scot Wortley, 'Police Use of Force in Ontario: An Examination of Data from the Special Investigations Unit, Final Report' (2006). Research project conducted on behalf of the African Canadian Legal Clinic for submission to the Ipperwash Inquiry: African-Canadians are only 3.6

percent of the Ontario population, but they represent 12 percent of civilians involved in SIU investigations, and Aboriginal people are only 1.7 percent of the provincial population, but they represent 7.1 percent of all civilians involved in SIU investigations.

4. Data from the World Values Survey (collected between 2005 and 2008) says 80 percent of Canadians reported having a 'great deal' or 'quite a lot' of confidence in police. In Stephen Goudge et al., *Policing Canada in the 21st Century: New Policing for New Challenges/The Expert Panel on the Future of Canadian Policing Models* (Council of Canadian Academies, 2014), p. 58, www.scienceadvice.ca/uploads/eng/assessments%20and%20publications%20and%20news%2 0releases/policing/policing_fullreporten.pdf.

5. By second generation, I mean children born in Canada to one or both foreign-born parents. By third generation, I mean children born in Canada to Canadian-born parents.

6. Jeffrey G. Reitz and Rupa Banerjee, 'Racial Inequality, Social Cohesion, and Policy Issues in Canada,' in *Belonging? Diversity, Recognition and Shared Citizenship in Canada*, ed. Keith G. Banting, Thomas J. Courchene and F. Leslie Seidle (McGill-Queen's University Press, 2007), pp. 489–545.

7. Nazilla Khanlou, 'Psychosocial Integration of Second and Third Generation Racialized Youth in Canada,' *Canadian Diversity*, www.metropolis.net/pdfs/vol_6_2_spring08_e.pdf.

8. Wesley G. Skogan, *Police and Community in Chicago: A Tale of Three Cities* (Oxford University Press, 2006), p. 6.

9. Peter K. Manning, *Police Work: The Social Organization of Policing* (Waveland Press, 1997), pp. 11–13.

10. 'Tavis Police Program Failed Toronto, Says Community Organizer,' CBC News Toronto, September 11, 2015, www.cbc.ca/news/canada/toronto/tavis-police-program-failed-toronto-says-community-organizer-1.3224064.

11. Peter K. Manning, *Democratic Policing in a Changing World* (Routledge, 2011), pp. 22, 48.

12. Stephen J. Schulhofer et al., 'American Policing at a Crossroads: Unsustainable Policies and the Procedural Justice Alternative,' *Journal of Criminal Law and Criminology*, vol. 101, no. 2 (2011), pp. 335–374.

13. Manning, *Democratic Policing*, pp. 12, 19.

14. Prince Albert is the third-largest city in Saskatchewan, with a population of 35,552 (2011 census).

15. Chad Nilson, *Risk-Driven Collaborative Intervention: A Preliminary Impact Assessment of Community Mobilization Prince Albert's Hub Model* (Community Mobilization, Prince Albert, 2014), p. 75.

16. Ibid., p. 35.

17. A decrease of 25 percent in 2012 alone, the largest reduction since 1998 (PACM, 2013); Goudge et al., *Policing Canada*, p. 106.

18. Constance Rice and Susan K. Lee, 'Relationship-Based Policing: Achieving Safety in Watts' (President's Task Force CSP Policy Brief), advancementprojectca.org/wp/wp-content/uploads/2015/09/imce/President's%20Task%20Force%20CSP%20Policy%20Brief%20FINAL %2002-27-15.pdf.

19. 'Community Safety Partnership: Collaboration for Safer Neighborhoods' (Urban Peace Institute), www.urbanpeaceinstitute.org/new-page-1/.

20. Police Resources in Canada Statistics Canada (2012); Crime Severity Index Statistics Canada (2014 c).

21. S. Ng and S. Nerad, *Evaluation of the FOCUS Rexdale Pilot Project* (Delivered to the City of Toronto and Toronto Police Service. Toronto, Ontario: Vision & Results Inc. & SN Management, 2015).

22. Goudge et al., *Policing Canada*, p. 75.

23. Ta-Nehisi Coates, *Between the World and Me*. (Spiegel & Grau, 2015), pp. 78–79.

Three Questions about Carding, Idil Burale

1. Betsy Powell, 'Most of Toronto's Newest Police Don't Live in Toronto,' *Toronto Star*, February 11, 2016.

Designing Dignified Social Housing, Jay Pitter

1. City of Toronto, 'Executive Summary to Transformative Change for TCHC: A Report from the Mayor's Task Force on Toronto Community Housing' (January 2016), p. 4.

2. Richard Buchanan, 'Human Dignity and Human Rights: Thoughts on the Principles of Human-Centered Design,' *Design Issues*, vol. 17, no. 3 (Summer 2001), pp. 35–39.

3. Reinhold Martin, Jacob Moore and Susanne Schindler, *The Art of Inequality: Architecture, Housing, and Real Estate* (Columbia University Press, 2015), p. 10.

4. Ibid., p. 11.

5. John C. Bacher, Preface to *Keeping to the Marketplace: The Evolution of Canadian Housing Policy* (McGill-Queen's University Press, 1993), p. viii.

6. Emily Badger, 'How Section 8 Became a Racial Slur: A History of Public Housing in America,' *Washington Post*, June 15, 2015.

7. Clare Cooper, 'The House as a Symbol of Self,' in *Environmental Psychology: People and Their Physical Settings*, eds. Harold M. Proshansky, William H. Ittelson and Leanne G. Rivlin (Holt Rinehart and Winston, 1976), pp. 435–448.

8. Jane Jacobs, *The Death and Life of Great American Cities* (The Modern Library, 1993).

9. Walter S. Keseredy, Shahid Alvi, Martin D. Schwartz and Barbara Perry, 'Violence Against and the Harassment of Women in Canadian Public Housing: An Exploratory Study,' *Canadian Review of Sociology*, vol. 36, no. 4 (November 1999), pp. 499–516.

10. Philippe Bourgois, *In Search of Respect: Selling Crack in El Barrio* (Cambridge University Press, 1999), p. 215.

11. 'Great Divide of Extremes and Disparity,' *Hamilton Spectator*, August 25, 2010.

12. Gary W. Evans, 'The Built Environment and Mental Health,' *Journal of Urban Health: Bulletin of the New York Academy of Medicine*, vol. 80, no. 4 (2003), pp. 536–555.

Reconsidering Revitalization, Jay Pitter and Sandra Costain

1. Dan Levin, 'In Toronto, a Neighborhood in Despair Transforms into a Model of Inclusion,' *New York Times*, February 28, 2016.

Model Citizens, Andrea Gunraj

1. 'NIA Profiles,' City of Toronto, www1.toronto.ca/wps/portal/contentonly?vgnextoid=e0bc186e20ee0410VgnVCM10000071d60f89RCRD.

2. 'Jane Jacobs,' Project for Public Spaces, www.pps.org/reference/jjacobs-2/.

3. John Rennie Short, 'Civic Engagement and Urban America,' *City*, vol. 5, no. 3 (2001), pp. 271–280.

4. 'Diversity Leads: Women and Visible Minorities in Senior Leadership Positions: A Profile of the Greater Toronto Area (GTA),' Diversity Institute, Ryerson University (2014), www.ryerson.ca/content/dam/diversity/reports/DiversityLeads2014_KeyPreliminaryFindings.pdf.

5. L. S. Tossutti, Mark Wang and Sanne Kaas-Mason, 'Family, Religion, and Civic Engagement in Canada,' *Canadian Ethnic Studies*, vol. 40, no. 3 (2008), pp. 65–90.

6. Yvonne Lai and Michaela Hynie, 'Community Engagement and Well-being of Immigrants: The Role of Knowledge,' *Canadian Issues* (Summer 2010), pp. 93–97.

7. Marty Martinson and Meredith Minkler, 'Civic Engagement and Older Adults: A Critical Perspective,' *The Gerontologist*, vol. 46, no. 3 (2006), pp. 318–324.

8. Ann-Marie Field, 'Counter-Hegemonic Citizenship: LGBT Communities and the Politics of Hate Crimes in Canada,' *Citizenship Studies*, vol. 11, no. 3 (2007), pp. 247–262.

9. Dave Meslin, National Speakers Bureau, nsb.com/speakers/dave-meslin/.

10. 'Feeling Congested,' City of Toronto, www1.toronto.ca/wps/portal/contentonly?vgnextoid=3649837c1b915410VgnVCM10000071d60f89RCRD.

11. Toronto Youth Equity Strategy (City of Toronto).

12. Robert D. Putnam, *Bowling Alone: The Collapse and Revival of American Community* (Simon & Schuster, 2000).

13. Brenda O'Neill, *Human Capital, Civic Engagement and Political Participation: Turning Skills and Knowledge into Engagement and Action* (Canadian Policy Research Networks Inc., 2006).

14. Parissa J. Ballard, Laura Caccavale and Christy M. Buchanan, 'Civic Orientation in Cultures of Privilege: What Role Do Schools Play?,' *Youth & Society*, vol. 47, no. 1 (2015), pp. 70–94.

15. O'Neill, *Human Capital*.

16. Ballard et al., 'Civic Orientation.'

17. Kelly LeRoux, 'Nonprofits as Civic Intermediaries: The Role of Community-Based Organizations in Promoting Political Participation,' *Urban Affairs Review*, vol. 42, no. 3 (2007), pp. 410–422.

18. Tossutti et al., 'Family, Religion, and Civic Engagement.'

A Tale of Two – or Three – Cities, Mariana Valverde

1. City of Toronto, Riverside Heritage District Study, 2014, p. 12.

Mobility in the Divided City, Eric Mann

1. Greater Toronto Transportation Authority, 'The Big Move: Transforming Transportation in the Greater Toronto and Hamilton Area' (Government of Ontario, 2008), p. 8, www.metrolinx.com/thebigmove/Docs/big_move/TheBigMove_020109.pdf.

2. Cherise Burda, '2014 Home Location Preference Survey: Understanding Where GTA Residents Prefer to Live and Commute' (Pembina Institute, 2014), www.pembina.org/pub/2014-home-location-preference-survey.

3. J. David Hulchanski, 'The Three Cities Within Toronto: Income Polarization among Toronto's Neighbourhoods, 1970–2005' (Cities Centre, University of Toronto and St. Christopher's House, 2010), www.urbancentre.utoronto.ca/pdfs/curp/tnrn/Three-Cities-Within-Toronto-2010-Final.pdf.

4. Paul Krugman, 'Inequality and the City,' *New York Times*, November 30, 2015.

5. Ray Chetty and Nathaniel Hendren, 'The Impacts of Neighborhoods on Intergenerational Mobility: Childhood Exposure Effects and County-Level Estimates' (Harvard University and NBER, 2015), scholar.harvard.edu/files/hendren/files/nbhds_paper.pdf.

6. Douglas Young and Roger Keil, 'Reconnecting the Disconnected: The Politics of Infrastructure in the In-between City,' *Cities*, vol. 27, no. 2 (2010).

7. 'Toronto Rental Market Tightens as Condo Leases Reach New Record,' *Urbanation* (2015), www.urbanation.ca/news/87-toronto-rental-market-tightens-condo-leases-reach-new-record.

8. Jason Furman, 'Barriers to Shared Growth: The Case of Land Use Regulation and Economic Rents' (The United States Government, 2015), www.whitehouse.gov/sites/default/files/page/files/20151120_barriers_shared_growth_land_use_regulation_and_economic_rents.pdf.

9. John Sewell, *The Shape of the Suburbs: Understanding Toronto's Sprawl* (University of Toronto Press, 2009), p. 221.

10. 'Live Where You Go: Encouraging Location-efficient Development in Ontario' (Pembina Institute, 2012), www.pembina.org/pub/2354.

Toward More Complete Communities, Alina Chatterjee

1. Ashante Infantry, 'Non-profit Market 707 Finds Success Thinking Inside the Box,' *Toronto Star*, June 2, 2015.

2. Ibid.

3. Jennifer Bain, 'Learn to Make Kanto's Tapsilog, a Filipino Breakfast of Champions,' *Toronto Star*, September 23, 2015.

4. Miki Nomura, 'Gushi Brings Japanese Streetfood to Toronto,' *Nikkei Voice*, July 25, 2013.

5. Suresh Doss, 'Toronto Popup Bombay Street Food Is Opening a Restaurant on Bay Street,' *Post City Toronto*, January 13, 2016.

6. Cara McKenna, 'Shipping Container Housing Being Rolled Out across Canada,' *Toronto Star*, May 3, 2015.

Going Beyond Representation, John Lorinc

1. Chris Selley, 'In Battle with Uber, Toronto Taxi Industry Seems Determined to Lose Respect,' *National Post*, February 3, 2016.

2. Government of Canada, 'Who Drives a Taxi in Canada?' (2012), www.cic.gc.ca/ENGLISH/RESOURCES/research/taxi/sec02.asp.

3. Myer Siemiatycki, 'Governing the Immigrant City: Immigrant Political Representation in Toronto,' *American Behavioral Scientist*, vol. 55, no. 9 (2011), pp. 1214–1234.

4. Caroline Andrew, John Biles, Myer Siemiatycki and Erin Tolley, eds., *Electing a Diverse Canada: The Representation of Immigrants, Minorities and Women* (UBC Press, 2008).

5. Ibid., p. 15.

6. Michael McGregor, Aaron Moore and Laura Stephenson, 'Toronto Election Study,' www.torontoelectionstudy.com.

7. David Rider, 'Council Defies Ford on Contracting Out Cleaners,' *Toronto Star*, April 11, 2012.

Conclusion, J. David Hulchanski

1. Richard G. Wilkinson, *The Impact of Inequality: How to Make Sick Societies Healthier* (The New Press, 2005), p. 23.

2. Ratna Omidvar, 'Sticky Fingers and Social Glue,' December 2011, maytree.com/policy-and-insights/opinion/sticky-fingers-and-social-glue.html.

THE CONTRIBUTORS

Noreen Ahmed-Ullah spent twenty-two years in Chicago, mostly as a staff reporter with the *Chicago Tribune*. She covered the Chicago Public Schools, the third-largest public education system in North America, and later worked as a foreign correspondent after 9/11, travelling through Afghanistan and Pakistan, reporting on political turmoil and Islamic extremism. She now calls Brampton home and loves writing about issues such as urban development, gentrification, ethnic communities and racial and socio-economic disparity.

Sarah Beamish was born in Melfort, Saskatchewan, on nêhiyaw (Plains Cree) land. An activist, artist and writer since childhood, she now works in social justice and public-interest litigation in Toronto and serves on the International Board of Amnesty International. She hopes to be a good ancestor one day.

Idil Burale is a community advocate, media commentator and associate at the MaRS Solutions Lab. Since 2012, she has been working toward improving police-community relations with Positive Change TO, an ad hoc advocacy group dedicated to addressing the root causes of violence in Toronto. Idil has also been an advisor to the Toronto Police Service's PACER project, as well as two other policing task forces, and also helped create the TPS's Somali Liaison Unit in Rexdale.

Alina Chatterjee is Team Lead for Neighbourhoods at United Way Toronto and York Region. With a strong background in equity work, fundraising and program development, she has worked with the Scadding Court Community Centre, Toronto Community Housing, Regent Park Neighbourhood Initiative, Alexandra Park Community Centre and as executive assistant to city councillor Kristyn Wong-Tam.

Denise DaCosta is a writer and artist living in Toronto.

Nicholas Davis, an accomplished journalist with twenty-seven years of experience in radio, television and print, is the CBC's Manager of Program Development. During seventeen years at the CBC, he has covered everything from crime to arts to the Olympics. As senior producer for *Metro Morning*, he was part of the team that made the program the number-one morning show in Greater Toronto. Nicky has won many awards, including a 2006 Gabriel for a story on Holly Jones. He lectures to aspiring reporters at several journalism schools, and coaches basketball at Sheridan College.

Beyhan Farhadi is a doctoral candidate in the Department of Geography at the University of Toronto and a secondary school teacher with the Toronto District School Board. Though she is currently researching geographies of education, her training and engagement with multiple disciplines and methodologies have resulted in unconventional professional trajectories, of which this project is part.

Andrea Gunraj is a Torontonian engaged in community development work, particularly in the areas of safety, equity, and gender-based violence prevention and education. She is a writer and author of both fiction and non-fiction and loves to explore stories of racialized people connecting with each other across time and space.

J. David Hulchanski has been a professor of housing and community development at the University of Toronto's Factor-Inwentash Faculty of Social Work since 1997. He holds the faculty's Dr. Chow Yei Ching Chair in Housing and served as the director of the Centre for Urban and Community Studies from 2000 to 2008. David is currently the principal investigator of a seven-year study of neighbourhood change in six major Canadian cities.

Sofia Ijaz is a refugee lawyer and human rights activist. She was raised in Toronto by her mother and grandparents, migrants from Pakistan. As part of her advocacy for refugee and prisoner rights, Sofia has lived and worked in Occupied Palestine, the U.S., the Hague and Syria.

Ian Kamau is an artist, writer, designer and city builder who grew up in the St. Lawrence neighbourhood of downtown Toronto. His parents, both pioneering filmmakers, emigrated from Trinidad in 1970. Ian has fifteen years of community development experience, a degree in fine arts and design, and a lifelong passion for arts as a tool for social transformation.

Asmaa Malik is an assistant professor of journalism at Ryerson University. She was most recently deputy managing editor at the *Montreal Gazette*, where she also wrote a monthly column on how online networks influence our off-line relationships. She previously worked at the *Toronto Star*, where she was weekend features editor, and her work has also appeared in the *Washington Post* and *NOW* magazine.

Eric Mann is an architect and an urban planner at DIALOG Inc., a Toronto-based integrated design firm active in Canada and abroad. His recent work includes project management for the master planning and design of new mixed-income, mixed-use communities, as well as urban planning of LRT transit corridors in Ontario and Alberta.

Shawn Micallef is a *Toronto Star* columnist, co-owner and an editor of *Spacing* magazine, co-founder of the mobile phone public space documentary project [murmur] and instructor at the University of Toronto. He is the author of *Stroll: Psychogeographic Walking Tours of Toronto* (Coach House Books, 2010), *Full Frontal T.O.: Exploring Toronto's Architectural Vernacular* (Coach House Books, 2012) and *The Trouble with Brunch: Work, Class and the Pursuit of Leisure* (Coach House Books, 2014), and was the Toronto Public Library's non-fiction writer-in-residence in 2013.

Taha Muharuma documents the soul of the city through street photography, portraiture and commercial photography, along with a new passion for teaching kids around the city his Mobile Photography 101 course. Candid, soulful moments are the foundation of every frame.

Paul Nguyen is an award-winning activist and filmmaker from Toronto's Jane-Finch area. In 2004, he created Jane-Finch.com to change negative stereotypes about his community. His grassroots project quickly became a national success story. He is a public speaker and media commentator on race, crime and youth issues.

.Ryan Paterson has worked for over fifteen years in the space where art, culture, community, social change, media, technology and commerce intersect. He is co-founder of Manifesto, a socially minded arts and culture animator best known for its annual festival, and creative director with Isobar Canada.

Karen Pitter is a registered social worker with a professional interest in mental health. She is currently establishing a telephone-based service for members of the Black community who are not comfortable with traditional first points of contact for mental health services.

Doug Saunders is the *Globe and Mail*'s international affairs columnist and writer, and the author of the migration-themed books *Arrival City: The Final Migration* and *Our Next World* (Knopf Canada, 2010) and *The Myth of the Muslim Tide: Do Immigrants Threaten the West?* (Vintage, 2012). He is currently working with the World Bank on a study of barriers to labour-migrant integration in Western cities.

Fatima Syed is a graduate of the Masters of Journalism program at Ryerson University, and has a BA in International Relations and English from the University of Toronto. She has written about immigration-related issues for the *Ryerson Review of Journalism*, the *Globe and Mail* and rabble.ca.

Rebeka Tabobondung is the editor-in-chief of MUSKRAT, an online Indigenous literary arts and culture publication. She is also a documentary filmmaker, cultural producer, poet and Indigenous knowledge researcher working with the Well Living House at St. Michael's Hospital in Toronto. Rebeka's latest research and film work documents traditional birth knowledge from Wasauksing First Nation, where she is also a member.

Mariana Valverde is a professor of criminology and socio-legal studies at the University of Toronto and the author of six books, including *Everyday Law on the Street: City Governance in an Age of Diversity* (University of Chicago Press, 2012). She is currently researching local infrastructure partnerships.

Nana Yanful is a criminal defence lawyer practicing at Simcoe Chambers in Toronto. She has a background in diversity and equity education and likes to philosophize and debate about race, policing and the law. Visit www.yanfullaw.ca.

THE EDITORS

Jay Pitter established a career as a public funder and then a communications and public engagement director before earning a graduate degree at York University's Faculty of Environmental Studies. Her passion for inclusive city-building led her to research site-specific narrative, environmental design, crime prevention through environmental design (CPTED) and urban place-making. Throughout her career, Jay has spearheaded noteworthy projects with organizations such as the Ontario Arts Council, Toronto Community Housing Corporation, Toronto Police Service, the City of Toronto, the Toronto District School Board and DIALOG, a national architecture firm. Her work has increased knowledge transfer, revenue, profile and partnerships through the co-creation of inclusive, safe and vibrant places. She has been a guest lecturer at the University of Toronto, York University, Centennial College and Seneca College, and was recently a faculty member at the University of Guelph-Humber. Jay has also written for *Spacing*, CBC Radio, *The Walrus* and the *Toronto Star*.

John Lorinc is a Toronto journalist, author and editor. He has written extensively about urban and municipal affairs in general, and Toronto in particular, for a range of publications, including *Spacing*, the *Globe and Mail*, the *Toronto Star*, *The Walrus* and *Toronto Life*. He has also reported on business, energy, education and the environment for publications such as *Canadian Geographic* and the *New York Times*' Green Inc. blog. John is the author of three books, including *The New City: How the Crisis in Canada's Urban Centres Is Reshaping the Nation* (Penguin, 2006). He contributed essays to all five volumes of Coach House Books' uTOpia series and co-edited *The Ward: The Life and Loss of Toronto's First Immigrant Neighbourhood* (Coach House Books, 2015). He has received numerous awards for his journalism. John lives in Toronto with his wife, Victoria Foote, and their two sons, Jacob and Samuel.

ACKNOWLEDGEMENTS

To the Creator, the source of every good deed and gift; John Lorinc, an insightful urban affairs writer, for generously inviting me to collaborate with him; Alana Wilcox and her team at Coach House Books, a small yet powerful press, for their incredible support of this project; the contributors, for their unyielding commitment and expertise; my daughter and great love, Kirsten Breanna Azan, for inspiring me daily; and my second-grade teacher turned lifelong mentor, who taught me radical city-building and humanity.

– Jay Pitter

I am grateful to the many editors who allow me to write about this city and cities in general, but especially my colleagues at *Spacing*, the *Globe and Mail*, the *Toronto Star* and *The Walrus*. I also have the great fortune of being able to draw on the insights of a wide range of sources who, for lack of a better term, could be described as urbanists, but are, in fact, people who just love cities as much as I do. Last, I'd like to thank Andrea Addario, a friend and colleague, who posed some tough questions at the front end of this project that remained top-of-mind throughout.

– John Lorinc

Typeset in Whitman and Benton.

Printed at the old Coach House on bpNichol Lane in Toronto, Ontario, on Zephyr Antique Laid paper, which was manufactured, acid-free, in Saint-Jérôme, Quebec, from second-growth forests. This book was printed with vegetable-based ink on a 1965 Heidelberg KORD offset litho press. Its pages were folded on a Baumfolder, gathered by hand, bound on a Sulby Auto-Minabinda and trimmed on a Polar single-knife cutter.

Edited by Jay Pitter and John Lorinc
Copy edited by Stuart Ross
Designed by Alana Wilcox
Cover by Ingrid Paulson

Coach House Books
80 bpNichol Lane
Toronto ON M5S 3J4
Canada

416 979 2217
800 367 6360

mail@chbooks.com
www.chbooks.com